Hmong at the Turning Point

Yang Dao, Ph.D.

Edited by Jeanne L. Blake

WorldBridge Associates, Ltd.

Minneapolis

Library of Congress Catalog Card Number 92-060020

Yang, Dao, 1943-
Hmong at the Turning Point/Yang Dao; Jeanne Blake
p. 184 cm. 26
Includes bibliography and index. 1. Hmong (Asian people)—
Laos. 2. Hill farming—Laos. 3. Laos—Economic conditions.
4. Laos—Politics and government. 5. Vietnamese conflict,
1961-1975—Economic aspects—Laos. I. Blake, Jeanne, 1948-
II. Title.
DS555.45.H55Y36 1993
ISBN 0-9632149-9-3

Published in the United States of America by WorldBridge
Associates, Ltd., 3249 Hennepin Avenue South, Minneapolis,
MN 55408 USA

Book design, composition, typesetting, printing and binding
by Bolger Publications-Creative Printing, Minneapolis MN
Printed and bound in the United States of America

In loving memory of my mother, Mrs. Ker Her (Yang), in the fond hopes that I can be and become the son she wished me to be.

CONTENTS

PART ONE

Hmong Society
The Hmong and Their Environment

1   THE NATURAL ENVIRONMENT

Terrain and Climate — Topography 4 • Soil 4 • Climate 4 • Natural Resources — Forest Resources 6 • Mineral Resources 7 • Hydroelectric Resources 7 • Transportation Systems 7

2   THE HMONG

The Hmong Population   Demographics — Population Estimates 12 • Age and Sex Distribution 13 • Distribution — Geographical Distribution 14 • Settlement Patterns 17 • Population Changes — Demographic Changes 18 • Migrations 19

Social and Political Organization   Traditional Organization — The Family 22 • The Clan 23 • Moving Toward Modern Patterns of Government — Hmong Under the French Protectorate 25 • Administrative Organization in Independent Laos (Regional Administration 27 • Administration of Rural Areas 28 • Administrative Decentralization 29)

3   HISTORICAL BACKGROUND

Struggle for Hegemony 36 • Hmong Uprisings in Laos — The Revolt of the Hmong *kaitong* 36 • The "Madman's War" 36 • The Hmong and the Laotian Nation — The Problem of the Ethnic Minorities 38 • The Hmong in the Laotian Travail 39

ACKNOWLEDGEMENTS

Since 1975, more than 80,000 Hmong from Laos have been resettled in the United States. Their presence here has raised many questions about their history, their culture and traditions, and their future. Public officials, educators, business people, church members, social service providers and interested individuals have sought accurate information about the Hmong. Hmong people themselves, particularly the young, uprooted from their natural environment, are in search of their cultural identity. *Hmong at the Turning Point* is the result of the constant interest and encouragement of these friends, new and old, throughout the world.

Written, as it is, out of my own experiences and that of my relatives, colleagues and fellow countrymen, both Hmong and non-Hmong, *Hmong at the Turning Point* owes a debt of gratitude to every person who has touched my life. The largest and least able to be repaid is to my parents, Her Ker, my beloved mother, who encouraged and supported a son pursuing a wholly unfamiliar path, and Yang My Nou, my father, who continues to be, even today at 80 years of age, a unique and inexhaustible resource on Hmong culture, traditions and music. My most heartfelt love and gratitude must go to my wife, Ly Mo, who throughout our lives together, which have spanned countries and continents, has, through her unceasing efforts and firm belief in me and in our people, made it possible for me to achieve the education, the experience and the time out of which this book has come. I will never forget the openness and wisdom with which Mr. Tougeu Lyfoung, among others, has, through the years, so generously provided me with valuable first-hand information about events which took place before I was old enough to appreciate them. My appreciation also goes to the University of Minnesota, whose warm welcome brought me from Paris to the United States in 1983, and to the Social Science Research Council, which provided financial support during my early days in this country. I am particularly grateful to Jeanne Blake, my editor, whose commitment, patience and dedication have been so essential to both the beginning and the completion of this book. Finally, I would like to thank my family, Robert Yang, Jeanne Blake and the many other relatives and friends who have provided financial and other support during the project.

EDITOR'S NOTE

An accident of fate first introduced me to the Hmong. In 1981, I committed to providing in-home language tutoring to a family of Hmong Cha from the Sayaboury region of Laos, then living in Saint Paul, Minnesota. Through their patient efforts and those of all of my students and their families, I gained whatever fluency I now have in the Hmong language and whatever knowledge, however incomplete, of this complex culture.

In 1988, it was my honor and privilege to be asked by Dr. Yang Dao to work with him on the rewriting of his book, *Les Hmong du Laos Face au Developpement*, first published in Laos in 1975. Updated and enlarged as *Hmong at the Turning Point*, the book provides an excellent introduction to the traditional life of the Hmong of Laos and to their place in the social and economic milieu of this critical region. Its focus is on *development*: the development of the traditional Hmong subsistence economy into the beginnings of a cooperative market economy, the destruction and subsequent metamorphosis of this market economy into a transitory wartime economy, and, finally, a integrated plan for the development of the plains and mountains of northern Laos. Delayed as it has been by national and international events, the time is now right for this vision of peace and cooperation. We hope that *Hmong at the Turning Point* will provide a common starting point for all those who are committed to the restoration of the Kingdom of a Million Elephants.

Working on this book has been a rich and rewarding experience. It has given me the opportunity to learn, many times through the voices of the actual participants, about critical historical and political events which shaped the lives of the Hmong in Southeast Asia. It has provided a counterpoint to the perspectives of my rural Hmong friends. Not least, it has given me the chance to build a friendship with the delightful Yang family. Being an outsider was both a hindrance and a help: a hindrance, in that I was unable to supply facts or offer interpretations based on personal experience; a help, in that I was able to spot inconsistencies, mistranslations and omissions not obvious in the original text. Though great care has been exercised throughout, I apologize in advance for the many errors that certainly remain, both those of substance and those of style, for which I alone take complete responsibility.

Like the author, I owe debts of gratitude too numerous to mention. First, to my beloved grandmother, now deceased, who was responsible for my meeting this fascinating people and who was so loved and respected by them. To my parents and sisters, for their patience and understanding with my Hmong pursuits over the years. To friends also involved with the Hmong, for their constant support and encouragement during this and many other projects. To my professional colleagues, for their endurance in listening to endless tales of discovery and for providing the lights of objectivity and balance when I most needed them. To my Hmong friends and relatives, for their generosity in sharing their unique points of view and for insisting on correct language and cultural performance from such a slow learner. Finally, to Dr. Yang Dao, for his confidence in me, however meagerly justified.

INTRODUCTION TO
THE SECOND EDITION

Amidst the popular euphoria of the spring of 1975, the first edition of this book, *Les Hmong du Laos Face au Developpement (The Hmong of Laos in the Vanguard of Development)*, was born. Sponsored by the Asia Foundation and published by Siaosavath Publications, its existence was to be as brief as that of a mayfly, swept away by the violent wind of the Laotian revolution and forgotten in the desperate rush to save life, family and nation.

Today, after 18 years, the book, revised, updated and augmented, has come back to life with the same intensity and with improved accuracy and completeness. Rechristened *Hmong at the Turning Point*, it recounts the tumultuous history of the Hmong people of Laos, the beginnings of their transition to a modern society, the destruction of these by their involvement in the "secret war" in Laos, and their tragic exodus following the withdrawal of the United States from Indochina.

Hmong at the Turning Point presents an overview of the Hmong way of life as it existed in the mountains of northern Laos prior to 1975. It is my hope that my inside perspectives will bring about a better understanding of these "montagnards" on the part of Americans and other foreigners, whose knowledge to date has been based largely upon more or less solid journalistic reporting. Long called "barbarian," "primitive," and even "uncivilized," the Hmong are shown to be a people like all others, aspiring to peace, working toward progress, and cherishing freedom and liberty.

The last four decades have truly constituted a turning point for the Hmong in Laos. They have striven conscientiously for social change through education, for economic progress through technological improvement, and for public status through political involvement. The third attempt at Laotian national reconciliation, which brought a glimmer of hope to their dreams, was brutally shattered. Under communist domination, Laos, already profoundly affected by a quarter-century of fratricidal war, was plunged into economic and social chaos. The Hmong, along with all Laotian citizens, are still suffering in the aftermath of this disaster. Without a rational, well-planned development effort, this crisis will persist and worsen, eventually jeopardizing the future of the country.

Hmong at the Turning Point offers such a development plan, based on the economic, social and political integration of the plains and mountain regions of Laos. Peace and democracy are the two tools essential to the successful implementation of the plan. Laotian leaders everywhere must seize their unique chance, offered by today's climate of international detente, to bring about a true Laotian reconciliation, the *sine qua non* condition for permanent security and prosperity in Laos.

FOREWORD (FIRST EDITION)

In this book, my friend Yang Dao presents his magnificent work on the problems of development among the Hmong people in northern Laos. They are very difficult problems indeed. The Meo, or more correctly, Hmong, some of whom I was able to meet around Cha Pa [North Vietnam] in 1931, have seen their traditional economy shattered on all sides: first by a population explosion which no longer allows the long forest fallow period that used to restore fertility to the lands, and then by the fratricidal war in Laos which has pointlessly slaughtered so many adults and even adolescents.

A new economy is taking hold. The valleys, certainly, can engage in intensive, continuous rice-growing of the kind done in neighboring Vietnam. Most of the rest of the land, however, comprises sloping highlands which must be tapped for other uses than simply forest: orchards and fruit plantations, permanent pasture where the forest does not grow back, bamboo for its myriad uses by an artisan class which must certainly be restored, and so on.

None of this can come to anything without the participation of the people concerned. The best suggestions of experts and policy makers, like Yang Dao, can be implemented on a broad scale only if they are reviewed, interpreted and, finally, reinvented and hence accepted by the peasants themselves. This assumes that they will have been educated, taught to read and write, and motivated, and that they will be able to form, by themselves, organizations which can truly represent them. Happiness for the people and prosperity for Laos, whose finding peace at long last makes my heart rejoice and fills me with hope, cannot be achieved without their active participation. They must organize their own cooperatives and participate directly, no longer simply through their leaders, in their country's economic life.

Given these conditions, Yang Dao's excellent monograph can perform the greatest of services by showing the nation's leaders, as well as the peasant organizations of the future, the possibilities, much greater than many of them think, for this splendid country.

René Dumont
PARIS
September 4, 1974

PREFACE (FIRST EDITION)

This book is the fruit of direct personal experience throughout my childhood and youth, supplemented by research conducted in my country, Laos. The study was made during a time of civil war, under conditions limited geographically to zones controlled by the Vientiane government and in time to the years preceding the destruction of the Sam Thong Center in 1970. Thus, the ethnographic present is the years 1969-1970. However, because the war was constantly introducing new and very important social and economic factors, later events are described wherever necessary.

Three foreign languages, Lao, Hmong and Chinese, are used in this book. Romanized spellings customary at the time of the original writing have been used for Lao words and place names. For Hmong, the romanization system devised by Barney, Smalley and Bertrais in 1953 has been used. Current English spellings of Chinese place names are used, followed parenthetically where necessary by their more familiar spellings.

To all those who helped, far and near, particularly to those of whose names discretion forbids the mention, I offer my sincerest thanks. I would like again to express my particular gratitude to Professor René Dumont (ret.) of the National Institute of Agronomy in Paris, who so kindly guided me throughout the original study.

INTRODUCTION (FIRST EDITION)

Situated in the heart of Southeast Asia, Laos has from time immemorial been a crossroads where races, civilizations, empires, interests and ideologies have collided. Its geographical position has made it the ramification point for migrations from south China which, over the centuries, have shaped the present-day countenance of ancient Lan Xang.[1] Although almost no organized human group exists that is truly ethnically homogeneous, Laos is, in our eyes, the very essence of a cultural mosaic, which makes this tiny country a perfect model for the study of diversity.

Laos has more than three million inhabitants belonging to 68 ethnic groups, each speaking its own language or dialect. The oldest ethnic element is made up of tribes traditionally subsumed under the name "Kha," a diverse group of some 700,000 people. The "Kha" belong to the Mon-Khmer family. More or less dispossessed, they live isolated from one another in the high valleys and are largely confined to itinerant denshering as a livelihood. Even today, their integration into the dominant (Lao) society is superficial at best.[2]

The Lao proper, who constitute the dominant ethnic group, belong to the branch of Tai who came originally from south China and whose southward migration was hastened in the thirteenth century by the thrust of Kublai Khan's Mongols. Driven out of China, they invaded Burma, Thailand, North Vietnam and present-day Laos, displacing the indigenous populations from the fertile valleys into the mountain highlands. It was at this time that these peoples were given the generic name of "Kha," meaning "slave," an epithet by which they are known even today.[3] The numbers of the new arrivals, the superiority of their social and military organization, and the richness of the lands they occupied gave them a monopoly on political power. Thus, the history of the Tai-Lao has been interwoven for seven centuries with that of Laos itself.

The third and most recently arrived ethnic group are the Sino-Tibetans: Mien (Yao), Hmong (Meo), "Lolo," and others. Fleeing the imperial yoke, these peoples poured in from the Chinese provinces of Sichuan (Szechuan), Hunan, Guizhou (Kweichow), Guangxi (Kwangsi) and Yunnan in the eighteenth and nineteenth centuries. Semi-nomadic tribes, they lived on the fringes of Lao society, which long considered them foreigners if not parasites. The newcomers settled throughout upper Laos where they engaged in itinerant farming and (particularly the Hmong) turned out to be excellent cattlemen. Often their concept of the world is limited to the horizon of their village or their mountains, since they have very little contact, aside from occasional trade, with the plains people.

Although the Lao, who gave their name to Laos, constitute the largest single ethnic element, "the proportion of ethnic minorities is far higher than the 15 percent found in Cambodia or in both Vietnams, to the point where one may well question whether they indeed make up more than half the population."[4] This hypothesis seems to be confirmed by the statement of Phoumi Vongvichit, secretary general of the Central Committee of the Neo

Lao Hak Sat, who estimates that ethnic Lao "comprise around 1.5 million inhabitants, or, in other words, a scant half of the total population; hence the minority nationalities play an extremely important role among the forces that produce and fight."[5]

FOOTNOTES:

[1] Lan Xang, or Kingdom of a Million Elephants, is the ancient name for Laos.

[2] In this book, "Lao" is used to designate the lowland Lao ethnic group and "Laotian" to refer to all citizens of the country of Laos.

[3] It is wrong to persist in applying the term "Kha," with its connotations of subjugation, to the indigenous Indochinese of our time. The Royal Lao Government should encourage ethno-sociological research in Laos aimed at a better understanding of the habits and customs of the different ethnic groups which make up the Laotian population and a better grasp of their deep-rooted and legitimate aspirations.

[4] Roland Breton, *Le Monde Diplomatique*, Paris, June 1970.

[5] Phoumi Vongvichit, *Laos and the Victorious Struggle of the Lao People Against American Neo-Colonialism*, Neo Lao Hak Sat Publications, 1968, p. 212.

THE HMONG

In the ethnic mosaic of the Kingdom of a Million Elephants, the Hmong hold the privilege of being the most recent immigrants. They generally settle on the peaks of mountains, far from the envious eyes of others. But just who are these Hmong?

Known as "Miao" or "Meo," appellations which the Hmong do not accept,[1] they number several million, scattered between the 16th and 30th parallels and between the 98th and 111th degrees of east longitude.[2] The vicissitudes of history uprooted them from the plains of the Huang He (Yellow) and the Yangzi (Yangtse) rivers in China and made them, unwillingly, into resigned mountaineers whose reserve has struck more than one observer. Generally peaceable but with a wild, proud spirit of independence, the Hmong people two centuries ago pulled up stakes from imperial China under expansionist pressure from the Han[3] and ahead of massacres of their members[4] and fled across the frontier from the sudden accelerations of history for which their archaic concept of the world had in no way prepared them.[5]

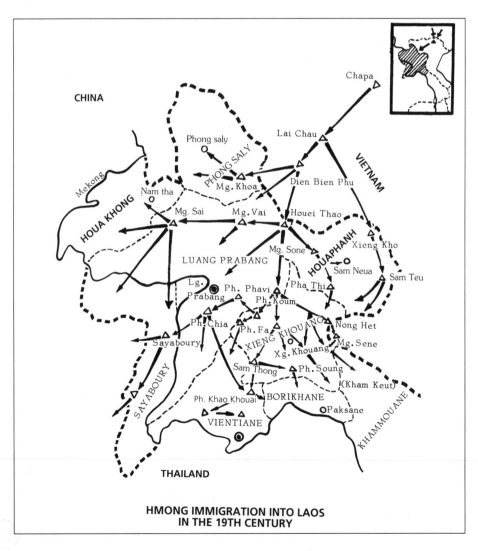

**HMONG IMMIGRATION INTO LAOS
IN THE 19TH CENTURY**

The Hmong migrated from north to south, from the climate of continental Asia toward the tropics, following the route taken by so many of Asia's peoples. If there was a difference, it was that the Hmong, as a rule, avoided the plains, content to move to other mountains when they no longer felt safe. Most of them settled in the highlands of southern China. Later, beginning in the nineteenth century, they infiltrated the entire northern half of French Indochina,[6] Thailand and Burma.

The Hmong arrived in Laos in the early 1800s. Their coming was a slow and peaceful process. Since they tended to settle in the highest of the mountain fastnesses, they did not disturb the Phouan[7] and Lao populations. Their choice of location seems to have been dictated by three main considerations:

HISTORY

The ancestors of the Hmong, tradition says, had lived in the plains along the Yellow River in China for several centuries before the arrival of the Han. As the crossroads of great migrations, these plains were not defensible. The Hmong, therefore, made an historic choice to take to the mountains, which were poorer but less accessible and easier to defend. For them, freedom and human dignity were worth more than any amount of fertile land.

CLIMATE

The oppressive heat of the tropical plains turned out to be very difficult for people like the Hmong, accustomed to the continental climate of central Asia, to tolerate. Furthermore, they were extremely susceptible to tropical diseases. It was only above 1,400 meters, the altitude limit of malaria, that they felt vigorous and healthy.

POLITICS

The plains and valleys of Southeast Asia were, for the most part, already settled and it would have taken a pitched battle to appropriate them. Since they were peaceable by nature and few in number, the Hmong were careful not to make enemies and consequent trouble for themselves. What they wanted more than anything else was the freedom for which they had always fought.

The settlement of the Hmong in Laos brings us to the subject of this book.

Part One is a study of the characteristics of the Hmong population living in this part of Southeast Asia. It looks at how and through what difficulties their society has evolved in its natural and human environments and how they came to be integrated into the Laotian nation.

Part Two examines the economic and social situations in which the Hmong people of Laos live. It comprises an analysis of the traditional self-sufficient society and its gradual metamorphosis into a society with a market economy, and an assessment of the unique situation created by the war now raging throughout the region.[8]

Part Three deals with the outlook for the future of the Hmong and other mountain peoples, already called upon to choose between a dying traditional economic system and a profound transformation of their subsistence economy, and to adapt as best they can to national and international economic circumstances. This part presents a plan for development of the mountain regions of Laos and, thereby, of a more effective national policy of economic integration.

A newly-written Part Four outlines the failure of the post-war attempt at Laotian national reconciliation and the historical exodus of the Hmong, subject to persecution if not outright genocide by the communist Pathet Lao government.

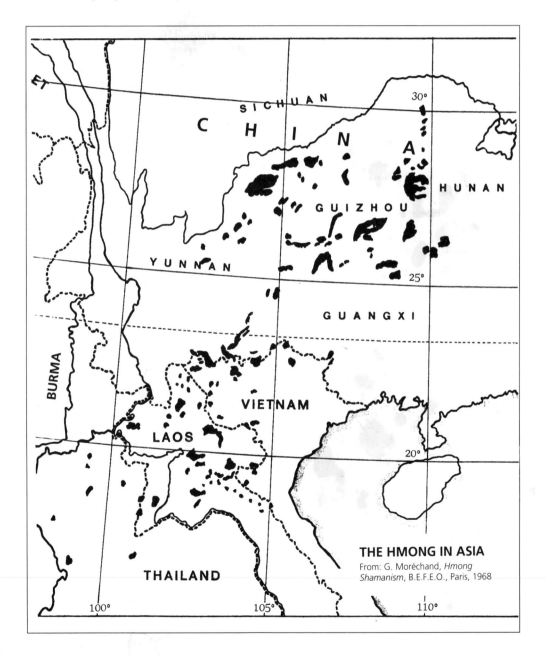

THE HMONG IN ASIA
From: G. Moréchand, *Hmong Shamanism*, B.E.F.E.O., Paris, 1968

FOOTNOTES:

[1] The word "Hmong" means man or human being. It is the name by which these people have always called themselves. The word "Miao," meaning barbarian, was used originally during the expansionist conquests of the Han dynasty to refer to all peoples of other than Chinese origin. Later, the epithet "Miao" was confined to certain refractory ethnic groups, including the Hmong, who fought against Chinese domination. Introduced in the late nineteenth century to French Indochina, "Miao" degenerated into "Meo," a derogatory term categorically denounced by the Hmong.

[2] The worldwide population of Hmong is estimated to be 6,000,000 (Miao) in the People's Republic of China (1990); 400,000 in North Vietnam (1986); 200,000-300,000 in northern Laos (1991); 80,000 in northern Thailand (1992; plus an additional approximately 40,000 living in refugee camps as of 1991); several thousand in Burma; 120,000 in the United States (1992); 13,000 in France (including 1,500 in French Guyana; 1992); 650 in Canada (1989) and 650 in Australia (1992).

[3] A name for the dynasty that ruled China from 206 B.C.-220 A.D., "Han" has come to be used as a general term referring to people of Chinese origin who speak Chinese and have a Chinese culture.

[4] Jean Chesnaux and Marianne Bastid, "China 1: From the Opium Wars to the Franco-Chinese War, 1840-1855," *Collection d'Histoire Contemporaine*, Hatier Université, Paris, 1969, p. 100.

[5] Jacques Lemoine, *A Green Hmong Village in Northern Laos*, Editions du Centre National de la Recherche Scientifique, Paris, 1972, p. 16.

[6] Vietnam, Cambodia and Laos.

[7] The Phouan or Tai Phouan, sometimes spelled Phuan, are an upland Tai ethnic group. They speak basically the same language, with certain tonal variations, as the lowland Lao, to whom they are related. They live almost exclusively in the Xieng Khouang plateau.

[8] Recall that the ethnographic present of Parts One, Two and Three is the years 1969-70.

PART ONE

Hmong Society

THE HMONG AND THEIR ENVIRONMENT

In Laos, the Hmong form a homogeneous ethnic group living in an area stretching from Houa Phanh to Sayaboury and from Phong Saly-Houa Khong to northern Khammouane. In short, they are scattered throughout northern Laos. No one can claim to know the Hmong, let alone understand them, without a comprehensive study of both their physical and human surroundings and the events of their history.

The *natural* environment creates the setting in which the Hmong develop; it is through his contact with nature that man shapes his character and forms his concept of the world. The essential features of Hmong sociology can be deduced from a study of their *human* environment. Finally, an *historical* overview provides a better understanding of the aspirations of the Hmong mountain people who are taking an active part on both sides of the current Laotian conflict.

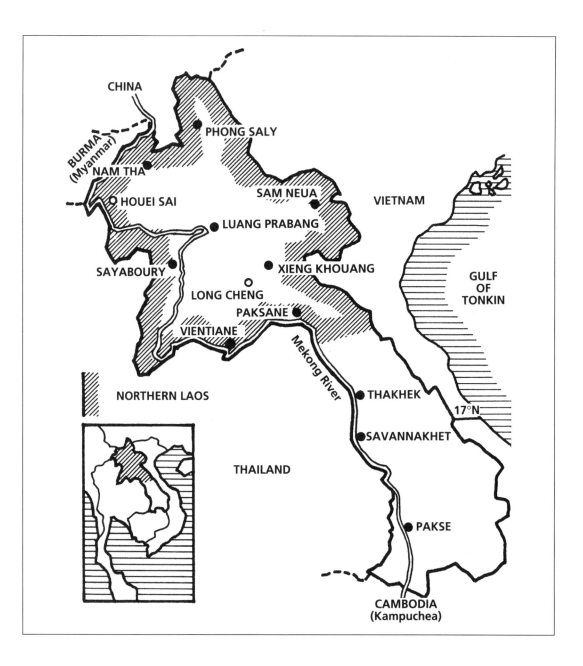

CHINA

BURMA
(Myanmar)

PHONG SALY

NAM THA

HOUEI SAI

SAM NEUA

VIETNAM

LUANG PRABANG

SAYABOURY

XIENG KHOUANG

LONG CHENG

PAKSANE

VIENTIANE

GULF
OF
TONKIN

NORTHERN LAOS

Mekong River

THAKHEK

17°N

SAVANNAKHET

THAILAND

PAKSE

CAMBODIA
(Kampuchea)

CHAPTER ONE

The Natural Environment

Bounded by North Vietnam, China, Burma and Thailand, northern Laos extends southward to the northern boundaries of the provinces of Vientiane, Borikhane and Khammouane. It covers an area of almost 130,000 square kilometers.

TERRAIN AND CLIMATE

TOPOGRAPHY   Northern Laos comprises a fairly complex terrain. The west (Luang Prabang, Sayaboury and Houa Khong provinces) is made up of mountain chains oriented northeast to southwest through which the Mekong River forces its difficult course. It is rugged country, with altitudes frequently exceeding 1,000 meters but rarely rising above 2,000 meters. In the north and east stands a vast range of crystalline-rock mountains interspersed with limestone plateaus at over 1,000 meters elevation. Some of the peaks in Houa Phanh province are just over 2,000 meters high. Between these two mountain ranges, which form an inverted V whose point coincides roughly with the extreme northern tip of Laos (Phong Saly province), lies the vast Phouan plateau of Xieng Khouang, which extends over 2,000 square kilometers at elevations of 1,200 to 1,500 meters. Phou Bia mountain (2,820 m.), located in the southernmost part of the plateau, is the highest point in Laos. South of Xieng Khouang is the plain of Vientiane, stretching along the Mekong River.

SOIL   The soil of northern Laos has the features and strata characteristic of soils subject to monsoon systems. In order of decreasing richness are sandstone soils, schists and soils derived from volcanic rocks (granite, phosphorus, etc.).

Alluvial Soils   Among the alluvial formations in the plains is a reddish-colored silt, a kind of dusty, rusty loam which is sterile. It plays a preponderant role in the distribution of the pseudo-steppes and forests in northern Laos and in the movements of people therein. There are also some fertile highland-derived alluvial soils, notably recent alluvia in the valleys.

Soils Built Up on Rocks   The mountainous terrain in the region from Xieng Khouang to Luang Prabang has peaks of about 1,500 to 1,700 meters. The order of soil types from top to bottom is sandstone, schist and limestone. Thus these peaks are often sandy, sometimes schisty. Here and there, where erosion has stripped away the sand and schist, rise limestone peaks more or less deforested by man.

CLIMATE   As part of the monsoon region of Asia, northern Laos has two main seasons: a dry, cool season (October to May) and a rainy, warm season (June to September). The period from November to January is a kind of intermediate season characterized by fog and rather low temperatures.

Temperature   Northern Laos has two distinct temperature zones: the Mekong valley plains and the mountains and plateaus.

The Mekong Valley   The plains of the Mekong valley are fairly hot, almost unbearable for mountain people. The temperature averages 25.7°C in Vientiane and 25.8°C in Luang Prabang. Cool air and chill winds from the northeast occasionally cause the temperature to drop to 10°C or even 5°C in Vientiane,[1] but in general the temperature varies little throughout the Mekong valley.

The Mountains and Plateaus   As the elevation increases, the temperature drops steadily and the vegetation undergoes marked changes. Around 800 to 1,000 meters, forests of pine and chestnut, orchards of peach and pear, and strawberry patches enjoy a more temperate climate. A comparison of the temperatures in the plains around Vientiane, the Luang Prabang valley and the plateau of Xieng Khouang illustrates this effect distinctly.

TEMPERATURE IN NORTHERN LAOS (°C)

MONTH	VIENTIANE (plain)		XIENG KHOUANG (1,200 m.)		LUANG PRABANG (valley)	
	Mean	Range	Mean	Range	Mean	Range
January	20.1	14.1	16.2	13.4	20.5	14.0
February	23.7	13.7	17.7	14.1	23.1	17.2
March	26.0	13.1	18.9	13.7	25.6	17.2
April	28.3	11.4	21.5	10.8	28.1	14.9
May	28.0	8.8	22.5	8.6	28.9	12.9
June	27.8	7.4	23.0	7.4	28.7	10.3
July	27.2	6.5	22.5	6.4	28.0	8.8
August	27.5	6.8	22.6	6.7	27.7	9.0
September	27.8	6.9	22.3	8.5	27.8	10.1
October	27.8	9.1	20.3	11.6	26.2	11.0
November	23.9	11.3	18.8	11.3	23.6	11.5
December	22.0	13.2	17.0	13.1	21.1	11.8
ANNUAL	**25.7**		**20.4**		**25.8**	

SOURCE: National Statistics Bureau of Laos

Winters are fairly severe in the mountains of northern Laos. Hoarfrost is a common phenomenon. In his monthly reports for 1939 and January 1940, the French director of the Xieng Khouang agricultural station reported temperatures as low as one -5°C and several -3°C. At Nong Het (1,500 m.), temperatures of -10°C have occasionally been recorded.

Rainfall   Annual mean rainfall for Laos as a whole is 1.5 to 1.7 meters, with considerable variation by region and elevation. On the plains, showers are often sudden, brief and violent. In the mountains, particularly toward the northeast, precipitation often takes the form of a persistent drizzle.

A study of contour and climate shows the very difficult conditions with which the Laotian people must constantly deal. Its mountainous character generally isolates northern Laos and favors ethnic segregation. Oppressive heat and humidity, particularly in the plains, contribute to the deterioration of arable land and other material elements. The resulting harsh working conditions threaten the health of the workers, reducing the length of time they can work and their efficiency while they do. Topographic and climatic conditions represent very serious obstacles, indeed, to the development of northern Laos.

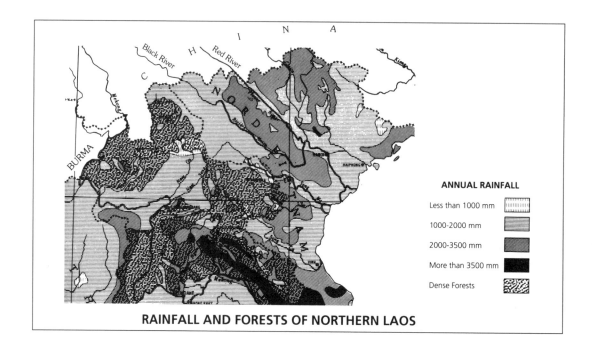

RAINFALL AND FORESTS OF NORTHERN LAOS

ANNUAL RAINFALL

Less than 1000 mm

1000-2000 mm

2000-3500 mm

More than 3500 mm

Dense Forests

NATURAL RESOURCES

The northern part of the kingdom is, however, rich in natural resources. Most of its territory is still forested, and the diversity of the forests is as important as that of the soils and climates.

FOREST RESOURCES

Teak   Teak, the object of large-scale exploitation in the forests of the royal domain of the north, is exported. It is sold on the world market as Siamese teak.[2]

Bamboo   Bamboo forests cover large areas both along streams and rivers and in certain other locations. Bamboo grows in many varieties, ranging from dwarf bamboos to giant species measuring more than 20 meters from ground to crown. However as yet there has been no systematic commercial utilization of these bamboo groves.

Rattan   Rattan grows in significant quantities but is generally used only on a family or local basis. It is just beginning to be exploited in the raw state.

Forest Products   A great many forest products such as sticklac, benzoin and various other resins could provide the basis for the development of trade.

The Xieng Khouang Plateau   The Xieng Khouang plateau deserves particular attention because of the variety of its forest products. Although the parts of the plateau lying below 500 meters (the Tha Thom area and the Nam Mo, Nam Khan and Nam Mat river valleys) yield forest products identical with those of tropical Laos, beginning at elevations of around 1,000 meters almost all the trees of temperate Europe may be found. One sees thriving forests of pine (more than 60,000 hectares) and oak, large stands of chestnut, wild apple, plum, peach and Chinese pear trees, grapes and wild hops. Forests of tea trees grow wild in the highlands, especially around Padong and Phou Sane.

MINERAL RESOURCES

Coal   Considerable deposits of anthracite have been found in the Nam Nhiep valley and in the Xieng Khouang region. There is known to be lignite in the upper Mekong valley and in Sayaboury province. Signs of coal deposits have been reported in Phong Saly and Luang Prabang provinces, in the Pak Lay region, and between the Mekong and Nam Lik rivers.

Iron   Large deposits of iron ore have been discovered in northern Laos. The main deposits lie between Xieng Khouang and Phong Savanh, where the metal content reaches as high as 70 percent, and in an area 50 kilometers to the south of Xieng Khouang.[3] Before these deposits can be mined, however, many problems, including that of transportation, will have to be solved.

Other Mineral Resources   Salt is found in the provinces of Houa Khong (around Houei Sai), Vientiane, Borikhane and Phong Saly. It is the object of a relatively brisk domestic trade. Gold is gathered in the provinces of Luang Prabang, Xieng Khouang and Houa Khong, where precious stones such as sapphires and zircons are also found. Deposits of copper, lead, antimony, zinc, silver and gypsum have been discovered in various parts of northern Laos. The question, however, is whether these deposits can be exploited economically.

HYDROELECTRIC RESOURCES

Northern Laos has a huge reserve of hydroelectric resources whose size and nature constitute a trump card of the highest order for its economic future.

> Thanks to the Annamite Range that runs from the northeast to the southeast of the country, Laos has at its disposal more than three million kilowatts of untapped water power from tributaries that empty into the Lao portion of the Mekong alone. More than two million kilowatts could easily be drawn from these tributaries at sites extremely favorable to the production of very low cost power. Each of the many waterfalls scattered throughout the country could provide power in amounts ranging from 10,000 to 200,000 kilowatts.[4]

It can thus be seen that the natural resources of northern Laos are both considerable in size and wide in variety. While exploitation of some of them has been slowed, even halted, by the current war, the development of most of them is hampered more by the absence of technically qualified people, by difficulties with financing and, above all, by the lack of adequate systems of transportation.

TRANSPORTATION SYSTEMS

Rivers   With the exception of its northernmost extremity, where the waters flow into the Black River of North Vietnam, northern Laos lies entirely within the drainage system of the Mekong River, either directly (upstream from Houei Sai and on the east bank of the river), via its tributaries (the Nam Ou, the Nam Suong and the Nam Khan), or, downstream of Vientiane, via the Nam Lik (a tributary of the Nam Ngum). While the Mekong is the main transportation artery for northern Laos, its tributaries also carry fairly heavy traffic during six months of the year. From June to November rafts regularly come down the swollen rivers, where many pirogues ply as well.

Roads The road system in northern Laos branches out from a central axis, RN 13,[5] which runs from Luang Prabang to the Cambodian border. During the rainy season, RN 13 is reduced to a dangerous mountain trail, particularly the section between Luang Prabang and Vientiane in the vicinity of Phou Khoune. It must be noted, however, that despite the war major improvements were made to the Vientiane-Luang Prabang portion of RN 13 between 1968 and 1971.

Branching off from RN 13 is RN 7, which serves Muong Soui, the Plain of Jars, and Vinh (Central Vietnam), with a branch running north from Ban Ban toward Sam Neua and another, at the Plain of Jars, running to Xieng Khouang and Tha Thom. A recently built road runs from Sam Thong to Long Cheng, Houei Kham and Muong Cha with a branch from Houei Kham to Ban Sone and Houei Mo, a small village located on RN 13. Finally, Chinese civil engineers are completing the paving of a "strategic road" to northern Laos. Christened the Mao Zedong (Mao Tse-tung) Road, it links the town of Meng La in Yunnan with Phong Saly province and continues on toward North Vietnam, with a branch at Muong Sai in the direction of Thailand.

A Tangled System of Trails The lack of roads is partially offset by a vast network of footpaths and horse tracks which link villages together, particularly in the mountains. Longer roads carrying more traffic connect one region to another.

Air Transport The precariousness of the roads, especially during the rainy season, and wartime insecurity have fostered the development of an airline system. Today every province has at least one airfield. The rapid expansion of air transport has not, however, been accompanied by reduction of fares, which are still exorbitant considering the meager resources of the average Laotian.

Because of the diversity of its climate, the extent of its habitable area and the wealth of its natural resources, northern Laos has always been the crossroads for invasions from south China and North Vietnam. Its natural environment forms the setting for the lives of a population diverse in ethnic origin, culture, habit and custom but nonetheless determined to share a common destiny.

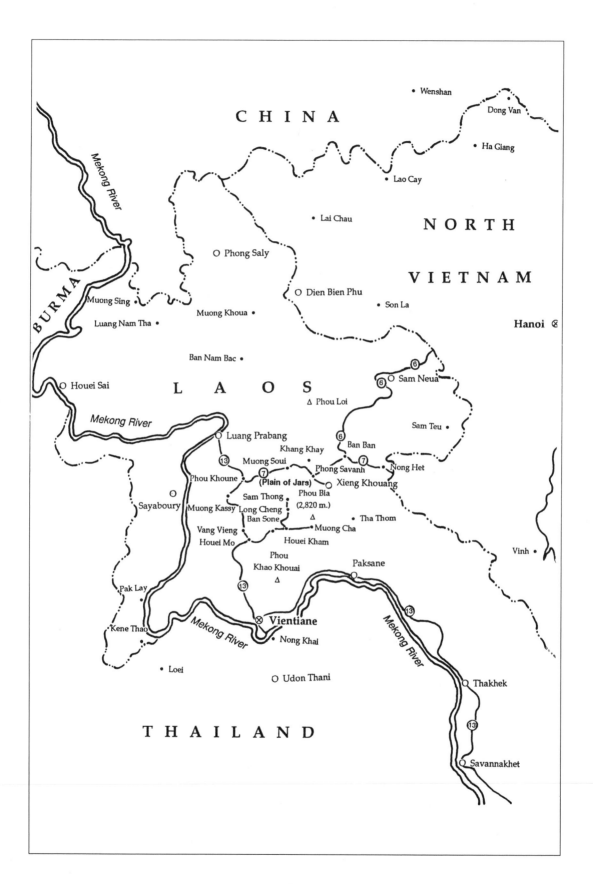

FOOTNOTES:

[1] Catholic Mission of Laos, *Geography of Laos*, Vientiane, 1961, p. 12.

[2] The name "Siamese" comes from Siam, the former name of the country of Thailand.

[3] Far Eastern Economic Review, *1968 Year Book*, 18 and 25 April 1968, p. 229.

[4] Pan Rassavong, "Economic Outlook for Laos," *La Revue Française*, No. 203, Paris, October 1967, p. 77.

[5] *Route Nationale* (National Road).

CHAPTER TWO

The Hmong

The Hmong have established themselves as best they can in this diversified setting, bringing with them a set of unique characteristics. This chapter will examine how this ethnic group has evolved and will continue to evolve in place and time, and try to grasp, in all its sociopolitical aspects, their deep aspiration to blossom within the harmony of a truly independent, free and democratic Laotian nation.

THE HMONG POPULATION

DEMOGRAPHICS

To our knowledge, determination of the Hmong population has never been the object of a serious study. It is difficult, if not impossible, to put an exact figure on this population, as it is on the population of Laos as a whole, since there has never been a census worthy of the name taken in the country.

POPULATION ESTIMATES

Under the French Protectorate   An ethnological study of the *Union Française*[1] estimated in 1937 that the Hmong population of all of Indochina numbered around 100,000 and that its annual growth rate was one percent.[2] Assuming that the estimate of total population provided at that time was approximately correct and that, given its very high birth rate, the actual growth rate of the Hmong population is closer to three percent, the figure for the Hmong population in Indochina as a whole 30 years later (1967) can be calculated as

$$100,000 \times (1 + 0.03)^{30} = 240,000.$$

This figure, which includes both North Vietnam and northern Laos, is greatly underestimated and seriously in error. North Vietnam alone has, as of today (1972), almost 250,000 Hmong![3] The *Union Française* estimate must be abandoned as a basis for demographic inquiry and other figures sought which more accurately depict the actual situation.

Since Independence   Since Laos became independent in 1954, a great many researchers, particularly the French, have taken an interest in studying the Hmong living there. In his book *Hmong Shamanism*, Guy Moréchand gave the figure of 60,000 as the number of Hmong living in Laos in 1968.[4] In fact this figure represented only the Hmong population in the single province of Xieng Khouang during the 1960s. Jacques Lemoine, in a study entitled *Social Organization in a Green Hmong Village*, estimated the Hmong population in Laos at 150,000.[5] Even this more generous figure still seems far too low.

What do the official statistics of the Royal Lao Government have to say on the subject? A document published by the Ministry of Economy and Planning states that

> the Mekong valley and the lowlands in general contain almost all the Lao, who comprise 63 percent of the some 2.8 million total inhabitants, according to estimates made in 1968. The highlands are populated by Proto-Indochinese groups designated generically by the

Lao as Kha (26 percent), groups who came originally from the south. They are also inhabited by peoples from the north, who have come across the Chinese border during the last century, principally the Meo and Yao,[6] who represent six percent of the population.[7]

The table below shows these figures, along with the corresponding absolute numbers. According to the official estimates, there are approximately 168,000 Hmong and Mien living in Laos (1969).

MAJOR ETHNIC GROUPS IN LAOS (1969)

ETHNIC GROUP	NUMBER	PERCENTAGE
Tai-Lao	1,764,000	63
Proto-Indochinese	728,000	26
Hmong and Mien	168,000	6
Others	140,000	5
TOTAL	**2,800,000**	**100**

SOURCE: National Statistics Bureau of Laos

In late 1969 and 1970, I conducted my own investigation in the mountains of northern Laos. The data I was able to collect differ significantly from the official figures.[8] First, it seems that the Mien are relatively numerous in Laos. Estimated at several tens of thousands, they live in fairly compact groups in the provinces of Houa Khong, Luang Prabang and Phong Saly. They have also established themselves in the regions of Sayaboury and Vang Vieng, north of Vientiane. As for the Hmong population, our best estimate is that it is somewhere in the neighborhood of 300,000, or about one tenth of the total population of Laos.[9] Analysis of their geographical distribution (discussed later in this chapter) provides a more accurate assessment of their actual numbers.

AGE AND SEX DISTRIBUTION

Gross Age A 1970 survey of 341 families totaling 3,165 people in Xieng Khouang province yielded the figures shown below for the age distribution of the Hmong population of northern Laos.

AGE DISTRIBUTION OF HMONG SURVEY SAMPLE (1970)

AGE	NUMBER	PERCENTAGE
Under 15	1,574	49.7
15 to 59	1,545	48.8
60 and over	46	1.5
TOTAL	**3,165**	**100.0**

If adults ages 15 to 59 are taken as an approximate equivalent of the working population, the proportion of this group to the total population assumes particular significance, especially when expressed as the load per working individual. The figures, if reliable, seem to indicate that among the Hmong the ratio of workers to non-workers is very close to 1.0; in other words, that for every active worker there is one non-worker. It must be pointed out, however, that in Laos, particularly among the Hmong, children start to work at the age of eight or ten, if not earlier, and that many young people, especially girls, are carrying a full adult work load by the time they reach 14 years of age. These people should also be considered part of the working population, which would increase the worker/non-worker ratio somewhat.

The Age Pyramid   The 1970 survey also shed some light on the age structure of the Hmong population of northern Laos. The data are illustrated in the age pyramid below.

AGE PYRAMID OF THE HMONG IN LAOS (1970)

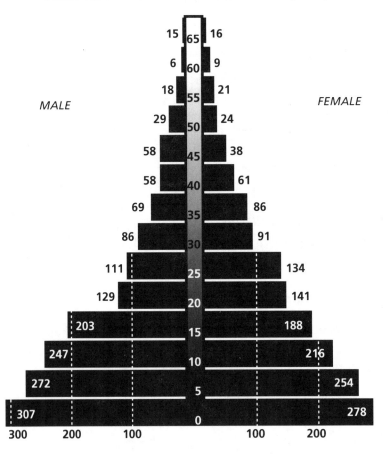

DISTRIBUTION

GEOGRAPHICAL DISTRIBUTION   Some sketchy censuses taken by Lao and Hmong military leaders on behalf of the Vientiane government showed the geographical distribution of Hmong indicated in the following table. The Hmong are most numerous in the provinces of Xieng Khouang, Luang Prabang and Houa Phanh. They live in more or less scattered groups in the western provinces of Sayaboury and Houa Khong. These provinces (particularly Sayaboury) as well as Vientiane province are taking in large numbers of refugees from the northeastern part of the kingdom. Finally, the southern provinces of Borikhane and Khammouane are frontier areas for the Hmong in their southward migratory thrust.

HMONG POPULATION DISTRIBUTION IN LAOS (1968)

PROVINCE	AREA (km.²)	TOTAL POPULATION (Est.)	HMONG POPULATION (Est.)
Xieng Khouang	19,500	193,000	75,000
Luang Prabang	37,200	400,000	60,000
Houa Phanh	16,300	187,000	55,000
Sayaboury	18,400	188,000	30,000
Houa Khong	12,900	127,000	25,000
Phong Saly	15,800	112,000	20,000
Vientiane	14,400	312,000	15,000
Khammouane	26,400	229,000	8,000
Borikhane	6,200	45,000	5,000
TOTAL	**167,100**	**1,793,000**	**293,000**

SOURCE: National Statistics Bureau of Laos

Proper censuses were taken in the Xieng Khouang region in 1968. The province chief, Chao Saikham, kindly supplied the following results:

POPULATION BY DISTRICT AND ETHNIC GROUP (XIENG KHOUANG, 1968)

DISTRICT	TAI-LAO	KHMOU[10]	HMONG
Muong Khoune	22,463	—	
Muong Kham	33,991	—	—
Muong Mok	20,328	—	—
Muong Pek	5,788	—	—
Muong Pang Say	—	12,453	—
Muong Xieng Hong	—	—	17,552
Muong Vieng Fa	—	—	18,858
Muong Vang Say	—	—	22,109
Muong Nong Het	—	—	7,173
Muong Ngat	—	—	9,789
TOTAL	**82,570**	**12,453**	**75,481**

SOURCE: Xieng Khouang Provincial Office.

Three observations must be made regarding the figures in the two tables. First, the 1968 provincial census figures should not be considered definitive. They vary markedly with time, over the course of months and years, according to fluctuations in the political and military situation. Some very large population shifts, compelled by war and insecurity, are still going on in the region. Hmong living in areas outside the control of the Royal Lao Government are represented incompletely or, in some cases, omitted entirely. Second, although the various ethnic groups, highly diverse in language, habits and customs, are commingled geographically, they are not so administratively. Each of them is administered directly by district chiefs belonging to the same ethnic group, who are, in turn, supervised by the governor and the regional military commander. Finally, notable by their absence from the tables are the large numbers of Chinese, Indians and Vietnamese who were present in the province prior to 1960. These foreign colonies were either evacuated to Vientiane or "rescued" by Pathet Lao[11] and North Vietnamese troops, who have been solidly entrenched in the Plain of Jars since January 1961.[12]

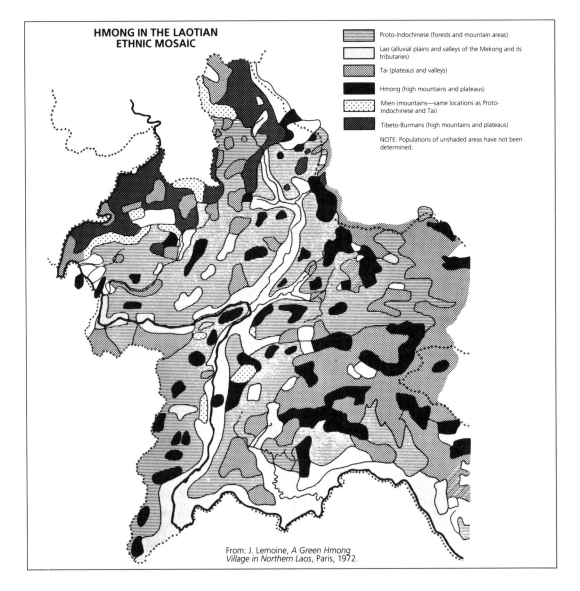

HMONG IN THE LAOTIAN ETHNIC MOSAIC

Proto-Indochinese (forests and mountain areas)

Lao (alluvial plains and valleys of the Mekong and its tributaries)

Tai (plateaus and valleys)

Hmong (high mountains and plateaus)

Mien (mountains—same locations as Proto-Indochinese and Tai)

Tibeto-Burmans (high mountains and plateaus)

NOTE: Populations of unshaded areas have not been determined.

From: J. Lemoine, *A Green Hmong Village in Northern Laos*, Paris, 1972.

SETTLEMENT PATTERNS　　The vast majority of Hmong (around 99 percent) live in rural areas. The beginnings, as yet embryonic, of urbanization can, however, be detected.

The Rural Setting　　The distribution of the Hmong population, like Laotian populations in general, is characterized by a very wide scattering of rural settlements, due primarily to the country's low population density (12 inhabitants/km.^{2} [31/mi.^{2}]) and to the life patterns of some strata of its population. The description that follows is that of the rural settlement pattern as it existed in normal times and as it can still be found in the provinces of Houa Khong, Phong Saly, Sayaboury, in some parts of the Luang Prabang mountains, and on the Phou Khao Khouai (Buffalo Horn Mountain) plateau north of Vientiane. This description is of particular significance since, for some eleven years now, war has profoundly disturbed the social structures of the populations of northeastern Laos, particularly in the provinces of Houa Phanh and Xieng Khouang.

Villages in Laos, especially in northern Laos, are typically inhabited by members of a single ethnic group. It is extremely rare to find a village in which different ethnic groups live together. Villages are connected to one another by trails, which the people keep in fairly good repair. During the rainy season, when vegetation is profuse and the forests are crawling with leeches, villagers do as little traveling as possible.

Mountain villages are generally smaller and the population more dispersed than in the plains. This configuration is largely attributable to the widespread practice of "slash-and-burn," or *rai*, agriculture, an extensive method of cultivation.[13] Located in relation to rice, corn and poppy fields, Hmong villages contain an average of 10 to 20 houses. Those having more than 50 houses are a rarity. Villages are often several hours', sometimes even several days', walk apart.

Because of the instability of village location, which changes periodically as fields become more and more distant, the Hmong in Laos have never cared much about building fine houses, since they will, in most cases, be used only temporarily. Built directly on the ground, with rough plank walls and grass-thatched or wooden-shingled roofs, Hmong houses have not changed much for centuries. Photographs of houses taken in 1920 are almost indistinguishable from those taken in 1970!

Since 1946 a few Hmong have entered the civil service and many more have sought out irrigated fields on which to settle down. Residential stability has enabled a good many of them to improve their dwellings. Some have adopted the Lao-style house on stilts; the more wealthy have built European-style houses. More and more, having a fine house is becoming a symbol of prestige and social advancement among the Hmong.

Urban Development　　As their economy gradually ceases to be limited to the family and village setting and as secondary and tertiary economic activities begin to emerge, people find a need to move together into large villages or towns whose growth, no longer bound to cultivated fields, can continue virtually without limit. This is the phenomenon of urbanization as it is occurring all over the world, including Laos, a phenomenon which has extended even into this country's highest mountains.

Since World War II the penetration of education into the mountain regions has brought rapid development to the Hmong. One sees more and more Hmong officials working side by side with their Lao counterparts in the various administrative offices of the provinces of northern Laos, most notably in Xieng Khouang. At the same time, a growing number of Hmong merchants are competing with Lao, Chinese and Vietnamese merchants. A new social class has been born, hastening the urbanization process which began, for the Hmong, in the outskirts of the city of Xieng Khouang (in the Phia Wat,[14] Wat Kang and Public Works Department neighborhoods) and at Lat Houang, a large cosmopolitan town which had a population of 1,500 in 1960.

Since 1961 the war has caused major population shifts and created a number of towns such as Pha Khao (pop. 7,000), Sam Thong (pop. 15,000)[15] and, above all, Long Cheng (pop. 30,000).[16] The growth of such centers inevitably requires the provision of a number of services: administration, health care, trade, education, etc. These services are all the more necessary since the occupants of these centers (mostly officials and military personnel) live on wage income.

These large population concentrations are, however, simply the result of refugees seeking a measure of security. They cannot form the basis for urban development, partly because of their temporary nature and partly because of their geographic location – mountainous terrain without adequate means of transportation. They will disappear spontaneously with the return of peace. The Hmong, after all, like the Laotian people in general, belong to the rural environment with which they live in close communion. But urbanization has taken hold of the mountain peoples' ways. They are now aware of the need to change their traditional societies and adapt them to the exigencies of modern life.

POPULATION CHANGES

DEMOGRAPHIC CHANGES

Birth Rate   Under normal peacetime conditions, the birth rate among the Hmong is relatively high: 45 to 53 per 1000.[17] This high rate is due partly to the fact that it "is subject only to the unfettered workings of nature and, insofar as the health of the population of child-bearing age is improving and free of the ancient epidemic scourges, the rates are reaching record highs."[18] It is also due to the attitudes of the Hmong themselves, for whom having many children is a blessing. It is common even today to find women who have had ten, twelve or even more children.

The birth rate is dropping significantly in some regions of the kingdom such as the northeast. The decline coincides with the spread of the war that has raged there for more than ten years. A survey of 3,165 refugees from Houa Phanh and Xieng Khouang provinces taken in 1970 showed a birth rate of 37 per thousand.[19] The reason for this lower rate was that almost all of the able-bodied men were either in the army or in the resistance forces and that many of them had died.[20]

Mortality Rate   The unhealthfulness of certain mountain regions infested with *Anopheles* mosquitoes, ignorance of basic concepts of hygiene, and the persistence of an archaic mentality all contribute to a relatively high mortality rate, particularly infant mortality, among the Hmong. Besides these factors, they have been stricken with the greatest plague of the century: war.

A survey of 1,065 Hmong in the Sayaboury region taken between January 1968 and January 1969 recorded a death rate of 17 per thousand.[21] The rate is certainly much higher in Houa Phanh and Xieng Khouang provinces, perhaps as high as 20 to 25 per thousand or more. The effects of war, malnutrition and the illnesses caused by repeated uprooting are incalculable and would explain the high mortality rate in northeastern Laos. However, it is an exaggeration to say that "the [Hmong] population has been half decimated by the war."[22] The presence of the Lao, Phouan and Khmou who are fighting alongside the Hmong is often, through ignorance or pretense, ignored, with the result that in this part of the country all war casualties are considered to be Hmong.

Growth of the Hmong Population   Taking all of these factors into account, the growth rate of the Hmong population in northern Laos can be estimated to have been around 25 to 30 per thousand in 1970. The growth rate was probably lower in the extreme northeast, a region especially hard hit by the war.

MIGRATIONS   From the time they were driven from the plains of the Huang He River in China, the Hmong have never known a stable existence. They have continually adapted to new geographic, climatic, economic and political situations. Their relatively recent mode of semi-nomadic farming,[23] their systems of social organization, the often catastrophic epidemics and that eternal plague of war maintain a constant state of migration among the Hmong, thus their wide dispersion across Southeast Asia. Maps of the distribution of Hmong settlements in Xieng Khouang province in the 1920s, the 1950s and in 1968-69 provide a typical example.

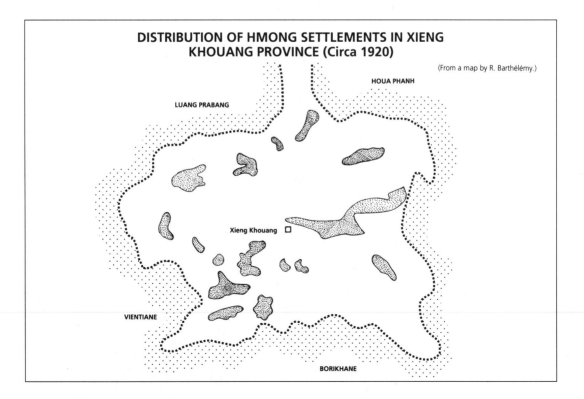

DISTRIBUTION OF HMONG SETTLEMENTS IN XIENG KHOUANG PROVINCE (Circa 1920)

(From a map by R. Barthélémy.)

HOUA PHANH

LUANG PRABANG

Xieng Khouang □

VIENTIANE

BORIKHANE

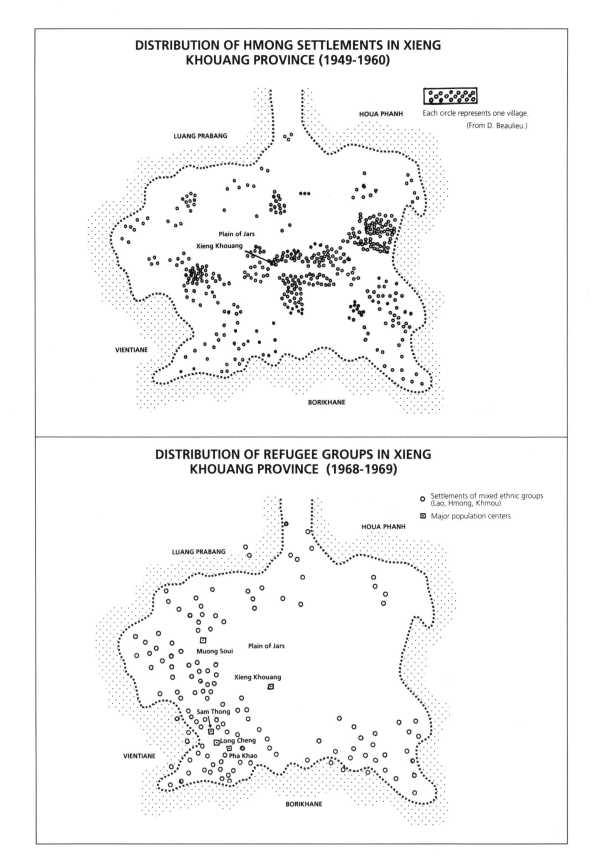

DISTRIBUTION OF HMONG SETTLEMENTS IN XIENG KHOUANG PROVINCE (1949-1960)

HOUA PHANH

LUANG PRABANG

Each circle represents one village.

(From D. Beaulieu.)

Plain of Jars

Xieng Khouang

VIENTIANE

BORIKHANE

DISTRIBUTION OF REFUGEE GROUPS IN XIENG KHOUANG PROVINCE (1968-1969)

○ Settlements of mixed ethnic groups
(Lao, Hmong, Khmou)

▣ Major population centers

HOUA PHANH

LUANG PRABANG

Muong Soui

Plain of Jars

Xieng Khouang

Sam Thong

Long Cheng

Pha Khao

VIENTIANE

BORIKHANE

Migrations Due to Agricultural Practices   As we will see in Chapter Four, the *rai* system of agriculture generally practiced nowadays by the Hmong in Laos requires a balance among arable land, population growth and forest fallow period. If this equilibrium cannot be maintained, regular movements of the population to new locations will be required.

Migrations Due to Patterns of Social Organization   Hmong political and social organization is based primarily on the clan and the extended family. All of the people in a specific clan (having the same patronymic) share ties, duties and special taboos which are very important in traditional ceremonies of ancestor veneration and particularly in funeral rites. This is why Hmong always try to live near fellow clanspeople while at the same time maintaining close ties with other clans from which they have taken wives. If they feel too isolated, Hmong will leave a village dominated by another clan, taking their goods and livestock with them, in search of their *kwv tij*, relatives whose ties with them are of clan membership rather than merely of blood. Thus social organization, bound up with religious practices, constitutes a very real factor in Hmong migrations.

Migrations Due to Epidemics   In the absence of modern medicine, catastrophic epidemics of smallpox and malaria often sweep like "evil spirits" through entire villages, nearly decimating them. For the Hmong, who understand nothing about these swift deaths which spread like wildfire to engulf whole regions, the only way to appease the evil spirits is to leave the area, but not before sacrificing chickens, pigs and even buffalo to the spirits as amends to them for "trespassing on their sacred sanctuary" and as entreaties to desist from pursuing the people further with their curses. This explains why entire villages are sometimes seen wandering along the mountain trails, driving their pigs and cattle ahead of them, carrying whatever is left of their belongings, in quest of other less hostile "country" where they can live their lives normally, without being beset by misfortune and mourning.

Migrations Due to War   War and the insecurity it causes constitute the last and by far the most important and most violent factor underlying large Hmong migrations. The first such displacement took place in Xieng Khouang province during the First Indochina War, which went on for eight years between the French and the Viet Minh movement[24] and ended with the historic battle of Dien Bien Phu and the 1954 Geneva agreements. But the largest and the most painful so far, was, without a doubt, the exodus that followed the resumption of hostilities in northeastern Laos in 1961. It affected almost the entire populations of the provinces of Houa Phanh, Luang Prabang and, above all, Xieng Khouang, the location of the famous Plain of Jars.

By early 1969 the whole of western Xieng Khouang province, particularly the southwest, was one huge refugee camp for Lao, Phouan, Tai Deng,[25] Khmou and Hmong from Houa Phanh province and the Phouan plateau. Dozens of centers set up to accommodate these refugees dotted the mountains of this region. The largest was Long Cheng, which in November 1969 had nearly 30,000 inhabitants, 60 percent of them Hmong, 20 percent Phouan and Tai Deng, and 20 percent Khmou. Sam Thong, the second largest town, had a population of 15,000, of which 50 percent were Hmong, 40 percent Phouan and Tai Deng, and 10 percent Khmou.

What we saw with our own eyes in the Long Cheng-Sam Thong region[26] contradicts the somewhat tendentious opinions reported in the press that the transfer of these populations was nothing but a CIA maneuver designed to corral the Lao populations along the lines of the strategic hamlets in South Vietnam. The truth is that for the Hmong, as for all the populations of northeastern Laos, the political situation compels constant movement as battlefields move and areas under rocket and artillery bombardment shift. In all of Laos, only Sayaboury province continues to enjoy relative stability. The people there still seem to be living at peace. Because of its fortunate geographic situation, it offers, for the moment, hospitality to those who have lost everything and left everything.

SOCIAL AND POLITICAL ORGANIZATION

Hmong social and political organization is based on structures that are at once traditional and modern.

TRADITIONAL ORGANIZATION

The Hmong mentality has, through the ages, been profoundly steeped in the concept of group. What counts is most often the group – the family, the clan – rather than the individual, whose sojourn on earth is a brief one.

THE FAMILY   The entire group of people who are descended from a common ancestor live together insofar as possible and form a community of interests which girls are the only ones to leave, when they marry and enter a similar community. Thus very large families of ten, twenty or more people may be found living under the same roof and under the leadership of the beloved "pater familias." A recent survey found that the average size of the basic social unit among the Hmong was 6.5 persons.[27] A comparable number for highly developed countries is around 3 or 4.

Among the Hmong, polygamy, early marriage (especially of girls) and certain other cultural practices profoundly affect the matrimonial structure of the population. The proportion of married men and women approaches 100 percent. Most marriages occur between the ages of 18-20 for boys and 14-16 for girls. This precocity is explained not only by physiology but by sociological and economic considerations as well. A married couple are considered "mature" people worthy of some respect; the arrival of children further increases their social status. Emancipating the Hmong woman will, of necessity, involve delaying the age of marriage. Young educated Hmong do, in fact, tend to marry later, but the influence of this factor is still minimal and, at the moment, is seen only in certain urban areas such as Vientiane, Luang Prabang, Sayaboury and Long Cheng.

Although monogamy is the general rule, polygamy is still a fairly widespread phenomenon among the Hmong. A survey taken in the Hmong village of Ban Houei Souai, located about 32 kilometers from the town of Sayaboury, showed that, of a sample of 54 married men, 45 (83%) had one wife, eight (15%) had two, and only one (2%) had three wives.[28] Polygamy generally begins about the age of thirty, a point at which the gender ratio has dipped in favor of females. The war is contributing to the spread of polygamy: since the beginning of their extensive participation in the conflict in 1961, it has created thousands of widows among the Hmong.

An analysis of spouse selection reveals some specific features of Hmong sociology. Among the Hmong, members of the same clan, being considered "brothers and sisters," cannot marry. On the other hand, a fairly high degree of consanguinity does exist due to the relatively frequent practice of marriage between cross-cousins (the daughter of a brother to the son of a sister or vice-versa). The practice of the levirate, now dying out, allows a younger brother to marry his widowed sister-in-law for reasons of inheritance and clan solidarity.[29] Finally, a feature common to all of Laos is the rarity of intermarriage between different ethnic groups.

The spread of education into every social and economic stratum is playing a role of the greatest importance in the mental transformation of all of the Laotian populations. The trend toward delayed marriage and the increasing frequency of mixed marriages between ethnic groups, particularly between Hmong and Lao and Hmong and Khmou, are some of its earliest indications. Education will probably lead to a decline in the incidence of polygamy as well.

THE CLAN   In addition to the ubiquitous family group, the Hmong are divided into patrilineal clans. There are 19 such clans in Laos: the Chang, Cheng, Chu, Fang, Hang, Her, Khang, Kong, Kue, Lor or Lo, Ly or Lee, Moua, Phang, Tang, Thao, Vue, Xiong, Vang and Yang. Children are considered members of their father's clan and take its name. The mother is of no consequence insofar as clan membership is concerned; she counts for nothing in the handing down of the family name. The clan is thus made up of a male ancestor, his sons and daughters, and the children of his sons.

An important difference between the family and the clan can be seen at once: the family has a fairly elastic character while the clan is a fixed entity. Divorce and migration may scatter the family, but clan ties are permanent. Every individual automatically takes the patronymic name at birth, bears it until death, and, if a man, passes it on to his children. However, because of the practice of clan exogamy, the same rule that cements the unity of the group also leads to its partial dissolution when its daughters marry.

From this stems a corollary: the clan, though excluding half of the blood relatives, is nevertheless a much more inclusive group than the family in that it actually recognizes bonds of common ancestry. Whereas in Western societies a third or fourth cousin is practically nonfunctioning as a member of the family, for the Hmong, thanks to the permanent nature of the clan bond, even the most distant clan relative is always considered a member of the same unit. He is called by a name which he shares with all its members, allowing no doubt as to his clan affiliation.

The feeling of community that emerges is reflected in kinship terminology. Clan members of the same generation call each other brothers and sisters. From there it is only a short step to the feeling that marriage between members of the same clan is somehow incestuous, leading to the Hmong practice of clan exogamy. The clan form of social organization creates among the Hmong a system of traditional leadership based essentially on its influence.

The Clan System of Leadership   It is striking, upon first glance, how, in traditional Hmong society, women are relegated entirely to the background in matters of politics. Only men participate in meetings having to do with the governance of the group. The Hmong woman never takes part in these discussions, which often directly affect her interests, and she cannot vote in an assembly, which she may attend only as an observer. This results in severe inequality between the genders, an inequality which educated Hmong women are denouncing more and more energetically as they demand their rights.

Traditionally, Hmong society requires that males, the agents of hereditary transmission of the ancestral line, play the principal roles. One finds here an egalitarian concept of society but one that is not without a relative hierarchization. The coexistence of an authoritarian system and a democratic one can be explained by family-based conceptions of society. Authoritarian powers correspond to those which, in the bosom of the family, are devolved upon the father. Egalitarian relations among children, on the other hand, are the very image of the modern concept of democracy, whose essential attribute is equality among individuals. In assemblies and meetings, however, the old men always cast the deciding vote. More experienced and wiser, they are generally listened to and their advice is almost always followed. In the words of a Hmong proverb, "They have eaten more rice [an allusion to age], they have seen more things, and they have done more thinking." But the authority of the old is coming under increasing challenge from the young to whom education has opened up wider horizons.

Hmong leaders are chosen by group suffrage. They are nominated from among the clan's most intelligent, capable, generous, influential and, generally, oldest members. If some disagreement within the community produces two candidates for the honor, an election is held in which only the village elders and adult males take part. The person who receives a majority of the votes becomes chief.

Traditionally, every village or hamlet is led by a headman, assisted by one or more notables, preferably chosen from among the spokesmen of the village's families or clans. The headman is the guest of honor at most ceremonies surrounding births, marriages and deaths and presides over rites honoring the village's patron spirit. With the aid of his advisers, he finds amicable settlements for disputes among members of the community. He organizes collective work on projects of common interest such as the building of bamboo aqueducts (which deliver water to the door of every house for the needs of its inhabitants and, on occasion, for the operation of rice mills), the building of houses (the entire village usually lends a hand in building a new house for one of its members), the maintenance of the inter-village trails, and so on.

In Hmong society there is a definite and well-respected hierarchy. It governs various groups ranging from an agglomeration of a few hamlets to all the villages in a territory of some size. According to Moréchand, "A clan chief can rule over an entire region, thanks to the influence he acquires through the mediation of his clan and his clientele."[30]

An Example of Clan Governance: The Hmong Administration at Nong Het in the Nineteenth Century   After leaving south China and coming through the "country of the Tai" in North Vietnam, the Hmong settled in the principality of Xieng Khouang in northeastern Laos.[31] They accepted the jurisdiction of the Phouan princes who reigned over the region. Little by little, the peaceable temperament and loyalty of the Hmong won the confidence and favor of the area's rulers, who granted them local administration, supervised by the authorities in the Muong Kham district where the immigrants had established compact settlements. It was at this time that the heads of the great Hmong families in the Nong Het mountains, a region bordering Vietnam, were recognized with the official title of *kaitong*.[32] Lor, Ly, Yang, Vang, and Moua *kaitong* governed their respective clans. Heads of families of lesser importance were called *photong, chongkone, chongcha* and *xaophay*.[33] In return, the Hmong officials had to pay the Phouan authorities regular tribute in the form of game (boars, deer, etc.), bear gall (highly prized in traditional medicine), elephant tusks and honey, as well as some of their small livestock (pigs, capons) and a few kilograms of opium.

These administrative measures were, for the most part, wise and realistic. They did nothing more than render the Hmong more confident and more receptive to gradual integration into the communities of the Phouan principality of Xieng Khouang. As time went by, however, major reforms brought about profound changes in the administrative structures set up by the Phouan authorities in the Hmong mountains.

MOVING TOWARD MODERN PATTERNS OF GOVERNMENT

The vicissitudes of history gradually led to the creation, alongside traditional Hmong structures, of another form of administration patterned along more modern lines. This form first appeared under the French protectorate and is still evolving within the developing Laotian nation.

HMONG ADMINISTRATION UNDER THE FRENCH PROTECTORATE

Appointment of the First Hmong *Tasseng*   Negotiations between the Franco-Lao authorities and Hmong leaders following the first Hmong uprising in 1896 led to the appointment of Moua *kaitong* as the first Hmong *tasseng* (sub-district chief). It was his duty to govern all the Hmong *kaitong* and other chiefs in the principality of Xieng Khouang. However, it was the bloody rebellion of 1919-1921 which, more than anything else, led the General Government of Indochina to make sweeping changes in the administration of the Hmong populations in North Vietnam and northern Laos.

Autonomous Administration   "Laos," wrote R. Barthélémy, head of the Civil Services in Indochina, in 1922,

> is apparently organized for administrative purposes as though it were populated solely by Laotians.[34] The laws are Laotian and so are the officials who apply them; and the Provincial Council, the embryo of our future Consultative Chamber, has never included a single repre-

sentative of the mountain races. Fixed in the valleys from the beginning because of logistic necessity, we have little by little centralized the indigenous administration into the hands of those who were nearest by. And yet several races live in Laos, and how very different they are in customs, language, habitat and religion! Our spirit of centralization, when it impelled us to impose Laotian law on everyone, impelled us into injustice!

Again, it was in a spirit of exaggerated simplification that we set up the pagoda schools; by making the monk an official teacher, we gave the Buddhists a total monopoly on education. This oversimplification, on the contrary, increases our administrative difficulties because, to all those non-Buddhists who live in the mountains and are still illiterate, orders can only be transmitted verbally; they are ill-understood and often even ill-transmitted.

We have unknowingly, in our obsession with centralization, created an aristocracy of peoples; but what mindless misery we have made for the second-rank races for whom it is so very difficult to come to us!

And yet sometimes they will break out ... (The Hmong rebellion of 1919-1921) was a warning. Let us bear this sincerely in mind. It is permissible to err but not to persevere once one has recognized one's error. Let us voice the wish:

1. That the Provincial Council must have a representative of each race;

2. That each race have its own officials, elected or chosen from among its members;

3. That teachers from all the races be trained and schools be set up in the mountains outside the pagodas;

4. That there be no centralization of the courts, that the local laws remain in effect so that every man will be judged by his peers, according to ancestral custom, with simply a provision for appeal to the French authorities on a voluntary basis.[35]

To what extent was this wish granted? We know that until 1945 the provincial councils contained not a single representative of the ethnic minorities, a fact that remains true in most of the provinces of present-day (1970) Laos. Furthermore, no mountain schools were built until 1939 and even then only in Xieng Khouang. Only points two and four were partially implemented.

"In order to deprive them [the Hmong] of any pretext for revolt in the future," a special administrative statute granted them district and local autonomy without Vietnamese, Tai or Lao intermediaries, which was what they had been demanding. "The Government of the Protectorate has decided that the Miao race will henceforth not be subordinate to any other race. The Miao will therefore govern themselves in the future, like the Laotians, the Tho[36] and the Annamites,[37] under the supervision of the Government of the Protectorate...," wrote F. M. Savina, a French Catholic missionary to Vietnam and Laos, in 1930.[38] It was not until then that there began to be large numbers of Hmong *tasseng*, or subdistrict chiefs, all across the northern part of French Indochina: in the regions of Dong Van, Ha Giang and Dien Bien Phu in North Vietnam and in the Muong Ngoi (Luang Prabang) region and on the Xieng Khouang plateau in northern Laos.

Prior to World War II there were 17 Hmong *tasseng* in Laos, all of them in Xieng Khouang province. This number rose to 24 under the administrative decentralization policy. At that time, the political ladder of the Hmong rose no higher than sub-district chief. The mountain peoples of the other provinces of Laos had to be content with *nai ban*, or village chiefs, who reported directly to Lao *tasseng*. Their situation has not changed greatly since then, with the exceptions of Houa Phanh province, which, along with one Hmong *chao muong* (1966-68), has now been granted Hmong *tasseng* and *nai kong* positions, though only since 1961, and then only for patently political reasons,[39] and Sayaboury province, which also has one Hmong *chao muong*. Similarly, Phou Khao Khouai in Vientiane province recently had a Hmong *tasseng* appointed, with authority over all the Hmong villages in the government-controlled zone of that region.

The Khmou, or "Kha," are, in general, one of the most underprivileged ethnic groups in Laos. They are flagrantly discriminated against in every area; their integration is seldom considered desirable by the dominant society, which continues to treat them with disdain. It is essential that the leaders of the country adopt a more understanding attitude toward this group and take measures to close the social gap between the plains dwellers and the mountain peoples, who are all too often neglected. This gap, which was not nearly so visible only fifty years ago, has widened with the growth and development that have benefited all but exclusively the plains populations. If this situation is allowed to continue it could have very unfortunate consequences for the future of the Laotian nation.

ADMINISTRATIVE ORGANIZATION IN INDEPENDENT LAOS

Since 1947 the kingdom of Laos has had a constitution. It calls for the integration of the Hmong, Khmou, Mien and other ethnic minorities into an independent Laotian nation and sets forth a policy of administrative decentralization tailored to the country's geographical configuration. This decentralization "will facilitate administration and guarantee the individuality of each province. It will also be the inhabitants' chance to manage their own affairs in the setting of their local communities."[40] Let us see how the Laotian administration functions and to what degree there is effective participation by all Laotian ethnic groups.

Regional Administration

Khoueng (Province)   Laos is made up of 16 provinces, or *khoueng*, each with its own governmental authorities: the *chao khoueng* (province chief) and the provincial advisory council. Appointed and removed by royal decree, the *chao khoueng*, with guidance from the Minister of the Interior, acts as general manager of the government officials in his province, represents the national interests, and exercises administrative supervision over the communities in his territory. The provincial advisory council, of which the *chao khoueng* is the president, is not a permanent assembly. It holds one mandatory session annually for the Oath of Allegiance ceremony and can be summoned into extraordinary session by the *chao khoueng*.

Muong (District)   Laotian provinces are divided geographically into districts (*muong*), each headed by a *chao muong*. The task of the *chao muong* is to provide direct contact between the provincial government and the rural population through elected officials (*tasseng* and *nai ban*). *Chao muong* are nominated by the *chao khoueng* and confirmed by the Minister of the

Interior. Depending on the distribution of the population, a *muong* may be further subdivided into two or three *kong* headed by *nai kong*, who assist the *chao muong* in his administrative duties. The *nai kong* are appointed by the *chao muong* and confirmed in their offices by the *chao khoueng*.

Administration of Rural Areas   Each *muong* typically contains several sub-districts which are themselves made up of several villages.

Tasseng (Sub-District)   At the head of each sub-district (*tasseng*) is a sub-district chief, also called a *tasseng*. *Tasseng* are elected by the village chiefs and members of the village councils of the sub-district and confirmed by the *chao khoueng* of the province. A sub-district advisory council assists the *tasseng* with administration. A *tasseng* may have jurisdiction over some 1,000 to 4,000 people living in 30 or more villages.

Ban (Village)   Villages, typically comprising 15 to 150 households, are under the authority of village chiefs, called *nai ban*, elected by universal adult male suffrage and confirmed by the *chao muong*. In each village there is an advisory council over which the village chief presides.

ADMINISTRATIVE ORGANIZATION:
MUONG VANG SAY
(Xieng Khouang Province, 1973)[41]

SUB-DISTRICT (*tasseng*)	# OF VILLAGES	POPULATION
Pha Say	35	3,334
Pha Phay	21	1,477
Na Vang	37	4,015
Pha No	21	1,635
Pha Pong	29	3,127
Muong Pha	33	2,367
Pha Khao	13	1,195
Phou Sangob	23	1,052
Pha Lou	16	1,407
Thong Hak	15	1,216
Phou Khe	20	1,478
Phou Houa Sang	12	887
Tham Heup	24	2,746
TOTAL	**299**	**25,936**

This is the Laotian administrative structure as described on paper. In practice it operates quite differently. It turns out that not all *khoueng* have functioning provincial councils and that there are also a good many *muong* and *tasseng* without advisory councils. Furthermore, the actual power is in the hands of prominent local families whose "feudal" nature the Pathet Lao so roundly condemn. Democracy has never existed in Laos, where "the elephant's foot crushes the bird's beak." This thousand-year-old Lao proverb is an incisive statement of a social problem that may well impede the country's future for years to come.

Equally deplorable is the incompetence and professional irresponsibility displayed by various government officials. Most officials have had no instruction in civil administration, and staff training leaves a great deal to be desired.[42] The lack of anything like a registry office (for births, deaths, etc.) speaks volumes about the administrative chaos in Laos, where corruption, the "shameful disease," is far from unknown. When Phoumi Vongvichit speaks of a "rotten, unjust" society, he is not engaging in mere demagoguery.[43]

Given these conditions, is it proper to conclude that the decentralization policy in Laos has been a failure? What impact has it had on the minority ethnic groups as a whole? Is it contributing to ethnic integration and nation-building?

Administrative Decentralization Policies and the Laotian Minorities

The administrative decentralization policy is not being implemented to the same degree everywhere in the country. Long confined to the plains regions, it is now beginning to reach the hitherto neglected mountain areas. An exception is the Xieng Khouang plateau, where the Hmong have long fought for recognition of their rights.

The demands of the Hmong, whom World War II suddenly wrenched out of their accustomed isolation, led in 1947 to the establishment of new Hmong *tasseng* and of two Hmong *nai kong*, a position reserved until that time for plains people. Even more significant was the appointment of Touby Lyfoung as deputy to the *chao khoueng* of Xieng Khouang and, as such, "*Chao Muong* of the Meo Population."[44] This process accelerated with the election of Toulia Lyfoung to the Constitutional and National Assemblies and the appointment to the King's Council of Tougeu Lyfoung,[45] who later succeeded his brother Toulia in the National Assembly and who, for the majority of years since 1960, has been the Director General of the Ministry of Justice in the Royal Lao Government.

Access to public office for Hmong has been a very important milestone on the road to integration of the ethnic minorities into the Laotian nation. This integration has, however, encountered many obstacles and difficulties due to the plains peoples' attitude of superiority and the resulting frustration of the mountain peoples, who are, on the whole, still living on the fringes of the dominant society. "Theoretically," writes Bernard Fall,

> Laos operates on the basis of equality extended to the mountain tribes. In reality, there has long been severe discrimination practiced against them in the areas of education, public works and access to public employment. Meanwhile, the measures that have been taken, such as the inclusion of Meo leaders like Touby Lyfoung in the government administration, have been nothing more than last-minute palliatives.[46]

The following are a few illustrative examples, the first of them related by Touby Lyfoung himself.

The Khmou leaders of the Luang Prabang region, having long since realized that the Lao *tasseng* under whose jurisdiction they operated not only paid practically no attention to their lot but were, in fact, heavily exploiting them, decided one day in 1948 to go to the royal capital and ask that the *tasseng*, all of whom were Lao merchants living in the city, be replaced by leaders of their own ethnic group. Their request was flatly denied, and the provincial authorities of Luang Prabang actually had the Khmou notables arrested. It took all of Touby Lyfoung's influence to persuade the court to free the innocent prisoners. That was done immediately, but there the matter rested.

The "Tougeu Affair" was another symptom of Laotian social uneasiness. It broke out in October 1964 and took on astonishing scope, triggering a general strike among court officials all over the kingdom. Its gravity may be summarized in the following words, taken from a letter addressed to Tougeu Lyfoung and signed "The Deputy to the Chairman of the Officials' Strike Committee":

> The Meo have no right to work as officials of the Ministry of Justice. They are foreigners.[47] Living in the mountains, they are too ignorant to work with the Lao. To be worthy of the name, Laos must be ruled and governed by the Lao. The Meo have no country; they live as parasites on Laos. We ask you, Mr. Tougeu Lyfoung, to resign your office (as Director General of Justice)....[48]

Prince Souvanna Phouma, prime minister of the Royal Lao Government, after conferring with political and military leaders, could find no professional fault with Tougeu Lyfoung and, furthermore, threatened the striking court officials with dismissal if they did not return to work. Tougeu Lyfoung was made special advisor to the Minister of Justice and, in 1967, was persuaded by Prince Souvanna Phouma to resume his position as Director General of Justice.

"The minorities," writes Touxoua Lyfoung, a master's degree candidate at the Bordeaux University School of Law and Economic Sciences,

> have never sought to challenge political power. They placed their trust in those whose duty it was to govern the country. All they asked, and all they still ask, is *justice*, a more equal justice.... In Attopeu province, the Kha account for 80 percent of the population, yet there has never been *a single* Kha province chief. The same holds true for Luang Prabang, where the Kha make up 45 percent of the population, exactly the same as the Lao, and for Xieng Khouang, where the Meo comprise more than 50 percent of the population.[49]

The current war has prompted the Royal Lao Government to adopt a more flexible policy toward the ethnic minorities in order to compete with the Pathet Lao, each side seeking to consolidate its military and political positions. This is the reason for the creation, in Xieng Khouang province, of five new *muong*, four Hmong and one Khmou. Hmong and Khmou have become more involved in national political affairs. Touby Lyfoung, a Hmong, served as Minister of Justice (1960), Minister of Social Welfare (1961-1963) and Minister of Health (1963), becoming Inspector General in the Ministry of the Interior in 1965.[50] In 1972, a Hmong and a Khmou from Xieng Khouang province and a Hmong from Houa Phanh province were elected to the National Assembly in Vientiane. With the exception of the two Lyfoung brothers, however, since 1964 (to 1973) there have been no representatives of the ethnic minorities at the highest executive levels of the Royal Lao Government.

For its part, the Neo Lao Hak Sat[51] boasts of "the elaboration of a union, an identity of views among the nationalities on the basis of equality and mutual assistance." Its central committee includes Faydang Lo(bliayao) and Sithon Kommadam, representatives, respectively, of the Hmong and the Lao Theung[52] populations living in the so-called "liberated zones." But what real power do these representatives of the people have in so centralized and rigid a system? What assessment can be made of freedom of expression, the fundamental condition for human fulfillment? Will democracy be better implemented in that part of Laos than in the country as a whole?

In order to permit the entire Laotian population, whether plains dwellers or mountain people, to derive full benefit from the administrative decentralization policy the Royal Lao Government asserts that it intends to pursue, we would take the liberty of expressing the following hopes:

- that all *chao muong* and *nai kong* be elected by electoral colleges consisting of the sub-district chiefs, the village chiefs and the members of the village councils of each district,

- that all *chao khoueng* be elected by electoral colleges consisting of all the district chiefs, their *nai kong* assistants, the sub-district and village chiefs, and all members of the provincial, district and local councils in the province, and

- that the major ethnic groups be represented at the highest executive levels of the Laotian government.

One cannot "integrate a master and a slave" without first changing their social status. National integration cannot be simply a relationship of authority and ethnic domination. It must reflect the *determination of all ethnic groups to live together on the basis of equality*. The problem of equality is of utmost importance to the prospects for the development of Laos. All the rebellions waged in the past, whether by the "Kha" in the south[53] or the "Meo" in the north, have been aimed not at independence but at that same equality, the basic principle of a genuine modern nation.

FOOTNOTES:

[1] French Union, association of former French colonies.

[2] Leroi Gourhan and P. Poirier, *Ethnology of the French Union*, Vol. II, Presse Universitaire de France, Paris, 1953, p. 647.

[3] The estimated Hmong population in North Vietnam in 1986 was approximately 400,000, living in nine provinces of northern Vietnam. (*The Minority Ethnic Groups of Vietnam* [Foreign Language Edition], Hanoi, 1986.)

[4] Guy Moréchand, "Hmong Shamanism," *Bulletin de l'Ecole Française d'Extrême-Orient* (BEFEO), Volume 16, Paris, 1968, p. 60.

[5] Jacques Lemoine, *Social Organization in a Green Hmong Village*, doctoral dissertation, College of Liberal Arts and Humanities, University of Paris, 1968.

[6] The Yao actually call themselves Mien or Iu Mien, which means man or human being.

[7] Laos, Department of Planning, "Laos in 1969: A Geographical and Historical Presentation; Economic and Financial Situation," *1969-1974 Master Plan*, Vientiane, July 1969, p. 2.

[8] This investigation was limited to areas of the country controlled by the Royal Lao Government. Estimates based on observations in these areas have been corrected to account for the approximately 1/3 of the Hmong population living in areas presently under the control of the Pathet Lao.

[9] The figure of 600,000 Hmong suggested by *Actualité* (a Lao-language magazine) is an obvious exaggeration. ("The Meo Nationality in Laos," *Actualité*, No. 13, Vientiane, 1971, p. 41 ff.)

[10] Commonly subsumed under the designation "Kha," the Khmou actually number around 23,000 in Xieng Khouang province. Half of them seem to have been included in the population estimates of the four Tai-Lao districts.

[11] Lao State or Land of the Lao. Founded in 1950 by Laotian communists (including Prince Souphanouvong), the Pathet Lao was a military and political resistance movement associated with the Viet Minh. The term came to be synonymous with the Laotian communist party (actually named the Lao People's Party). Throughout the 1960s and 1970s, the Pathet Lao, with advice and material assistance from the Soviet Union and the People's Republic of China and troops from North Vietnam, led the armed resistance against the US-supported Royal Lao Government and eventually took over the country of Laos in 1975.

[12] North Vietnamese intervention in Laos has been publicly denounced on several occasions by Prince Souvanna Phouma, head of the Royal Lao Government.

[13] Is this book, the term "rai" is used to describe both the extensive mode of cultivation itself and a field in which this type of agriculture is practiced.

[14] "Wat" is the Lao term for a Buddhist temple compound.

[15] In March 1970, Sam Thong had a 200-bed hospital, a large elementary school and a high school, all of which were completely destroyed by the war.

[16] Population figures as of 1969.

[17] Khammeung Tounalom (Chief Surgeon, Sene Souk Hospital), personal communication, Sam Thong, 1969.

[18] George Pierre, *Panorama of the Present-Day World*, Presse Universitaire de France, Paris, 1965, p. 19.

[19] Cf. p. 13.

[20] According to one official source, from 1961 to 1975 the war in the Second Military Region (Xieng Khouang and Houa Phanh provinces) resulted in more than 15,000 casualties among government troops alone, half of them Hmong and the rest Lao and Khmou. Hmong and Lao observers, however, reported as many as 30,000 casualties among General Vang Pao's troops, with the result that boys as young as 12 years old were drafted into the war effort.

[21] Survey conducted by the Muong Phieng Health Service at the request of the author.

[22] Jean-Claude Pomonti, *Le Monde*, Paris, October 21, 1970.

[23] It is said that in ancient times the Hmong were sedentary farmers on the plains of the Huang He (Yellow) River in China.

[24] The Viet Minh, short for Vietnam Dôc Lâp Dông Minh (League for the Independence of Vietnam), was a communist-led umbrella organization founded in 1941 by Ho Chi Minh to fight for the independence of Vietnam, first from the Japanese and then from the French. Although formally absorbed into the Vietnamese Communist Party in 1951, elements of the Viet Minh continued to play a major part in the military and political upheavals in South Vietnam (through the Viet Cong), Laos (through the Pathet Lao) and Cambodia (through the Khmer Rouge).

[25] The Tai Deng (Red Tai), like the Phouan, are an ethnic group related to the lowland Lao. They speak a language similar to Lao and live in the highlands.

[26] Personal visit, 1969.

[27] Cf. p. 13.

[28] Muong Phieng Health Service survey, 1968-69.

[29] Marriage of an older brother to his younger brother's widow, however, is strictly prohibited.

[30] Moréchand, *Hmong Shamanism*, p. 65.

[31] The Hmong settled in other areas besides Xieng Khouang, but the Hmong on the Phouan plateau of this region were to play a particularly important historical role.

[32] The term "kaitong" is a Chinese-Vietnamese honorary title equivalent to the present-day position of *tasseng*, or sub-district chief, in Laos.

[33] Honorific titles of lower rank than *kaitong*.

[34] The term "Laotian" here means the Lao ethnic group rather than Laotian citizens, since the nation of Laos had yet to be born.

[35] R. Barthélémy, "Comments on Administrative Decentralization and a Racial Policy for Laos," in *Comptes Rendus et Rapports du Congres de l'Organisation Coloniale*, Vol. I, 1922, pp. 139-140.

[36] A branch of the Tai.

[37] An historical name for the Vietnamese.

[38] F. M. Savina, *History of the Miao*, Imprimerie de la Société des Missions Etrangères de Paris, Hong Kong, 1930, p. 238.

[39] Cf. note 44 below.

[40] Lebel de Chateauvieux, *Commentary on the Laotian Constitution*, Report No. 11, Institut International d'Administration Publique (IIAP), Paris, 1948, p. 28.

[41] Xiong Pao Ly (former *nai kong* in the Muong Vang Say district), personal communication, Saint Paul, Minnesota, February 1992.

[42] It is not only the ordinary people, government staff and mid-level officials who are lacking in civic spirit, but even more so the top leaders of the country, whose national consciousness has yet to be proven.

[43] Vongvichit, *Laos and the Victorious Struggle*, p. 180.

[44] In 1966 the position of *Chao Muong* of the Meo Population was abolished and replaced by five Hmong *chao muong*.

[45] The King's Council is the quasi-legislative upper house of the two-part National Congress. Its functions are to review and amend legislation originating in the National Assembly (the lower house), submit it to the King and advise him on its ratification.

[46] Bernard B. Fall, "The Problem of Governing Ethnic Minorities in Cambodia, Laos, and Both Zones of Vietnam," in *Political Problems of Poly-ethnic States*, P/PR/12, p. 28 ff.

[47] The Laotian constitution explicitly states the contrary.

[48] Anonymous letter, Vientiane, October 29, 1964.

[49] Touxoua Lyfoung, "An Opinion on the Problem of Ethnic Groups in Laos," *L'Etudiant Lao* (Lao Students' Bulletin, Bordeaux Section), Paris, 1971.

[50] A nephew of Faydang Lobliayao, Touby Lyfoung was later appointed to the King's Council (1973) and served as Deputy Minister of Telecommunication in the Provisional Government of National Union (1974-1975). After the fall of Laos, he was imprisoned in a Pathet Lao re-education camp in Vieng Say (Sam Neua), where he is said to have died in 1979.

[51] Lao Patriotic Front. Founded in 1956 after the secret formation of the Lao People's Party (the Laotian communist party) the previous year, the Neo Lao Hak Sat was the political arm of the Pathet Lao (the military arm was the Lao People's Liberation Army). It was a legal political party in Laos and was succeeded by the Lao Front for National Reconstruction (Neo Lao Sang Sat) in February 1979.

[52] Lao Theung, sometimes spelled Lao Theng, is a generic term for Laotians of Mon-Khmer origin who were traditionally uplanders and practiced slash-and-burn agriculture. The corresponding term for Laotians of Sino-Tibetan origin living in the mountains (Hmong, Mien, etc.) is Lao Soung and for lowland Lao and related upland Tai peoples, Lao Loum.

[53] The 1901-1910 and 1934-46 rebellions of the Bolovens "Kha," headed first by Ong Keo and later by Kommadam, father of Sithon Kommadam, resulted in the overhaul of the system of heavy taxation and forced labor to which they were subject at the time.

Historical Background

A series of struggles and rebellions have punctuated the history of the Hmong in Laos. Today, however, as citizens of the Kingdom of a Million Elephants, though they still go on fighting as do all the ethnic groups on both sides, they do so for the national independence of Laos.

STRUGGLE FOR HEGEMONY

Though the arrival of the Hmong in Laos did not disturb the plains dwellers, it did trouble the Khmou people in the mountains. The Khmou, who had for centuries ruled over the heights of the Xieng Khouang plateau, certainly did not view without concern this intrusion by strangers planning to settle down in the region. At the beginning of the nineteenth century, a blood feud broke out between the Hmong and the Khmou over who should exercise hegemony in the mountains. In the end, the flintlock rifle, introduced from China, gave the Hmong the advantage. The Khmou, armed only with sabres and crossbows, were defeated and many of them driven back into the mountains of Luang Prabang. Those who remained decided to live as good neighbors with the Hmong, and peace reigned over the mountains of Xieng Khouang.

But no sooner was one trouble settled than another came along to take its place. Such was the situation in the nineteenth century, which witnessed the bloodiest Hmong uprisings in the history of Laos.

HMONG UPRISINGS IN LAOS

The establishment of the French protectorate in Laos in 1893 and the economic consequences which that entailed soon aroused discontent among the Hmong. The heavy-handedness of the authorities was simply a match to powder. Two Hmong uprisings took place during this period.

THE REVOLT OF THE HMONG KAITONG   In 1896, a new tax system, which the Hmong *kaitong* deemed undemocratic, was imposed. They refused to collect the burdensome taxes from their people, who had not even been told about them in advance. The reaction of the local Franco-Lao authorities was to send the *garde indigène*[1] into the mountains around the Xieng Khouang plateau to intimidate the Hmong. The Hmong *kaitong* organized a resistance force and attacked the *garde* at Ban Khang Phanieng, 20 kilometers east of Ban Ban. Word of this attack reached the high French authorities, who immediately ordered a cease-fire. The Hmong, anxious to live in peace, accepted at once and delegated Moua *kaitong* to enter into negotiations at Ban Ban with the Commissioner of the Government of the Republic of France in Xieng Khouang and the Lao *chao muong* of Ban Ban. The peace made there lasted nearly 25 years before it was shattered by another revolt, this one far more serious and bloody.

THE "MADMAN'S WAR"   Known as the *"Guerre du Fou,"* or "Madman's War," the Hmong rebellion which broke out in July 1919 in Lao Cai province in North Vietnam would ignite all of northern Indochina within a few short weeks. Extremely violent repressive measures were taken by the French forces, who, with their superior firepower, successfully drove the Meo from stronghold to stronghold, harassing them without reprieve, surrounding them and decimating them so swiftly that within a month all the units had either been destroyed or had surrendered, that Batchay,[2] in rout, was abandoned by the last survivors, and that in March 1921 the column could be disbanded.[3]

The widespread nature of the insurrection and the bloody repression prompt a search for the causes of the rebellion of 1919-1921, the truth about which is still far from elucidated by historians. Le Boulanger emphasizes the "fanaticism of suspicious tribes, superstitious to excess, blindly obedient (like the Kha of the south to the *phou-mi-boun*) to leaders who impressed them with practices of the lowest kinds of witchcraft."[4] The Hmong, however, offer an explanation quite unlike that of Le Boulanger, who tries to justify the savage actions of the French and local authorities. According to the elderly Hmong I interviewed, it was the tyranny, the extortion, the misappropriation of tax monies and the injustices of every kind, of which the Hmong were always the victims, which drove them to revolt as the only way to make themselves heard.

The testimony of Colonel Henri Roux, a good friend of Blia Yao Lo (Lobliayao), the well-known Hmong leader of the Trân Ninh plateau,[5] follows that same line:

Certainly, the Luang Prabang Court always showed themselves generous toward the Meo. But there were petty local chiefs, always lazy, often greedy, to whom the Meo were nothing but a fine cow which they could milk mercilessly. At times, the Meo's warlike temperament would be aroused, and there were good reasons for that: exorbitant taxes, stiff levies on opium, horses requisitioned and not paid for. And always these petty chiefs brandished the bogey of the French government before the unfortunate Meo. But one day the cup overflowed and, notwithstanding the bogey, rebellion broke out.[6]

Reverend F. M. Savina, a witness to the "Madman's War," documented the causes of the Hmong rebellion in a lengthy, classified official report to the French Government in Indochina. In his report Savina wrote:

The revolt having broken out openly, we [the French] could do nothing but defend the Tai and the Lao against the Meo. As could be foreseen, the Meo turned themselves immediately against us and the Annamites [Vietnamese] who accompanied us, which only lengthened the rebellion. Without our intervention, the Meo would quickly have prevailed over the Tai and the Lao.[7]

Father Savina raised several questions about this Hmong rebellion:

Seeing that the Meo hated the Tai and the Tai hated the Meo, I asked myself why. Seeing that the Tai duped the Meo and the Meo did not dupe the Tai, I asked myself why. Seeing that the Tai possessed their own land and were governed by chiefs from their own ethnic group, whereas the Meo did not possess land and were obliged to obey foreign chiefs, I asked myself why. Seeing that the Meo complaints remained unanswered indefinitely in administrative offices, I asked myself why. Seeing that the Tai always prevailed against the Meo, even when they were obviously in the wrong, I asked myself why. Seeing that some [French] officials treated the Meo like strangers, I asked myself why. Seeing that no official was ever able to or wanted to learn the Meo language, I asked myself why. Seeing that the

Protectorate administration established schools everywhere in Indochina but never in the Meo villages, I asked myself why. I have met many officials in my life, but I have never met them on the paths leading to the Meo villages, I asked myself why. In trying to solve this racial equation which contains several unknowns, I came to know the true causes of the current Meo uprising.... An entire people does not become fanatic overnight without apparent reason, following the voice of the first sorcerer who comes along; and mere neglect has never pushed to rebellion an entire group of people, composed of different tribes, separated from each other by a hundred kilometers....[8]

Pachay (Batchay) Vue and Shong Zer Lo, the two principal leaders of the rebellion of 1919-1921, were, say the old Hmong, far from being madmen. Pachay Vue was the son of a notable family from the Hmong village of Na Ou in the Muong Theng (Dien Bien Phu) district, where his uncle, Shong Tou Vue, was the village chief. Shong Zer Lo, who came from Xieng Khouang, was the son of *kaitong* Nyia Her Lo, half-brother to *kaitong* Lobliayao, father of Faydang Lobliayao. They had risen up against the injustice whose victims had invariably been they and theirs. Some Hmong shamans, more or less mad, did in fact take advantage of the turmoil to expand their power and influence, hence the terms "Madman's War" or "Crazy War," expressions which lead to confusion and obscure the true significance of this Hmong insurrection.

It was after this bloody uprising, prime responsibility for which must be placed on "greedy local chiefs," that the French administration in Indochina decided to grant special administrative status to the Hmong. For a time thereafter, political stability prevailed in the Hmong mountains. It remained essentially undisturbed until the Japanese occupation of March 1945, which sounded the death knell for the *pax gallica* and rudely awoke the nationalist sentiments of the Indochinese peoples even as it paved the way for revolution.

THE HMONG AND THE LAOTIAN NATION

The presence of ethnic minorities invariably poses problems in a country like Laos, where these people constitute almost half the population. What are these problems and what are the political aspirations of the Hmong, who are Laotian citizens, in the current conflict between the warring princes of the kingdom?

THE PROBLEM OF THE ETHNIC MINORITIES After the defeat of Japan in 1945 and the return of the French to Indochina, the road to independence for Laos was prepared by Constitutional Assembly elections, where some 45 seats were to be filled. The opportunity was then or never for the ethnic minorities to claim equal rights and to assert their points of view. Representing the Hmong, Toulia Lyfoung ran and was elected in Xieng Khouang province. There were no candidates from the other ethnic minorities, who were not even informed of the elections. The struggle promised to be a difficult one for the only deputy speaking on behalf of all the ethnic minorities.

In the Constitutional Assembly, Toulia Lyfoung quickly raised the issue of the status of the ethnic minorities, an issue which the Assembly preferred to ignore. "The minorities issue," wrote Lebel de Chateauvieux, "has been shamefully neglected. Half or more of the population of Laos is Kha, Lu, Yao, etc., who are completely different from the Lao.... It is crucial that their existence be taken into account; the claims and demands of the Meo representative illustrate the importance of the problem."[9] The ethnic minority issue was settled at the constitutional level by Article 4 of the Laotian Constitution adopted on March 10, 1947, which stated, "Any and all individuals belonging to races permanently settled in Laotian territory and possessing no other nationality shall be [considered] Laotian citizens."[10]

In addition, the Hmong deputy requested that the minorities, particularly the Hmong, be governed by leaders of their own ethnic groups and expressed the hope that Ethnic Minorities Affairs offices would be set up wherever there were sizable populations of ethnic minorities. (Prior to 1945, ethnic minorities were not allowed on *khoueng* staffs.) These demands were partially satisfied with the implementation of an administrative decentralization system as stipulated in the Constitution. "It will constitute an excellent guarantee for the minorities, in that they will be represented on a pro rata basis in the provincial assemblies."[11] The extent to which the decentralization policy was actually implemented nationwide has already been demonstrated!

Despite all these measures, Laotian unity was still a long way from realization. The conflict that has gone on for almost 30 years is tangible proof of the fragility of the political structures set up in Laos.

THE HMONG IN THE LAOTIAN TRAVAIL
The historical background of the war now raging in Laos has been the subject of numerous works; we confine ourselves here to clarification of the political positions of the Hmong, inextricably caught up in the Laotian turmoil.

Unity among the Hmong, as among the Lao, had no solid foundation upon which to be built. Family rivalries which had long opposed the Ly and the Lo clans were a determining factor when, at that moment in Laotian history when the split occurred between the so-called revolutionary forces and the so-called government forces, a choice had to be made.

At the beginning of the conflict which followed closely upon the end of World War II, Touby Lyfoung, head of the Ly clan, opted for the Lao royal family of Luang Prabang, who favored a return of the French with provision of a new status for Laos, which, among other things, embodied a pledge of its total, though gradual, independence. He explained his position by saying, "The King is the true leader of Laos. The Hmong, who are his subjects, owe him obedience and loyalty."[12] General Vang Pao was later to remind the Hmong of their loyalty to the crown when he ordered a royal residence built at Long Cheng, where, since 1964, the king and queen have come every *chiang* (New Year) to visit the displaced populations.

Faydang Lobliayao, chief of the Lo family, sided, on the other hand, with Prince Souphanouvong, leader of the Pathet Lao, who, with the support of the Viet Minh, fought first against the French return to Laos and then against the Vientiane government, whom they called "vassals of the foreigners." Nevertheless, the Laotian revolutionaries have continued to claim to be "respecters of the throne," the symbol of Laotian unity! Faydang Lobliayao is currently vice president of the Neo Lao Hak Sat, the political wing of the Pathet Lao.

The diametrically opposed political commitments of these two Hmong leaders led inevitably to the split of some of the Hmong into two "enemy" camps: on one side the pro-government supporters of Touby Lyfoung and on the other the pro-Pathet Lao backers of Faydang Lobliayao. The majority of the Hmong in the kingdom, however, remained outside of the conflict, going about their peaceful lives in the mountain highlands, which representatives of the Laotian government seldom bothered to visit.

The year 1960 was a major turning point in contemporary Laotian history and in the destiny of the Hmong in the kingdom. A coup d'etat, headed by Captain Kong Le,[13] touched off major events that were to shake Laotian society to the core. Little by little, the entire eastern part of the country was set aflame in a devastating, murderous war from which no one could escape. The ethnic minorities found themselves caught up, against their will, by the force of events, on both sides of the conflict that, for eleven years, has been and still is sowing death and destruction among the Laotian populations. "We are fighting," one Hmong explained, "because they drove us out of our lands and out of our villages, and because they have forced us to live in misery. Our country is all of that [gesturing toward the Xieng Khouang plateau] and we shall defend it at all costs."

In the current war in Laos, the Hmong General Vang Pao has received much attention both for himself and for the "Meo," largely because of the strategic position of the Second Military Region which he commands.[14] Contradictions around this subject abound, often resulting from mistaken, false or biased information. Some of these may be very dangerous to the country's future as a nation. An accurate explanation of the situation is required in order to better understand the Laotian tragedy.

Jacques Decornoy has, on many occasions, spoken of the "Meo mercenary army" under General Vang Pao. He is, however, quite careful to specify the "special forces" when speaking of the Lao in southern or central Laos.[15] Why this difference in terminology to describe identical status? Is the reporter for *Le Monde* ignorant of the fact that the "Meo" as well as the "Kha" and the "Yao" are all Laotian citizens with exactly the same rights as the Lao? Or is he attempting to divide Laotians by arousing ethnic antagonism?

Elsewhere, in *Laos: Special War Versus People's War*, these lines appear: "To fight the Lao dug in in the mountains, the Americans count on their special commandos recruited from among the minority living in the region, the Meo."[16] Is this the truth that Wilfred Burchett seeks to confirm when he writes, "They (the Meo) were encouraged to commit atrocities against the Lao Loum[17] and against others so as to make them culpable and to terrify them with the idea of what would happen to them if they were themselves ever defeated or captured. It was burned into their brains that they must kill or be killed."[18] And what conclusion should be drawn about the contention that, "integration into the Laotian nation of the Meo minorities, who have been fighting an intense war *for their own interests* for many years, poses a delicate, if not insoluble, problem to the Vientiane government [emphasis added]"?[19]

First of all, it must be recognized that the "star-studded" General Vang Pao is an officer in the Royal Armed Forces (FAR) and that his military forces – regular as well as "special" forces – are not made up exclusively of "Meo," as certain overly-tendentious reporters and writers imply. During a visit to Long Cheng and Sam Thong in 1969, we spoke with many Khmou, Phouan and Lao troops. According to an official source, the Hmong comprise only about 60 percent of the troops which the Royal Lao Government has placed under the command of General Vang Pao.[20] Vang Pao's general staff, then set up at Sam Thong, consisted of officers of various ethnic groups (Lao, Hmong, Khmou), headed by Colonel Tiao Monivong, a member of the Lao royal family of Luang Prabang.

Under these circumstances, it would be difficult, if not impossible, for the Hmong to "vent their hatred on the Lao and others" and to commit the atrocities to which Burchett refers. Indeed, if the Hmong actually did practice such savagery against other Laotian ethnic groups, their bases at Sam Thong and Long Cheng would long since have been destroyed without it being necessary to call on Pathet Lao and North Vietnamese troops to do the job! What Lao or Khmou (of which there are plenty at both Long Cheng and Sam Thong) would have tolerated such "barbarism" on the part of the Hmong? In fact, while the Laotian and American air forces played an important role in the defense of Long Cheng, it was the solidarity and determination of the pro-government Lao, Hmong and Khmou that finally made it possible to repel the Pathet Lao and North Vietnamese attacks of 1970, 1971 and 1972 against this stronghold, considered the key point defending the approaches to Vientiane.

One may, with some justification, wonder whether such talk of "atrocities" may have been cunningly bandied about in order to cast an unfavorable light on the present position of the Hmong, who constitute, on both sides of the fighting, a real national force, and to set Lao against Hmong in a sinister scheme to destroy the already unstable Laotian nation. Furthermore, it is difficult indeed to understand Brossollet and Joyaux's argument that the Hmong are waging an intense war for their own interests and that they are a threat to Laos's future. Such an unfounded assertion by such eminent people could well harm not only the Hmong but the Laotian nation as a whole.

The truth is that the war now going on in Laos far exceeds the capability of the Hmong to wage and, indeed, may well escape the control of the Pathet Lao and the Vientiane government. It is now in the hands of the major powers: the People's Republic of China, the Soviet Union and the Soviet bloc countries, who have thrown their support behind the Pathet Lao; and the United States of America, which, with massive amounts of money, food, materiel and advisory assistance, notably that of the Army Special Forces (the so-called "Green Berets"), is backing the Royal Lao Government. The divided Laotian people are merely pawns in the struggle by the great world powers for hegemony in Southeast Asia. These powers alone hold the key to the future of this sorely tried little kingdom.[21]

The Laotian people, majority as well as minority, have nothing to gain from this war, which can only weaken their country's position. On the contrary, they have everything to gain by joining together to build a common future, in mutual understanding and tolerance, in mutual assistance and national accord. As for the Hmong, their fortunes have long been tied to those of the Laotian nation for which they are living, fighting and dying.

FOOTNOTES:

[1] Paramilitary troops, led by French officers, recruited mostly from among the Vietnamese but also from among the local populations (sometimes called *Gardes Indochinois*).

[2] Batchay (or Pachay) Vue, whom the Neo Lao Hak Sat has elevated to the status of a national hero, was one of the principal leaders of the insurrection.

[3] Paul Le Boulanger, *History of French Laos*, Plon, Paris, 1931, p. 357 ff.

[4] Ibid. The *phou-mi-boun*, practitioners of traditional magic, gave their name to a rebellion in 1901 by the Lao Theung on the Bolovens Plateau against French taxation and forced labor.

[5] Trân Ninh is the Vietnamese name for the province of Xieng Khouang.

[6] Henri Roux and Chu Van Tran, "Some Ethnic Minorities in Northern Tonkin," *France-Asie*, Nos. 92-93, Saigon, January-February 1954, p. 404.

[7] Jean Lartéguy, *The Fabulous Adventure of the Opium People*, collab. Yang Dao, Presses de la Cité, Paris, 1979, p. 96.

[8] Ibid.

[9] Lebel de Chateauvieux, *Commentary on the Laotian Constitution*, p. 28.

[10] Laos, *The Laotian Constitutional Assembly (March 15-May 10, 1947)*, Imprimerie Française d'Outre Mer, Saigon, 1949, p. 101.

[11] Laos, *Laotian Constitutional Assembly (March 15-May 10, 1947)*, Staff Communique No. 9, Vientiane, April 8, 1947.

[12] Touby Lyfoung, personal interview, 1970.

[13] Neutralists led by Captain Kong Le of the Second Royal Lao Paratroop Battalion seized key government and communications centers in Vientiane on August 8, 1960, leading to a complex succession of short-lived governments. Although allied for a time with the Pathet Lao and actually supplied with arms from the Soviet Union, by 1964 most of Kong Le's neutralists had been forced to ally themselves with the Royal Lao Army.

[14] After joining the "Meo" popular resistance forces at a very young age, in 1947 Vang Pao, in his late teens, joined the Royal Laotian Gendarmerie and later enlisted in the Royal Armed Forces (FAR) when it was established in 1949-50. He attended the Laotian Corporals' School in Luang Prabang and the Laotian Officers' School at Dong Hene and took the Laotian Battalion Commanders' course in Vientiane (in 1956 or 1957). In 1975 he held the rank of Division General in the Royal Armed Forces.

[15] Jacques Decournoy, *Le Monde*, Paris, 1968-72.

[16] Anonymous (Les Etudiants Lao Patriotiques?), *Laos: Special War versus People's War*, Git-le-Coeur, Paris, 1970, p. 17.

[17] The lowland Lao.

[18] Wilfred Burchett, *The Second Indochina War: Cambodia and Laos*, Seuil, Paris, 1970, p. 109.

[19] Guy Brossollet and François Joyaux, "Laos," *Notes and Documentary Studies*, No. 3.360, La Documentation Française, Paris, October 20, 1969, p. 10.

[20] Second Military Region staff, personal interview, 1969.

[21] An upcoming book will examine the secret war in Laos from the Hmong perspective.

Hmong Socioeconomic Patterns

THE HMONG ECONOMY AND ITS EVOLUTION

The demands imposed by the natural environment, the need to adapt to new economic conditions in order to survive, and the political circumstances which are toppling old structures are all factors which help to explain the complexity of the present-day Hmong village economy. This economy looks less and less like it did only twenty years ago, but that does not mean that it has found a new equilibrium. Old, secure structures are crumbling, sometimes quite suddenly, as in northeastern Laos, devastated by more than ten years of war; new ones have not yet emerged. The Hmong village economy is in a state of transition, still burdened with the constraints and inertia of the past, yet constantly shaken by new forces which are leading to the development of new economic forms.

Part Two examines the *traditional* Hmong village economy, enclosed in its age-old socioeconomic structure (Chapter Four); the *transitional* village economy, gradually becoming part of a dynamic regional economy (Chapter Five); and the *wartime* economy typical of Laos today (Chapter Six). Study of these socioeconomic patterns provides a better understanding of the mental and psychological evolution of the mountain peoples in relation to the changes they are now experiencing and, as a result, forms the basis for realistic plans to integrate them into a national development strategy.

CHAPTER FOUR

The Traditional Village Economy

Three interrelated features characterize the traditional Hmong village economy: conservatism, insularity and inertia.

Socioeconomic Conservatism   As has already been shown, the social structure in Hmong village communities is tightly organized and hierarchical. The village is less a territorial collectivity bonded by economic interests than a family community in the broadest sense, that is, a lineage (with its ramifications) or an association of lineages. The oldest man in the oldest paternal line leads the community. He embodies traditional knowledge, he ensures the ties with the ancestors, he sees to it that customs are honored. He is the one who makes decisions about the division of labor, the agricultural calendar, and so on.

This Hmong social structure is linked both to a particular concept of people and things and to a specific agricultural technology. For Hmong peasants, nature represents not only richness and abundance but mystery and destructive forces as well. Traditions, customs, rules and proverbs sum up age-old wisdom to which every Hmong must submit under pain of the harshest sanctions. This sociological environment strongly favors the continuation of ancestral technology and the traditional cycle of cultivation. These traditions are, the Hmong peasants believe, the best and least risky way to assure themselves of a sufficient supply of food.

Economic Insularity   The insularity of the Hmong village economy is both a demographic and an economic phenomenon. It is a result of the very wide distribution of people over unequally hospitable geographic areas and stems from a vital ecological equilibrium that must be maintained. In Laos, particularly in the mountain regions, village economic insularity is further reinforced by the inadequacy of the transportation systems and the absence of interconnections between those that do exist.

This isolation also explains why subsistence agriculture is still the rule in most regions of Laos. In the mountains, the Hmong peasant engages primarily in swidden rice cultivation and in the raising of other food crops; it is to these fields that he devotes most of his time and effort. Scorned as an improvident and an idler is the man who does not cultivate his rice and look after his chickens and his pair of pigs! Hmong villages have been little affected by monetary influences. Self-sufficiency is carefully ensured, and trade in the hinterlands is based on barter. Only twenty years ago a Hmong peasant would have been scoffed at for taking his agricultural products to the regional market for sale.

To this negative attitude of the Hmong people must be added the distance and the cost of market goods. Why produce more than you can consume when you know that, because of the disastrous state of the roads, the Chinese or Lao merchants may decide to bypass your village entirely? Even where trails do exist, their deplorable condition makes it too costly to move goods out. It is not uncommon to find that, in the end, transportation costs exceed the price the goods would bring in the market. The only economically profitable crop is opium poppies. Opium packs a high value into a small volume. It long ago became the primary source of cash for the Hmong, who specialized in its production. Only ten years ago, poppy-growing was thriving all over the mountains of northern Laos.

Under these conditions, the Hmong village economy has almost no choice but to remain insular, and that insularity does not encourage growth. It is too much subject to the pressure of immediate basic needs, pressure which has increased recently due to the population explosion among the Hmong. Unknown and isolated, the village economy tends gradually to turn inward on itself unless some outside effort is made to break it out of its isolation.

Apparent Inertia   The fundamental feature of the traditional Hmong economy is that there is almost no potential for an increase in the economic yield per person. The traditional society does not have available to it the tremendous possibilities afforded by modern science and technology, nor would it know how to exploit them regularly and systematically if it did. The range of opportunities open to grandchildren is essentially the same as that which was open to their grandparents. Stability of needs and self-sufficiency: these are the basic traits of economic inertia.

This economic inertia is reflected in a seeming "allergy" to anything connected with increasing productivity, an attitude engendered by the security the traditional economic system provides. The Hmong farmer who knows the price of his own effort also knows from experience that there is a good chance it may be spent for nothing. He has no incentive to increase the productivity of his labor, because what he produces will, in peacetime, simply go to meet the needs of a self-contained economy with no channels to market; any unconsumed surplus would have nowhere to go. Cash incomes are, in general, low and are treated as marginal. Cash is used to buy salt, cloth, cooking utensils and the like. As we will see later, it is opium that plays the most important and widespread financial role.

Finally, the stagnant economy of traditional Hmong society is explained by the nonproductive consumption of the annual surplus. Families are usually able to produce somewhat more than they consume during a year. This surplus is used primarily to pay for family feasts (namings, weddings, etc.), curing ceremonies, funerals, and sacrifices to local spirits and to the ancestors. Solidarity requires that the entire village share in the joys and sorrows of each of its members; thus every feast and ceremony becomes an occasion for heavy spending. Numerous pigs and whole oxen may be devoured in the space of a few hours at a wedding or funeral. Imagine the economic catastrophe that entails for the family who must host such a ceremony!

To these more or less unscheduled outlays must be added those occasioned by the Hmong New Year, which occurs every year in late November or early December. The first few days of the new year are devoted to visits and receptions. Tradition requires that every family, in turn, invite the members of the community to a feast in honor of the new year. Fortunately, not everyone is able to accept all of these invitations. Neighbors, busy with their own domestic tasks or ritual ceremonies, usually just delegate one or two people per household to renew these old traditions, which have kept Hmong society alive down through the ages. As can be seen, the practice of traditional family, ritual and festive customs has as a consequence the siphoning off of family resources into nonproductive ends.

Having looked at its basic characteristics, let us now examine some of the problems posed by the traditional Hmong economy. We will look first at traditional agriculture and animal husbandry practices and then at the standard of living in the traditional society, a standard of living which is a direct result of the self-sufficient subsistence economy practiced by the Hmong mountain people.

PRODUCTION ACTIVITIES

The traditional Hmong economy is based primarily on a combination of agriculture and animal husbandry. While family-level animal husbandry certainly plays an important role in the subsistence life-style of the Hmong, most of their efforts are devoted to agriculture and are divided between food crops and industrial or cash crops.

AGRICULTURE

The most striking thing about the Hmong way of life is its mobility, due mainly to their practice of itinerant agriculture, which is the rule throughout the mountains of northern Laos. In this shifting system of agriculture, the soil is cropped constantly until decreasing fertility causes unacceptable lowering of yields. The fields are then abandoned for a period of time in order to allow the soil to restore itself.[1] While the old fields are lying fallow, the farmer must plant his crops in other places until, the soil having regained its fertility, he can move his crops back to the original fields. When all arable land within about two hours' walk of the village has been exhausted, however, the Hmong usually simply move villagers and domestic animals to a virgin area on another mountain, with no intention of returning. The itinerant system of agriculture is characterized by

- almost complete lack of working of the soil

- absence of fertilizer – successive crops are nourished by the store of fertilizing elements in the soil itself and from existing vegetation which is destroyed by burning prior to planting

- no attempt to control crop diseases and parasites.

The visible signs of shifting agriculture are the numerous *rai* – deforested patches of deep green to yellow, depending on age – found in the tropical forest.

The *Rai* and its Agricultural Techniques   A *rai* (rī) is a temporary, unirrigated field created by hasty cutting and burning, which clears the land and fertilizes it with ash. The so-called slash-and-burn system of agriculture is an extensive system based on a technical tradition necessitated by geographical and environmental conditions. The techniques used, the results achieved and the body of their conscious knowledge suggest that the Hmong peasants' adaptation to the environment of the mountains of northern Laos is at least as old as their first settlements there.

The selection of *rai* fields usually begins shortly before the New Year. Each village's selections are confined to its own territory, the territorial confines of a village being defined less by legal statute than by the maximum practical distance between dwellings and fields. (Theoretically, all land belongs to the king of Laos; the farmer who works it has the right to its use and profits.) The selection of *rai* depends on physical features as well. Slopes steeper than 25 percent grade, for example, cannot be cleared or planted without the soil, having been completely stripped of its natural protection by the hand of man, suffering extremely serious erosion during the great downpours of the monsoon season.

Once a family has chosen a field for planting, the land must be cleared. In February and March the trees are cut down, leaving stumps as much as a meter high standing. Clearing is an individual undertaking; neighbors cannot help each other because everyone is busy with his own *rai* at the same time. The topped trees and brush are left to dry and, in late March and April, are burned. The soil is then cleared of debris, the fertilizing ashes spread, and the field kept weeded until planting time. It usually takes about a month to prepare a *rai*. Preparation is faster and easier when the *rai* is in its second or third year of cultivation. All that need be done then is to cut down the rice stubble or cornstalks, grasses and brush and spread them out evenly so that they will dry enough to burn.

On each *rai*, unless it is quite close to the village, is a shelter or small house. At the peak of the agricultural season, Hmong farmers spend weeks at a time there, returning to the village only rarely. Near the *rai* house, the farmer builds a pigsty, a temporary granary for the season's crop, and a stable for the horses, which are put out to pasture.

No planting is done during the dry season that follows the first harvest on a *rai*. Before the onset of the next rainy season, a second planting is done, using more seed than was needed the first year. It is sometimes possible to get a third year of crops from a *rai*, but eventually the declining yield makes it necessary to leave the *rai* fallow or, as is more often the case, to abandon it altogether. The old rule of thumb was that the cultivation cycle of a *rai* lasted 14 or 15 years.

CULTIVATION CYCLE OF A *RAI*

First year	Rice or corn
Second year	Rice or corn
Third year	Rice or corn (broadcast) – *rai* often left fallow or abandoned
Fourth to 15th year	Left fallow or abandoned

In practice, the productive period of a *rai* is extremely variable. It is a function of yield – upon which the life of the community depends – and of geographical conditions. René Dumont writes:

> Tropical soils are, on the average, poorer than those of the European and North American plains, with the exception of those deriving from volcanic rock and recent alluvia, which are important exceptions. They are everywhere subject to degradation through intense leaching by warm waters, which carry off the minerals. The acid water soaks into the humus and turns the streams brown, as it does in Scandinavia. It quickly burns the organic matter. The process may go all the way to total destruction, as in the case of formation of ferrous or laterite crusts dried out (after being stripped of the topsoil that protected them) by their exposure on the surface to alternating wet and dry seasons.... Erosion is another mode of total destruction, promoted by the clearing of the soil by brushfires or by repeated and careless cropping.[2]

The *rai*, stripped of its protective forest, deteriorates rapidly through laterite formation. When a laterite layer is built up close to the surface, the soil loses all value and can no longer be planted.

The Hmong do not usually exploit a *rai* for more than three years in succession. The land, whether left fallow or abandoned, is gradually invaded by vegetation (sometimes brush, sometimes savannah or pseudo-steppe) which replaces the forest. If he is to survive, the Hmong peasant must go elsewhere, find a corner of the forest that has not yet been farmed and start a new crop cycle. The quest for crop land largely explains the mobility and wide dispersion of the Hmong. This geographical instability guarantees a relatively low standard of living, justifying the Hmong proverb that says,

> If you eat all you want, you grow fat;
> If you run, you grow thin.
> If you settle down, you grow rich;
> If you move about, you grow poor.

For the past twenty years or so, there has been evidence of a widespread desire for change among the Hmong. The uncertain nature of slash-and-burn agriculture, the growing pressure of overpopulation on the system of production relative to its ability to meet basic needs, the aspirations of the young for a better life: all these factors combine to entice the Hmong down from their mountain heights. In Xieng Khouang province, with the encouragement of the governor, Chao Saikham, and the "*Chao Muong* of the Meo Population," Touby Lyfoung, some Hmong have begun to undertake irrigated rice cultivation. The same thing has occurred spontaneously in Sayaboury among families living on the outskirts of the town. For its part, the Neo Lao Hak Sat has reportedly made some major agrarian reforms in the "liberated zones," thus enabling the mountain peoples to improve their standard of living steadily and rapidly. Chapter Five deals with this subject at length.

FOOD CROPS   To the Hmong, the major part of whose efforts are directed toward self-sufficiency, food crops are of utmost importance. The nutritional balance of their diet is a function of the yields of their food crops, yields which are always subject to the unpredictable external circumstances before which peasants are helpless.

Having known only irrigated rice cultivation in their native China, the Hmong, after migrating into the mountains of Southeast Asia, were forced to turn temporarily to the cultivation of corn, or *pob kws* as it is known by both the Hmong and the southern Chinese, the crop upon which they had relied to sustain them in bad times in their homeland. With the acquisition of dry rice cultivation techniques by the Hmong in the early part of this century, rice has once again supplanted corn as the staple food crop. Corn remains the second most important food crop, although nowadays it is used almost exclusively as feed for chickens, pigs and horses.

In addition to these two main crops, the Hmong raise a whole range of vegetables and related plants: cucumbers, melons, eggplant, Chinese mustard, onions, beans, soybeans, cabbage, ginger, parsley, chicory, yams, taro, manioc and sugar cane. To these must be added potatoes, which, introduced around 1920 by the French colonial administration, thrive fairly well in the mountains. Fruits, such as bananas, peaches, Chinese pears and papayas, also play an important part in the diet. Finally, foods obtained by gathering round out the Hmong diet: bamboo shoots, mushrooms, wild honey and others.

As can be seen, food crops are quite diverse among the Hmong, who are known for their energy and adaptability. Though there may be famine today in some of the mountain regions hardest hit by the war, it was unknown in those same areas a mere ten years ago. The Hmong have always prided themselves on being hard workers; to them, begging is a terrible shame. Ample proof of this diligence lies in a look at their agricultural calendar.

The Hmong Agricultural Calendar   The political situation and lack of time prevented a detailed survey of the Hmong agricultural calendar during my 1969 visit. The following calendar was developed by Jacques Lemoine for the Pha Hok region of Sayaboury province. It is accurate for most Hmong villages in northern Laos, give or take a week or so according to location.

THE HMONG AGRICULTURAL CALENDAR

First month[3]	Rice was harvested before the New Year celebrations in December. Now it must be threshed and brought home, along with the corn. The opium poppy fields are given a final weeding. The squash harvest begins.
Second month	All efforts are directed to milking the poppies. At home, the axes and brush knives are sharpened in preparation for clearing the *rai*.
Third month	The opium harvest is finished. Work begins on clearing parts of the forest for corn and rice *rai*. At home, women spin hemp, which will be used for skirts.
Fourth month	Completion of clearing the *rai* is followed by a month of idleness while waiting for the wood to dry where it has been cut. Most of the men use this slack time to make things for household use (feeding troughs, buckets, etc.), go hunting and do a little trading. Some use this time to bring in the last loads of corn.
Fifth month	The dry season has arrived. The *rai* is burned and the burnt-over fields cleared of debris. When the first rain comes, the corn is planted. In the same *rai* are planted pumpkins, banana trees, hemp and perhaps some papaya trees.
Sixth month	Rice is planted and in the same *rai* go eggplant, sugar cane, cucumbers, ginger, onions, yams, taro, manioc, beans, soybeans, and so on.
Seventh month	The rains have come. The corn is weeded, which it badly needs; then the rice is weeded. Tobacco is planted.

Eighth month	The opium *rai* is prepared: trees and brush are cut if necessary, followed by careful cleaning of the *rai*. Hemp is cut and peeled.
Ninth month	The weeds and grasses are turned under in the opium *rai*, then the early opium is planted. Corn harvesting begins. At home, Green Hmong (*Hmoob Ntsuab*) women prepare the indigo and decorate the hemp skirt cloth with batik designs.
Tenth month	Late opium is planted, some of it in the corn *rai*. Along with opium, chicory, Chinese mustard and parsley are planted. The rains become intermittent. The first clear days are used to harvest the first rice of the year.
Eleventh month	Rice and all the crops that were planted with it (melons, cucumbers, etc.) are harvested.
Twelfth month	The opium is weeded and red and white squash are harvested. The rice harvest is completed. At home, women are sewing and embroidering in preparation for the New Year.[4]

The work pace of the Hmong suggests that the hidden unemployment spoken of by many experts on developing countries is a relatively rare phenomenon in the Hmong mountains. The nature of the terrain, the uncertain weather conditions, and their archaic agricultural techniques often prevent these farmers from obtaining the results they anticipate from their labor. A study of the two main crops, rice and corn, illustrates this very clearly.

Rice   In Laos, the growing of dry-land rice is a significant and relatively recent innovation in the production patterns of the Hmong people. Dry rice growing is characterized principally by the lack of submersion or irrigation of the rice field. The crop depends entirely on rainfall; the grower does nothing to augment the natural water supply.

It is often said that the Hmong "plowed with fire and planted with spears," meaning that the Hmong knew only swidden agriculture. However, there are many indications that the ancestors of the Hmong were well acquainted with the art of flooded rice growing. One such indication is the presence in their current vocabulary of terms having to do with wet rice growing: for example, plow (*rab voom*), harrow (*rab phuaj*) and seedlings (*cov yub*). On the other hand, there is no specific Hmong word for *rai*, which they call *daim teb*, or "piece of land," though there is a term for flooded rice field (*liaj*). Furthermore, the fact that there is a Hmong name, *tus twm*, for the water buffalo (*B. bubalis*), an animal used exclusively in the wetlands of the plains, suggests that the Hmong people were once dwellers in the lowlands and paddies. The practice of irrigated rice cultivation continues today among the Hmong in China. Lemoine, citing Ivez de Beauclair[5] writes, "The Miao populations of Kweichow she visited cultivated only sticky rice and built rice fields on terraces irrigated with bamboo pipelines."[6]

How did the Hmong of Laos arrive at their present set of agricultural practices? To the political, climatic and historical reasons already discussed must be added ecological conditions. According to Pierre Gourou:

The mountain people are not ignorant, with the exception of a few backward Moi (Proto-Indochinese), of wet rice growing. They like to have flooded rice fields which yield their harvests regularly, year after year. But, on the one hand, sites favorable for establishing such paddy fields are rare in mountain country: the requisite slope, soil composition and water supplies are rarely found in combination. On the other hand, constructing and maintaining flooded fields takes considerable work, and the mountain people, weakened by fever, are not capable of such sustained efforts.[7]

In spite of the many difficulties, those Hmong who were able to construct flooded rice fields did so. In North Vietnam, Charles Robequain observed in 1929 that "[w]hen they [the Hmong] have a chance to set up irrigated rice fields away from other races, they quickly abandon their nomadic ways; they have already done so, for example, in Tonkin at Dong Van, Pak Kha, Cha Pa, Hoang Su Fi, etc....."[8] An elderly Hmong man, originally from Mu Cang Chai in Yen Bay province in North Vietnam, recalls the existence of two large Hmong villages, *Hav Tuam Tswm* ("Bamboo Valley") and *Tsev Kub Hnyiab* ("Burned Houses"), on either side of the clear, wide *Xov Moos* river, where, for generations, Hmong had grown irrigated rice.[9]

In Laos, the beginning of this century also witnessed a number of Hmong starting flooded rice culture in Xieng Khouang province. It is said that their efforts were rewarded with some very fine rice harvests. After a few years, however, decimated and disheartened by tropical diseases (malaria, etc.), the Hmong farmers decided to return, without regret, to the far healthier climate of their mountain homes.

The unavailability of suitable plains land, the prevalence of tropical diseases in the lowlands, and the unfavorable nature of the upland soil and climate explain why, when they first arrived in Indochina, the Hmong considered rice a luxury. They brought it out only for special occasions; corn was their dietary staple. Rice, produced by Lao growers, was generally purchased with opium, which, as we shall see later, was used as a medium of exchange.

Dry rice growing was, some 30 or 40 years ago, a development which turned the farm life and dietary habits of the Hmong in the mountains of Laos almost completely around after a period of having been dependent on corn. Apparently it was contact with Lao and Khmou farmers, who gave them seeds of mountain rice capable of being grown without irrigation, that launched the Hmong into dry rice cultivation on a massive scale. It was not until around the 1940s that the practice of dry rice cultivation spread to all Hmong villages and that the habit of daily rice consumption again became common among the Hmong throughout northern Laos. Dry rice growing was also unknown until quite recently among the North Vietnamese Hmong, specifically in the Viet Bac region. Today, however, eating corn has again become a symbol of poverty and misery.

Like their Khmou and Lao neighbors, the Hmong grow a wide variety of both glutinous and non-glutinous rices. Fluffy (non-glutinous) rice is the standard fare; sticky rice is used only on feast days, particularly the New Year, when it is eaten in the form of delicious rice cakes.

Size and Planting of Rice Rai   The area of rice *rai* varies considerably depending on available manpower and the age of the *rai*. The *rai* of extended families are larger than those belonging to smaller families. The age of a rice *rai* affects its ease of preparation and determines its yield. The average size of Hmong rice *rai* is between 0.7 and 1.5 hectares per family.[10]

Rice planting begins in late April and continues through the month of May. If possible, the work is done in teams comprised of an entire extended family (both men and women), several couples without children, or a group of small children working together. When one *rai* has been planted, the team moves on to the other members' *rai*. Planting may also be done by a single couple if necessary.

Making roughly parallel lines, a man with a dibble stick in each hand pokes holes in the soil at intervals of approximately 30 centimeters. A woman or girl walking behind him, holding in her fist grain from the shallow bowl she carries in her left hand, drops a dozen or so grains into each hole and covers it with her feet. A team can sow a *rai* in two or three days, whereas for a couple working alone it may well take a week or more. Three basketfuls of seed, or about 54 kilograms, are required to plant a half-hectare *rai*.

Harvesting and Threshing   The early rice harvest begins around mid-September. A small amount of rice, selected from among the riper heads, is harvested at this time. Using small, scimitar-shaped knives, the farmers cut the paddy high on the stalk, about 1.5 meters above the ground. The stalks, with the heads still attached, are dried either in front of the house in the sun or in a large cast-iron pan suspended above the family fireplace. Some of this rice will be set aside for sacrifices to the ancestors at the time of the "Eating of the New Rice" (*noj nplej tshiab*) celebration in October. On this occasion, a pig is killed and relatives and village neighbors invited to a feast.

The larger late rice harvest does not begin until late October or early November. The paddy is cut with a sickle at 20 to 30 centimeters above the ground. The stalks are gathered and laid on mats in the sun to dry. When fairly dry, they are stored temporarily in a loft.

When the harvest is complete, the rice is threshed with wooden staves. Lemoine has described this operation very well:

> Close to the granary on the *rai*, a wooden frame with a floor of bamboo latticework is set up. The dried rice stalks are tossed onto the threshing floor and the girls and women thresh it with six-foot-long wooden sticks. The grain falls through the lattice openings onto a mat below the threshing floor. When a sufficient amount has been threshed, the rice is loaded into baskets and taken to the winnowing floor. When there are only small quantities of rice, hand winnowing suffices. For large-scale winnowing, a ramp five to six meters high is built from tree trunks. A woman carries a basketful of threshed rice to the top and, leaning on the crossbeam that forms a kind of balustrade, she pours the rice out in a slow stream. As they fall, the grains shed their husks and any other debris, which is carried away by the wind. A little girl with a broom neatly separates the two.[11]

At the end of each day, the threshed rice is carried home in large baskets (approximately 18 kilograms capacity) on the backs of the men and women. Rice is also loaded into baskets on the back of a draft horse, if one is available. The rice is carried from the threshing site to a large granary on stilts, built close to the house. The dry rice is hulled as needed by the family, using a heavy foot-powered pounder which sometimes requires several people to operate. The task of hulling rice is usually assigned to women and girls.

Yield   Dry rice yields vary considerably with the regularity of rainfall over the growing season and the length of time a field has been worked. Lemoine reported that the average yield of 18 *rai*, which comprised the entire ricelands of the village of Pha Hok in Sayaboury province in 1965, was 2,935.6 kilograms per hectare.[12] Charles Pierson, a United Nations Food and Agriculture Organization expert who worked with the Royal Lao Government from 1967 to 1970, provided the following information on rice yields:

YEAR	YIELD
First year	3,000 kilograms/hectare
Second year	1,500 kilograms/hectare
Third year	600 kilograms/hectare[13]

This declining yield explains why rice is generally planted for only two seasons on a given *rai*. Planting a third crop means going hungry unless a newly cleared *rai* is planted as well to compensate for the scanty yield of the old one.

Production Cost   A look at the cost of production of a hectare of rice provides some idea of the profitability of working a rice *rai*. In 1969, we surveyed a rice *rai* belonging to the Kia Her family in the southern part of Xieng Khouang province. With the help of a son, Mr. and Mrs. Kia Her worked an area of about 1.5 hectares. According to Her, the harvest was 2,640 kilograms. Working the rice *rai* cost the family:

ACTIVITY	PRODUCTION COST
Preparation (1 hectare)	48 working days[14]
Sowing	12 working days
First weeding	19 working days
Second weeding	12 working days
Harvesting	15 working days
TOTAL	**106 working days**

"The Hmong working day begins with the 'first cock's crow.' If the daughter-in-law, the youngest wife, or the daughter has not arisen, she has until the second or third cockcrow, meaning sometime between four and five o'clock in the morning," says Lemoine.[15] However, the working hours of the Hmong farmer vary widely depending on the season and phase of the agricultural cycle. The average is around ten hours of work per day. It is important to note that in traditional Hmong society women work as much or more than men.

The time devoted to rice growing is usually greater than that needed to grow an equivalent area of corn. The main reason for this is that rice grows more slowly than corn and thus runs a greater risk of being smothered by weeds, which thrive during the monsoon rains. Long, arduous hours of weeding are required: two weedings for new *rai* which have first been completely cleared by burning, and three or even four weedings for second and third year *rai*. To the 106 working days required for the Hers' *rai* must be added the labor for threshing. Dumont's example from the North Vietnam delta is probably also valid for the mountains of northern Laos:

> A fairly strong man can thresh 50 to 200 kilograms a day, or even as much as 260 kilograms, if his field has yielded well and if the paddy is a variety that sheds its chaff readily. In addition to this must be counted the work of the helpers (women or children) who untie the sheaves and tramp the straw with their feet.[16]

At this rate, it would take at least nine days to thresh the harvest from a one-hectare rice *rai* in its first year of dry cultivation. Finally, transporting the rice harvest must be done on the backs of people or pack horses under very difficult conditions: poorly maintained trails, rugged terrain, often very long distances (one or two hours' walk) between the village and the fields. This can take from 10 to 20 days, depending on the means available (horses, helpers, etc.).

Corn The elderly Hmong in Laos say that when their ancestors left south China, the most valuable things they brought with them were cucumber and pumpkin seeds, peach pits and seed corn. At that time, corn was unquestionably the most important grain, for two main reasons:

○ The mountain regions which were still accessible to the Hmong immigrants were unsuited to the growing of irrigated rice. Furthermore, the newcomers knew nothing about mountain rice or dry rice agriculture. This hypothesis seems justified by the widespread consumption of corn by Hmong people at times in the past and by the relatively recent spread, in Southeast Asia, of dry rice growing on Hmong *rai*.

○ On the generally poor land available to them, corn grew splendidly and yielded good harvests. In the absence of rice, corn could provide adequate human nutrition and, at the same time, supply basic feed for the domestic animals the Hmong had brought with them on their long migration.

These two reasons explain why corn was for many years the staple of the diet of the northern Laotian and North Vietnamese Hmong populations. Its consumption was widespread enough to evoke comment from more than one foreigner traveling through the mountain regions of Indochina during the French colonial period. Pierre Lafont, commenting on the work of J. M. Halpern,[17] writes:

> We were astonished to read that rice was the main crop of the Meo, and that corn was only a secondary crop for them. Had the author read Condominas,[18] he would at least have learned that the basis of the Meo diet is corn rather than rice, and if he had spent a few days in a Meo village, he would have seen the preponderant place corn cakes occupy in the people's diet; these corn cakes are made with corn and no other grain.[19]

That observation, which was quite correct two decades ago, is no longer true today. With the introduction of dry rice cultivation everywhere in the Hmong mountains, corn has lost its preponderance over rice. Even so, large amounts of it are still grown because of its good nutritional qualities as feed for pigs and barnyard fowl.

Corn Cultivation   Corn is planted in April and May. It is rarely sown in a first-year *rai* but rather after one or two crops of rice, when the soil is already somewhat depleted. With a hoe in one hand and some grains of corn in the other, the farmer makes a depression six to ten centimeters deep in the black *rai* soil, drops in five or six grains of corn and covers them up with the back of the hoe. The distance between holes is about one meter; therefore some 9,500 to 10,000 holes, which will produce 35,000 to 45,000 stalks of corn, can be dug on a *rai* of one hectare.[20]

The more frequent the rain, the faster the corn grows, racing against the invading weeds that try to smother it. A month after planting, the area around each stalk of corn is carefully weeded with a hoe; two months later the corn is weeded again. The older the *rai*, the more weeds there are and the faster they grow. Weeding is a time-consuming and back-breaking chore for the mountain farmers.

Harvesting is done by breaking off the ears of corn and tossing them into a basket carried on the back, leaving the stalks standing. The corn is stored, on the ear, in huge baskets or in a granary. It is shelled with a hand sheller and ground in a large hand-powered stone mill as needed.

Size of Corn Rai   Corn *rai* are generally smaller than rice *rai*. Like rice *rai*, their area varies as a function of the available work force. A young household with two or three small children, for example, will generally plant only half or perhaps one hectare of corn per year, devoting the balance of its efforts to other food crops, primarily rice. It goes without saying that in the days when corn was the staple of the Hmong diet, the area planted in corn was at least twice what it is now; all efforts were concentrated on the corn crop, which in those days fed both man and beast.

Yield   The extreme variation of soil fertility with the age of a *rai* makes it difficult to calculate the yield of corn, like that of rice, with anything approaching accuracy. However, yields from mountain *rai* are, contrary to appearances, higher, at least for the first two years' harvests, than those of plains fields which are plowed but not fertilized. In a sampling of several *rai* in the Pha Hok region of Sayaboury province, Lemoine found an average yield of 4,456 kilograms/hectare.[21] Our own more limited survey of three corn *rai* in the Long Cheng-Sam Thong region gave an average yield of 22 quintals (2,200 kg.) per hectare. The yield declines sharply after the second year; the third year's harvest may be as low as 7.5 or 8 quintals (750 or 800 kg.) per hectare. At this point, if not sooner, the *rai* is abandoned and a new planting site cleared.

Production Cost   Our 1969 survey of an approximately one-hectare corn *rai* belonging to the Chong Khu family in the Phak Khe region of southern Xieng Khouang province yielded the following figures:

ACTIVITY	PRODUCTION COST
Preparation	42 working days
Planting	10 working days
First weeding	20 working days
Second weeding	12 working days
Harvesting	16 working days
TOTAL	**100 working days**

Working a one-hectare corn *rai* cost Mr. and Mrs. Chong Khu 50 days' work apiece, or a total of 100 working days. Since it was the first year this *rai* had been planted, its preparation time was fairly long (42 days). An old rice *rai* converted to corn would have taken only 10 to 14 days to prepare. Cutting the trees to clear the primary forest, very heavy work usually reserved for men, is responsible for most of this increase in preparation time.

The Khus' *rai* yielded 2,160 kilograms of corn. At first glance, the *rai* seems more profitable than an unfertilized lowland field (1,300 kg./ha.).[22] Such a comparison is misleading, however, in that it does not take into account, on the one hand, the four baskets (around 80 kilograms) of seed corn used and, on the other, the time taken to transport the harvested crop over long distances and very difficult terrain.

Our inquiry revealed that most of the Khus' corn crop was transported by a pack horse and the remainder on the couple's backs. The location of the *rai* allowed only two round trips between field and home per day. If, on each trip back from the *rai*, the horse carried 40 kilograms of corn and Chong Khu and his wife each carried 20 kilograms in their back baskets, the yield brought back to the village per trip would be

40 kilograms + 2(20 kilograms) = 80 kilograms

The quantity of corn brought home in one day would be

80 kilograms x 2 round trips = 160 kilograms

Getting in the entire corn crop would require

$$\frac{2{,}160 \text{ kilograms}}{160 \text{ kilograms/day}} = 13.5 \text{ days}$$

The net return on working the *rai* would be even lower if all hauling had to be done on the farmers' backs. In this case, it might take a month to get the entire crop back to the village.

These analyses of the productivity of rice and corn growing point up several serious challenges to the traditional Hmong subsistence economy as practiced in the mountains of northern Laos. First, both examples clearly demonstrate that the lack of an adequate transportation system is, and will continue to be for a long time to come, a bottleneck of considerable consequence to the economy of the mountain regions. Even more serious is the problem of long-term nutritional adequacy. Higher yields and greater productivity are needed to improve the quantity and, more importantly, the quality of the mountain peoples' diet. Such an improvement is a necessary condition for any increase in output, the basis of development. The present yields are made possible only by strong arms and an abundance of primary forest. Until there is an awakening of national consciousness, traditional Laotian society as a whole and that of the Hmong in particular can expect no better. Contributing to underdevelopment in every form are the negligence and indifference of a good many of the nation's leaders, less concerned with the lot of the people than with their own affairs, even though, without exception, they loudly proclaim their intentions to "pursue a social policy," "hasten economic development," and "defend democracy!"

Left to their own devices, Hmong farmers continue to live in an unending search for land to plant, land which is shrinking dangerously with each generation and with each political and military development. Population displacements caused by the war have forced hundreds of villages to resettle in less troubled areas, where ecological conditions are not particularly favorable. (These problems are discussed in detail in Chapter Six.)

Having studied the two main food crops raised by the Hmong, let us now look at some of the other crops they grow.

Other Food Crops   In addition to rice and corn, the Hmong grow a large variety of vegetables, mainly for family consumption. Some of the most important of these are:

Cucumbers   Highly valued by the Hmong, cucumbers are grown along with the rice and corn crops. Planted at the same time as corn and rice, they are harvested around October. Several species of cucumbers may be found growing in the same *rai*: Chinese cucumbers, larger than those found in Western countries, whose ripening flesh takes on a saffron yellow color; bitter cucumbers (*Monordica charantia*); and smooth, oval, melon-like fruits. These hardy Hmong cucumbers are generally immune to parasitic diseases such as rot, various cryptogamic infestations and attack by insects.

Squash and Pumpkins   Local varieties of squash, good-sized and quite tasty, grow in northern Laos, particularly in Xieng Khouang province. Squash are usually grown in gardens of about 20 by 30 meters, close to the house and fenced on all sides. They climb up trees, which act as living stakes. Pumpkins are planted in the *rai* with the corn. All are hardy varieties, free of disease.

Cabbage   The Hmong grow a variety of cabbages, ranging from Chinese mustard to cauliflower to the common head cabbage. These varieties thrive in the mountains. Chinese mustard is sown at the same time as the opium poppies and grows in the same fields. Head cabbage and cauliflower are kitchen-garden crops. They are used to make soup and may also be sautéed. Mustard is the only variety that is preserved. "First you make a kind of sauerkraut in brine, then you spread it out in the sun, hanging over bamboo poles. When dry, it will keep for several months."[23]

Beans   The Hmong raise a variety of bean with a very long pod (about 30 cm.). A soup made of these beans boiled without salt is a favorite of the Hmong, particularly during the hottest days on the *rai*. It is also used as a drink with meals.

Soybeans are a special favorite in Hmong gardening. The beans, first soaked in a bowl of water, are mashed through a hand mill; the soy milk that comes out is used as the base for curd. The soybean curd, or tofu, is not as high a quality as that made by the Chinese and the Vietnamese, but its consumption is widespread among the Hmong.

Potatoes   The potato grown by the Hmong is not native to the mountains of northern Laos; it was most likely introduced by the French sometime around the turn of the century. It is probably the Early Rose variety, now degenerated due, apparently, to a viral disease. The Hmong generally consider this potato a wild crop: potatoes left in the ground one year produce a crop the next, during the rains. Under ideal circumstances, potatoes are planted in late February and harvested in late May. The one great enemy of this crop is the red ant, which gnaws the young tubers.

Finally, in the Hmong garden may be found eggplant, onions, small tomatoes, various seasoning herbs (parsley, peppers, etc.) and something the Hmong call *kav ywm* (*Colocasia* sp.), a broad-leafed plant with edible stems.

Fruits   Fruits commonly found in a Hmong village include bananas, papayas and peaches. Bananas are picked green and buried in the rice stored in the granary next to the house, where they ripen slowly in the heat. Freshly gathered ripe papayas are a favorite of young and old; the yellow-fleshed fruits are delicious. Since there are always plenty of them growing wild, they are often picked green and fed to the pigs.

The peach is the one fruit the Hmong carried with them on their long migrations from China, through North Vietnam and Laos, into Thailand. These fruit are characterized by their large size; fine color; blunt shape; sweet, white, lovely-perfumed flesh; and brown, elongated, broadly-grooved free stone. They are of excellent quality when ripe (around the end of June).[24] "Hmong" peaches grow wild at elevations of 1,200 to 1,500 meters. However, peaches, like bananas and papayas, are not, strictly speaking, wild fruits. Very often there are peach trees growing in the sturdily fenced gardens almost every Hmong family tends.

To these fruits must be added the pineapple, which does fairly well at high elevations. In Xieng Khouang province, the Hmong and the Phouan also grow a variety of Chinese pear tree which bears very sweet and beautifully scented fruit. Many wild pear trees growing in the province produce much smaller fruit with sour-tasting flesh. Simple grafting could improve the quality of these wild pears. However, if they were to be grown on a large scale, they would become susceptible to the parasites and diseases so numerous in such climates.

At present, there is no methodical tending of these garden and orchard crops, although they could form the basis of commercial trade with a good potential for development. The markets are there: rising living standards have created an increasing demand for fruits and vegetables. However, development of these crops is hampered by the distance from towns, compounded by the lack of roads and transportation and by the lack of security created by the on-going war.

NON-FOOD CROPS   While food crops occupy a dominant place in the traditional Hmong economy, non-food crops also play a significant role. The most important of these are hemp, a crop grown for the production of textiles, and the opium poppy, grown primarily for trade and thus a significant source of cash for the Hmong farmer.

Hemp   In northern Laos, the Hmong grow hemp almost exclusively for their personal use; it is not the object of any trade. Hmong hemp grows to an average of three meters in height, sometimes reaching as high as five meters. According to Pidance, the species that reaches that height is *Cannabis gigantea*.[25] It is grown at elevations between 1,200 and 2,000 meters.

Choice of Land   Hemp is a demanding plant; it requires soil that is fairly rich in organic matter. The Hmong grow it on alluvial soils, in hollows, on particularly fertile old opium fields, on the sites of abandoned villages and in the family garden, where animal wastes can be brought to nourish it.

Hemp Cultivation   Hemp is sown around April, right after cutting and clearing. When the land is fertile enough, hemp is usually planted on an opium poppy *rai*, following the opium harvest. The seeds sprout seven to eight days after planting. The crop must be weeded two or more times. When the plants have grown to a height of eight to ten centimeters, they are thinned to allow each one a space of about eight centimeters square. Three months after planting, as soon as flowering is completed, the hemp stalks are harvested. Several stalks are left growing around the edges of the field to produce seeds for subsequent crops. The cut stalks are left lying in the fields, where rain and dew rett them naturally. All that need be done is to turn them over every other day or so for about a week until the process is complete.

An assessment of yield is difficult because of the general decline in hemp growing and the lack of security due to the war. The current situation prevented any on-site surveys during our field research. A study of the textiles of Trân Ninh (Xieng Khouang) reported a yield of about 3,000 to 3,500 kilograms of dried hemp stalks per hectare.[26]

Stripping is done by hand. Hmong women strip the stalk by pulling on the outer fibers, which are then knotted end to end. This primitive method of preparing the fibers for spinning is an extremely time-consuming chore for the Hmong housewife. The fibers are spun into thread which is wound into skeins, bleached in an ash-based bath, and softened by rolling between a board and a wooden cylinder. The softened thread is then woven, on a hand-made portable loom, into narrow lengths of white cloth for sewing into the family's clothing.

Production Cost   In 1905, Pidance estimated the production cost of a hectare of hemp as follows:

ACTIVITY	VALUE (piasters)[27]
Cleaning	6.00
Plowing	8.00
Planting and covering	2.00
Watching	2.00
Top dressing and weeding	8.00
Harvesting	2.00
Retting	15.00
Preparation of thread	15.00
Softening fibers	4.00
Pounding	10.00
Bleaching	3.00
TOTAL	**75.00**[28]

Current Trends   Twenty years ago, almost every Hmong woman wore skirts of hemp cloth; men's clothing was made of hemp cloth as well. Nowadays this fabric is used only to make the pleated skirts worn by Green Hmong women; White Hmong women have adopted trousers. This change is explained by the abundance of mosquitoes, which home in on the bare legs of Hmong women working in the fields, by the influx of foreign cloth of better quality at low prices, and, finally, by the long, hard work required to make Hmong hemp cloth. Cresson and Jeannin write:

> What long and weary toil, from the time the hemp is planted, this finery (the pleated, embroidered skirt) costs the Meo woman! No wonder it is her pride and joy. All year round, her whole life long, it keeps the Meo woman busy in the fields, along the roads and around the hearth. You can understand why you never see such a skirt for sale and why the Meo are so grudging about selling even the hemp cloth.[29]

In fact, the Green Hmong, the only ones who continue to grow hemp, are growing less and less of it. Green Hmong women are beginning to adopt trousers also. Competition from Japanese textiles has cut into hemp growing, which is gradually disappearing among the Hmong who are under the control of the Vientiane government. The Neo Lao Hak Sat, however, has reportedly restored traditional Hmong weaving to a place of honor in the "liberated zones," seeking in this way to assure "true economic independence, the basic condition for any real political independence." One wonders, though, whether it would not be better to replace hemp growing, which is not very profitable, with some more lucrative crop such as coffee.

Having examined hemp growing briefly, let us turn now to the opium poppy. What is its niche in the traditional Hmong economy? What has been and will be the development of opium production in Laos?

The Opium Poppy Opium poppy growing has, for more than a century, played a very important role in the traditional economy of the Hmong people. In this section, we will look at how poppy growing, which was foreign to imperial China, happened to take root in that country and how it became one of the main financial resources of the Hmong all across Southeast Asia.

Historical Background The opium poppy originated in the Middle East. It was known to the Greeks before the present era. Four centuries before Christ, Hippocrates recommended it as a remedy for some of his patients. The propagation of opium use, however, was due primarily to Arab physicians and traders. During the eighteenth century, the drug spread throughout all of northern India, where poppy growing was taken over and organized by the powerful East India Company. From there, the habit of opium smoking and the resultant scourge of opium addiction expanded into the Far East. In this way, the Indian drug reached China, where consumption soon increased prodigiously, generating tremendous profits for the British company at the expense of the health of the Chinese.

Concerned over deteriorating social conditions, Chinese authorities attempted to ban imports of the terrible drug. A vigorous campaign against opium smoking and the seizure of millions of pounds of illegal opium led to the so-called Opium War (1839-42) with England. The 1842 Treaty of Nanjing, though avoiding the explicit mention of opium, created five free-trade ports in China, which the British used largely to market illegal opium. Following a second defeat by England in 1858, the Chinese were forced to place an import duty on opium despite the fact that both the use and sale of opium were illegal in China at the time! All efforts to stamp out addiction, which had reached horrifying proportions, were in vain. Indeed, some Chinese leaders hoped not to wipe out addiction but to channel some of its enormous profits into their own pockets.

Apparently it was around this time that the ancestors of the Hmong, driven into the mountainous regions of southern China by the invading Han Chinese who had taken over their land, began to grow opium for the booming trade. They became specialists in this crop, which became a new source of income for them. However, most of the profits went not to the producers but to Chinese officials and military chiefs who enriched themselves on the labor of the peasants. This situation was mirrored in North Vietnam and northern Laos, to the profit of local chiefs and nobles, most of whom were true feudal lords. The practice of opium growing was handed down from generation to generation, across borders and countries, to our own time.

Cultivation and Yield Of all the crops grown by the Hmong, the opium poppy requires the most care and attention. The poppy is a very demanding plant: it requires rich, finely tilled soil, it flourishes only under certain conditions of moisture and sunshine, and it gives good yields only when properly handled. After generations of experience, the Hmong have learned to prefer the limestone mountains for poppy cultivation; the soil is more suitable and the exposure to the elements more favorable.

According to Fridman, the Hmong grow two varieties of *Papaver somniferum satigerum*.[30] One has pale mauve blossoms with large, oblong, fairly thin-walled capsules. Its milk is quite thin and gives a very low yield on coagulation. The other, more prevalent, has maroon-colored flowers and small to medium size, almost spherical, thick-walled capsules. It produces a creamy latex which coagulates quickly and gives a good yield.

The Hmong in northern Laos plant poppies at two times during the year, producing opium of different qualities: early opium and late opium. Early opium is sown broadcast in a corn *rai* about the time the ears of corn are ripe (late July-early August). The weeds are first pulled up and the soil lightly worked. An estimated three kilograms of seed are required to plant one hectare. Germination takes about ten days. The plants are thinned twice, at two-week intervals, and the more delicate ones removed, leaving a space of 15 to 20 centimeters between plants. The tall corn stalks (1.5 to 2.5 meters) shelter the poppies from the sun and smother any weeds which might harm them. By the time the ears of corn are harvested and the stalks removed, the poppy plants have reached four to five centimeters in height and are sturdy enough to stand up under the heavy monsoon rains. They blossom in October and November, and early opium is harvested until well into December. Early opium is not widely grown, however, since its quality is inferior to that of late opium. It is used only to tide the smokers over until the late opium harvest.

Late opium, the more important crop, is usually planted after the corn harvest. Beginning in July and August, when the rains have properly mellowed the soil, the opium *rai* is prepared. The cornstalks, which have been left standing after the harvest, are pulled up and burned in small piles in the field. Grasses are turned under and the soil is broken up by working with a hoe – a task that calls for considerable patience! Finally, the cornstalk ashes are spread evenly over the field. It is worth noting that working of the soil and the use of plant residue fertilizer are, unfortunately, practiced by the Hmong only in the cultivation of opium.

Late opium is planted in late August and early September. The seed is sown broadcast, like that of early opium. Weeding is done with the aid of a hoe. The first weeding takes place two months after planting, when the plants have not yet reached 20 centimeters in height. It goes on constantly until the poppies bloom.

Gathering of the latex begins in January and ends as late as March. The poppy capsules are cut around noon, when the sun is at its zenith. The opium knife consists of a small wooden handle, 15 to 20 centimeters in length, rounded and polished, at the tip of which three small copper blades are inserted parallel to each other about two millimeters apart.

On the first day, two cuts are made from top to bottom on opposite sides of the capsule. The action of the sun and the cool night causes the latex, flowing from the cuts, to coagulate quickly on the surface of the capsule. The coagulated droplets are gathered before sunrise the next morning using a small moon-shaped iron scraper. When the scraper is full, the latex is turned into a small bowl. This operation may go on until mid-morning, when the morning meal is eaten and the knife blades are sharpened in preparation for making new cuts, the latex from which will be collected the next day.

Each poppy fruit is cut four to six times, depending on its size. The second day's yield is less than the first, and each succeeding day's even smaller as the number of cuts increases. However, since the poppy plant continues to bear fruit, there may be capsules to cut for a month or more.

Opium *rai* vary greatly in size depending on the nature of the soil and the exposure to the sun. The average opium field is approximately half a hectare; it is rare to find one larger than a hectare. If the *rai* is small (a quarter-hectare or less), the farmer will probably have one or two more nearby.

The study of opium yields is not an easy task. Such inquiries often encounter hostile attitudes on the part of the Hmong, who will not allow anyone to make an accurate accounting. A former Inspector for Customs and Monopolies of French Indochina (Augier), estimated the yield at five kilograms per hectare. According to Marseille, former Commissioner of Agriculture, yields in Xieng Khouang province varied, according to the year and the *rai*, from five to ten kilograms per hectare. Boutin, a former official at Sam Neua, reported that the yield in Houa Phanh province was ten kilograms per hectare in average years and could reach as high as 18 kilograms in very good years.[31] Finally, Lemoine writes that in the Pha Hok region of Sayaboury province the average yield was 5.7 kilograms of raw opium per *rai*. According to Lemoine, a good *rai* would rarely yield more than 7.6 to 11.4 kilograms per hectare.[32]

Opium Production and Marketing   Estimating opium production in Laos has always been very difficult because of the wide dispersion of the population, the lack of an adequate infrastructure, and the continuing war. These factors have constantly hindered the task of the inquirer, who has also had to cope with mistrust on the part of the growers, often subject to oppressive taxation. During the colonial era, the French government confined itself to rough estimates. The Royal Lao Government has, since independence, done no better itself and generally simply refers to earlier French figures. The total annual opium production in Laos is usually given as 70 tons (1960).[33]

For generations, the Hmong, the Mien and some Phouan and Tai Deng have grown opium for their own use. Poppy growing was a necessity for the mountain peoples of northern Laos. Opium was not merely a source of revenue. Known from antiquity for its curative powers, opium was and still is a medical essential in many remote parts of the country.

It is to its effect on the central nervous system that opium (ingested or applied locally) – and particularly morphine given by hypodermic – owes its ability to soothe remarkably all kinds of pain, whether sudden and acute (gastric attacks, appendicitis, hepatic colic, nephritis, lead poisoning, neuralgia, painful insomnia accompanying acute inflammations) or chronic (ulcers, cancer, etc.). An analgesic and hypnotic, opium is also a very useful nerve sedative in mental disturbance, delirium, and nervous system disorders (epilepsy, eclampsia, chorea, etc.). It also soothes attacks of angina pectoris of aortic origin.... The excellent results sometimes achieved with the drug (particularly elixir of paregoric) in controlling diarrhea (simple diarrhea, catarrhal enteritis, typhoid fever) are the result of a three-fold effect: relief of pain, moderation of intestinal contractions, reduction of secretions....[34]

Opium has soothed physical pain and saved thousands of lives in these regions totally lacking any medical or health infrastructure. Its therapeutic effects led to its very quickly breaking out of the confines of personal use and becoming the object of local and international commerce. Opium trading had, and still has, many forms, ranging from legal marketing to smuggling.

During the colonial period, the purchase and sale of opium was operated as a legal monopoly held by the French Department of Customs and Monopolies under the order of February 7, 1899, which created the Opium Monopoly. That law, which was to regulate opium matters in all of Indochina for 50 years, contained a special provision for the Mien and the Hmong while at the same time enacting strict measures against fraud and smuggling.[35] Annual sales by the Opium Monopoly in its early years were:

YEAR	QUANTITY[36]
Prior to 1910	>110,000 kg.
1916	65,000 to 75,000 kg.
1916 to 1918	>115,000 kg.

This growth was no doubt due to the unusual conditions created by the world war, to the unprecedented prosperity from two consecutive years of bumper rice crops, to the enormous rise in exports, and to the presence of more than 50,000 Chinese laborers in northern Vietnam.[37]

Following the war, the Opium Monopoly's revenues remained relatively constant at between 60,000 and 70,000 kilograms of opium annually until 1930-31. French Indochina was, in its turn, hit by the Great Depression, which led to a considerable drop in opium sales by the Opium Monopoly. Its volume dropped to 28,458 kilograms in 1934; by 1938 sales had still not recovered to the level of 1930.

Income from opium enabled the French colonial government to show a healthy financial picture with budget surpluses. According to Dumarest, the overall budget of French Indochina, which was 20 million piasters in 1900, topped 100 million piasters in 1931-32.[38] The following percentages of net revenue derived from the opium monopoly, in which the steep decline of the early 1930s is evident, show that opium continued, nevertheless, to be a significant source of revenue in the overall budget of French Indochina.

YEAR	OPIUM REVENUES AS A PERCENTAGE OF TOTAL REVENUES[39]
1920	19%
1925	10.5%
1930	9.5%
1932	4.7%

Fridman gathered the following highly debatable opium production figures for the late 1930s and early 1940s:

YEAR	LOCAL OPIUM REVENUES[40]
1935	20 tons
1942	25 tons
1944	30 tons

The sudden acceleration in production beginning in 1942 is explained by the complete isolation of French Indochina from the rest of the world during World War II. Having been cut off from some of its major sources, the colonial government was in desperate need of revenue. Assuming a local consumption of five tons, the annual surplus of raw opium could have been as large as 15 to 25 tons during these years.

When World War II broke out and isolated Indochina from the rest of the world, the Opium Monopoly's stockpile quickly dwindled, causing both social and economic problems for the colonial government. First, opium had to be found to supply not only the users in the highlands of Laos and northern Vietnam but also the opium dens in Vientiane and, more critically, those in Hanoi, Haiphong, Saigon and Phnom Penh, where there were an estimated 100,000 to 150,000 Chinese and Vietnamese addicts living in 1936.[41] Secondly, opium was needed to supplement the colonial budget, now cut off from its major revenue sources. The French government turned to northern Laos and Vietnam; the Opium Monopoly made huge purchases in those areas. Despite an increase in production, the retail price of opium spiraled upward at a dizzying rate.

When the French government entered international talks on suppression of the use of opium, official purchases of opium again dropped sharply, without, however, affecting the cultivation and production of the drug. Marketing of the surplus was taken over by smugglers: Vientiane, Hanoi, Haiphong, Saigon, Phnom Penh, Bangkok and Hong Kong became the major markets. Profits remained fantastic: in 1952-53, a kilogram of opium bought for 3,000 piasters on the Xieng Khouang market would reap 7,500 piasters in Saigon.[42]

France's withdrawal in 1954 led to the end of their government-sponsored purchases of opium in Indochina, which broke up into independent states. After Laos became independent, the government was unable to control the production of opium being diverted into illicit channels, often covered up by some of the most highly placed people in the kingdom. This great opium rush would eventually contaminate the entire social spectrum, sucking in Chinese and Vietnamese merchants and officials, high and low, as well as dignitaries of the kingdom of Laos. A major share of the opium harvest went to the Viet Minh, who were willing to pay more for it than the Laotian government. The Viet Minh would then sell it on the major commercial markets of Southeast Asia, reaping the substantial profits it needed to buy arms.

The resumption of hostilities in Laos and the entry of the Hmong into the war have profoundly affected poppy growing. Since 1961, opium production in northern Laos has declined to an all-time low. Xieng Khouang province is no longer "the opium-growing country," regardless of what some foreign reporters, who have not set foot in the country for years, may say to the contrary. In 1960, opium which was sold openly on the Phong Savanh and Xieng Khouang markets for around 200 francs per kilogram (about $18.50/pound) would bring 5,000 francs in Saigon, 10,000 francs in Bangkok and 20,000 francs in Taipei.[43] The decline in opium production after 1961 caused a corresponding increase in its price. In 1969, a kilogram of opium sold for 26,000 kip[44] ($108) in Sayaboury, 30,000 kip in Vientiane, and more than 35,000 kip on the Sam Thong and Long Cheng markets.[45] Its price reached astronomical heights in the markets of Saigon, Bangkok and Hong Kong, reflecting the risks involved in smuggling it into those places.

In 1969 I traveled throughout the mountains of Xieng Khouang province and saw very few opium *rai*. It seems that a few years earlier General Vang Pao had asked the people in that part of the country to stop growing opium and concentrate on food crops and livestock. However, no suitable replacement crop has yet been suggested. War, insecurity and the difficulties of marketing opium (opium trade is theoretically illegal in Laos) are the main causes of the sudden decline in opium production in Laos.

Opium, nevertheless, continues to play an important role in the Laotian economy. At the end of 1970 a highly placed source in the kingdom stated, during a BBC London broadcast, that opium sales make up a substantial part of the national budget. Even so, it is important to realize that most of the opium goes into fraudulent or illegal smuggling operations often assisted or even organized by eminent persons within the country. In fact, since 1954 the opium monopoly has gradually passed into the hands of the prominent families of the kingdom, who share the lavish profits with their partners, powerful Chinese dealers in Vientiane, Savannakhet, Pakse, Luang Prabang and Xieng Khouang. French civilian pilots were no less involved in the drug traffic than are some American pilots today (1971). Two heroin manufacturing laboratories are said to be in operation in Laos, one in Luang Prabang and the other in Houei Sai. With protection from the highest levels, their opium supply comes mostly from the Golden Triangle area.

In view of various international drug control agreements, the disastrous effects of both drug addiction and drug trafficking, and the current pattern of opium production in the country, it may be questioned whether poppy growing will continue in Laos in the years ahead. A bill was passed in the National Assembly and approved by King Srisavang Vatthana on September 24, 1971, to ban, throughout Laos, the growing of poppies as well as the manufacture, consumption, sale, transport or possession of opium or its derivatives.[46,47] However, there have as yet been no viable suggestions of alternative cash crops. Under these conditions, the law, though enacted, will be neither realistic nor enforceable. This will remain the case as long as opium continues to be a major financial resource for a good portion of the Laotian population and as long as there is no realistic possibility of effective control over its production. The mountains of Laos are still and will continue to be a mystery to the government so long as they remain neglected.

LIVESTOCK

While agriculture is the major Hmong occupation, livestock also has a very important place in their traditional economy. Self-sufficiency needs and traditional ritual practices have maintained its role over the centuries.

Poultry Poultry raising is by far the most common type of animal husbandry practiced by the Hmong. Poultry is very closely tied in with the Hmong way of life. It is needed to nourish the new mother (who needs more protein than others), to call back the soul of a sick child, for the traditional marriage ceremony, and, finally, at the funeral, to give the dead a start on their way to build a new life. In short, poultry is indispensable to traditional Hmong existence.

A Hmong family will try, at all times, to maintain a flock of 10 to 30 roosters, hens and pullets.[48] The mountain climate and Hmong husbandry techniques combine to make Hmong poultry superior to that of the plains. A Hmong pullet, for example, is as large as a Western laying hen. The Hmong feed their poultry, mainly on corn and unhulled rice, twice a day, at sunup and sundown.[49] During the rest of the day, the fowl are allowed to wander at will around the yard and the areas close to the house, scrounging whatever they can to round out their rations. When they come home at night, they head straight for the henhouse, located close to their owner's house. This is why victims are always chosen at night for sacrifice on the morrow!

A Hmong hen lays an average of only 80 to 100 eggs a year, whereas a Western laying hen may lay as many as 200 or more. The eggs are carefully gathered and most are put into brood nests. Eggs are eaten only rarely, but many are used on the shaman's altar and in various ritual ceremonies. The Hmong regularly caponize young cockerels, producing capons weighing two to three kilograms. Capons are generally reserved for the New Rice festival and for the *tsiab peb caug*, or New Year feast. They are also used as gifts.

Hmong villagers also raise ducks when big enough streams, marshes or ponds are available. Before the outbreak of hostilities in 1961, the Hmong village of Khang Kho (in Xieng Khouang province south of the Plain of Jars) had a relatively large flock of ducks. Today they are raised almost everywhere in the Sam Thong-Long Cheng area and particularly in the Muong Phieng region of Sayaboury province.

Swine Swine are without a doubt the favorite livestock of the Hmong. Pigs provide not only meat but, equally important, fat, which is required for cooking and many other uses. Hmong raise two common breeds of pig: the spotted black-and-white variety common to all of Southeast Asia and another variety, probably European in origin, having long pink bristles like the pigs seen in Western countries. Adults of this latter variety are markedly larger and fleshier than spotted pigs. In Xieng Khouang province, we found an average herd size of five to ten pigs, including two sows and a boar, per family. Sows generally farrow once a year, producing an average of six young per litter.

Sows and their piglets are usually left to roam about at will. They spend their time in the bush, beneath the stilted granaries, or, during the rainy season, under the projecting eaves of the house. Some, earmarked for butchering, especially for the New Year holiday, are given a partially sheltered sty and proudly shown to visitors who happen by. Not all Hmong build pigsties; some let all of their pigs wander freely at all times. It is quite a spectacle to see the entire herd, large and small, come running in from all directions when their mistress calls them to feed!

Hmong women feed their pigs on corn, bran, banana leaves and the stems of wild banana trees in winter, and on bean leaves and bourbon palm stems during the rainy season. The pigs squabble noisily over their twice-daily rations, set out, at the same time as the chickens are fed, in one or more wooden troughs built in the small yard in front of the house. The animals can grow to a remarkable size, but, fat as they are, they provide little meat. The plains pigs, though smaller in size, are better for butchering.

The Hmong usually preserve whatever pork is not consumed during ceremonies and festivals. Two methods of preservation are used. In the more common method, pieces of fatty pork are salted and hung over the hearth, where they are cured slowly by the heat and the rising smoke. In the second method, the pork is boiled in a large pot until well done, chopped ginger added and the mixture boiled until all the water has evaporated, leaving only the meat, the fat and the ginger. This mixture is then packed into terrines, covered with banana leaves and stored near the fireplace. This second method has the advantage of preserving the meat longer (six months to a year).

Cattle and Water Buffalo   The mountains of northern Laos, thanks to their temperate climate, provide natural pastures for cattle. The morning dews and mists keep forage fresh at all times. Herds of zebu and water buffalo live in a semi-wild state in the forest bush and on old *rai*.

Husbandry of these animals, so vital for ritual sacrifices to the dead and to protective spirits, has declined considerably since the end of World War II. Elderly Hmong often speak with nostalgia of the "good old days [before 1940] when every family had a dozen oxen and buffalo." Cattle are disappearing; more than 25 years of war have decimated their numbers faster than normal reproduction can restore them. Before the resumption of local hostilities in 1961, there were sizable herds in almost every Hmong village. At that time, for example, the Hmong *tasseng* of Khang Kho kept several hundred oxen and water buffalo. Today this rare "capital on the hoof" has become a source of great pride for anyone who can afford it. In 1969 there was in the Sam Thong mountains a herd of more than 400 cattle and buffalo belonging to several brothers of an extended family. Another herd just as large grazed over the abandoned *rai* between Sam Thong and Long Cheng. In 1972 several herds of similar size were sighted in the grassy region of Muong Cha southeast of Xieng Khouang, an area distinguished for its cattle raising. These were only the remnants of much larger herds, having managed to escape from the devastating war that has raged for more than ten years in Xieng Khouang province.

Neither cattle nor water buffalo are given any particular care. They are allowed free range all year round, their owners coming out to check on them from time to time. Among the Hmong, as among the Laotians in general, there is little danger of theft. Periodically, when the pasture becomes depleted, relatives, sometimes several families, are mobilized to drive the herd from one mountain to the next. Shifting of herds becomes a real expedition!

As a rule, Hmong prefer cattle to buffalo, first because of the quality of their meat, and secondly because of their docile temperament, which buffalo, accustomed to living wild, do not usually possess. Buffalo can be quite dangerous; they will sometimes charge passers-by who disturb their peace and quiet. Capturing even an ox, much less a buffalo, under these conditions is no mean feat; it takes considerable skill and even more patience. Often the pursuer must use his flintlock rifle to bring down the maddened and therefore dangerous beast.

In traditional Hmong society, oxen and buffalo are not normally used as draft animals. Cattle raising is a response to a religious rather than an economic need. When calamity strikes a community, the Hmong turn to the ancestors, to heaven or to the local spirits to protect them. In return they promise one or more oxen or buffalo depending on the seriousness of the trouble. Such a promise is always kept if after making it there is an improvement in the situation or if things return to normal.

It is Hmong funerals, though, that entail the most exorbitant expenditures of cattle. "We have seen," writes Bernard Bourotte,

> two oxen killed on the fifth day after death, three more on the sixth, plus another in honor of the French visitors, and eight on the morning of the burial. The value of the cattle alone came to at least a thousand piasters.... The shades of these beasts will go along with the dead man while the meat will be eaten by those at the funeral. Eating and drinking is the main order of the day until the "raising of the body."[50]

The older the deceased person and the more influence he had, the greater the sacrifices will be. At the funeral, each of a person's adult sons, daughters (or sons-in-law) and a maternal uncle or his representative is obliged to kill an ox. Others are sacrificed by close relatives and friends who have come to pay their last respects. The lack of facilities for preserving or keeping meat often means a week of gorging on it followed by several weeks without eating any at all.

Horses   The horse also holds an important place in traditional Hmong society; this importance is reflected in the way horses are treated. Unlike cattle, which even during the worst weather of the year wander in a semi-neglected state through village and forest, every horse has a good tight stable near its owner's house. Every day tender hay or young cornstalks are gathered for the horse to eat. It is also fed paddy and ears of corn regularly. Before every long trip the horses' mangers must be kept full at all times. It is not unusual, when they will soon be required to travel long distances or subject to great exertion, for the master to get up several times during the night to feed his animals.

Of all domestic animals, the horse plays perhaps the most important role in Hmong economic self-sufficiency. Just as oxen and buffalo are indispensable for farm work on the plains, the horse is vital to agriculture in the mountains. Its use is almost universal in these regions, where topographical conditions and tradition rule out the use of draft animals for plowing or drayage. Every day during the harvest the horse carries two large loads of paddy or corn home from the *rai* in baskets slung with ropes from either side of its pack saddle. Even so, most of the hauling falls to people, as we saw earlier. During the slack period (late March and early April) the horse accompanies its master, acting as a casual traveling merchant, on long treks through the mountains, carrying the most diverse loads of cloth, yarn, clothing, cooking utensils, and so on.

The horse is, above all, a status symbol. The traditional Hmong social ladder is measured by the quality of one's saddle horse. The better off a man is, the harder he will try to buy a fine horse, which will be his pride and joy.[51] These animals, invariably well cared for, take almost no part in farm drudgery.

Goats   Finally, around most Hmong villages one sees herds of goats living in a semi-domesticated state. From time to time one is singled out and captured for a ritual sacrifice. Though they willingly eat it, goat meat is not relished by the Hmong, who much prefer either beef or pork.

In Laos, the Hmong seem to be in a most favorable position for animal husbandry to flourish. The mountain climate is more conducive to animal health than that of the lowland plains; the humidity makes for lush grazing and pastureland. However, the mountain people consume only a small proportion of the animals they raise. Most of them are used for religious and shamanistic purposes. Ancient pastoral methods, lack of infrastructures such as roads and bridges, lack of organized livestock markets, and, above all, lack of knowledge of the potential of the Laotian mountains combine to create a formidable impediment to the expansion of animal husbandry there.

HANDICRAFTS

Handicrafts are an important part of traditional Hmong society. They are all the more necessary in that Hmong settlements are so widely scattered and isolated. A Hmong must meet the vast majority of his needs with homemade craft objects. A farmer by vocation, he becomes a do-it-yourself carpenter, cabinetmaker and basket weaver during the slack times. In the old days, he made his own bowls and spoons of wood and wove sandals of hemp. An occasional expert weaver may still be found among the Green Hmong although, as we saw earlier, Hmong hemp cloth is steadily being replaced by imported textiles.

Almost every Hmong village has its blacksmith who, in exchange for a few ounces of opium, will turn out hoes, axes, brush knives, sickles and other farm implements. If he is especially skillful, he may also be a jeweler or a gunsmith. Nowadays in the shops of Long Cheng one finds Hmong necklaces, bracelets and rings done in amazingly fine silver. Flintlock rifles, though, are disappearing; these days they are made only on special order as gifts or souvenirs.

There are also makers of flutes, guimbards and *qeej*, the mouth organ that is the symbol of the Hmong people. Hmong culture is intimately bound up with these traditional musical instruments. On starry nights one can hear the sweet sounds of flutes and mouth harps waft by, laden with poetry, weaving young men and women together into the most charming of idylls. And at the close of life, the sound of the *qeej* accompanies a Hmong on his final voyage.

STANDARD OF LIVING

The study of subsistence activities leads into an examination of the Hmong standard of living. The choice of criteria for describing the standard of living in the mountains of northern Laos poses some complicated and delicate problems. For one thing, appearances can be very misleading; one cannot, without serious risk of error, rely on impressions alone. For another, a partial or incomplete study can, and often does, lead to erroneous interpretations. For example, in the same region a clinical survey may show an overall satisfactory state of health, while demographic data show an extremely high mortality rate between birth and the age of ten. These criteria, if considered individually, would certainly lead to contradictory conclusions. Such instances are by no means rare in Laos, where natural selection plays a very harsh role and where poor hygienic conditions combined with endemic diseases such as malaria, intestinal parasites, and so forth, cause very high infant mortality. Only the strongest and hardiest children survive.

With these considerations in mind, let us take a look at Hmong living standards on three levels: the biological, the economic and the social. These levels will not be studied exhaustively; rather, the most significant factors within each of them will be identified and examined.

THE BIOLOGICAL LEVEL

At the biological level, we will consider the state of health of the Hmong and other ethnic groups in northern Laos, the hygienic conditions in which their traditional societies operate, and the causes of the extremely high mortality rate, especially among children.

STATE OF HEALTH   In late 1969, Dr. Khammeung Tounalom, chief physician and surgeon at the Sene Souk Hospital in Sam Thong, summarized the health of the peoples of northern Laos as follows: "A person is born and grows up in an environment totally lacking in hygiene; he lives out his life in the same way his ancestors did."[52] Unhealthy living conditions and ignorance of the origins of the diseases that proliferate there and the ways in which they are transmitted are the real reasons for the curse that has long stricken northern Laos and has yet to be exorcised. This state of affairs explains the precarious state of health among the peoples as well as the very high mortality rate, particularly among children. Those infants who somehow manage to survive the critical first years of their tenuous existence acquire immunity to the many diseases to which they are exposed and along with it an astonishing physical stamina.

ENVIRONMENTAL CONDITIONS   Health and its preservation are closely linked to the ecological environment. The fate of a population is written there in advance, although subsequent improvements in sanitation and hygiene may modify the general health conditions somewhat.

Climate is one of the essential ecological factors. It affects health both indirectly and directly: indirectly, by determining to some degree the availability of food and by favoring or inhibiting the presence of germs and the spread of disease; directly, through its component factors (temperature, humidity, etc.), which, in Laos, include a relatively high mean temperature and a wide range of variation in weather conditions, particularly in temperature over a single day and in humidity from one season of the year to another. Some of these conditions unquestionably increase susceptibility to germs and diseases.

An important topographical factor is the formation of stagnant pools of rain water or water from overflowing streams, which are excellent breeding grounds for larvae of the *Anopheles* mosquito, the vector of malaria. This factor is particularly serious in the small valleys in which the Hmong sometimes locate their corn and rice *rai*. Here they come into contact with the mosquitoes and so fall victim to violent and sometimes fatal attacks of malaria.

The dwelling is another environmental factor. While it does provide some protection against the weather, lack of adequate facilities for removal of refuse in the village plays a role in the spread of certain infectious diseases, mainly by encouraging the proliferation of flies, which are a classic transmission factor in the spread of disease through food.

Drinking water is the vehicle for a number of disease-causing viruses (poliomyelitis, hepatitis), microbes and microorganisms (typhoid fever, bacterial and amoebic dysentery), and the eggs of intestinal worms. While the quality of the water supply (mainly spring water) in most Hmong villages is acceptable, it is far from adequate in quantity. The shortage of water undoubtedly plays a part, also, in the low level of personal hygiene and the high incidence of skin diseases: impetigo among children (generally beginning in the ear lobe and often spreading to the whole body), boils in adults, itching resembling the effects of scabies in nearly everyone, and many others.

Finally, diet plays a key role in the preservation of health and the maintenance of resistance to disease. Though fairly diversified, the Hmong diet is relatively poor nutritionally. Hmong daily meals generally consist of boiled rice and vegetables. Despite all the opportunities afforded by game and sacrifices, meat consumption is extremely low. What cattle there are are largely earmarked for religious and shamanistic propitiatory rites to ward off illness, though the consumption of the offerings by participants at these rituals assures most adults of at least a minimal amount of protein. We saw earlier how sickness and particularly death and funeral rites can wipe out capital accumulated by years of effort. The numerous pigs, cows and buffalo sacrificed, however, result in only a tiny share of meat for the family whom fate has chosen to host such often ruinous ceremonies. On days of mourning as well as on feast days such as New Rice, New Year, etc., large numbers of guests consume vast quantities of meat in a single sitting. At its conclusion, shares of meat must be offered to parents and kin as well as to those who assisted in preparing and carrying out the ceremony. Whatever is left, usually very little, will enrich the family's daily fare for the next week or so.

It is easy to see why the Hmong are vegetarians most of the time. It has been estimated that meat appears on the Hmong table only twice or three times a month on the average. Very poor families would seldom taste it at all were it not for the distribution of meat at feasts and rituals. This explains the chronic malnutrition among the Hmong as well as among the other underprivileged social classes in Laos. Actual deficiency diseases, however, are quite rare. "Our people are undernourished," says Dr. Tounalom, "but not to the point where they get sick from it."

ENDEMIC AND EPIDEMIC DISEASES Ecological conditions also influence the existence and extent of endemic diseases. Some, like cholera and plague, are relatively rare in the mountains; others affect nearly the entire population.

Malaria is perhaps the principal disease and morbidity factor in the upland valleys. Seasonal peaks of infant mortality are its direct result. As already mentioned, the shallow ditches on the edges of the *rai* are excellent breeding grounds for the *Anopheles* mosquito.

Amoebic dysentery and tuberculosis are other terrible scourges. Tuberculosis is now spreading at a dangerous rate in some regions of northern Laos. Traditional medicine is helpless against it. Without proper care, sufferers gradually exhaust themselves and then die suddenly. The risk of contagion is high; no public health measures have been taken to treat tuberculosis properly or to confine its spread.

Though lower in incidence, pneumonia, meningitis, smallpox and measles also cause large numbers of deaths each year, particularly among children. There are widespread reports of the spread of venereal diseases (syphilis and gonorrhea). On the other hand, Hansen's disease, one of the most difficult diseases to cure, is confined to only a few areas of the country.

CAUSES OF DEATH In Laos, where almost no reliable vital statistics are collected, particularly in the mountain regions, it is difficult to determine even the exact cause of a death, much less the proportion of deaths attributable to specific diseases. There is general agreement that most deaths are due to malaria, amoebic dysentery and pulmonary infections. However, accidental deaths (falls from cliffs or trees, hunting accidents, etc.) are fairly common. Individual and group hygiene (drinking water, refuse disposal, etc.) must also answer for some deaths. Many women, for example, die in childbirth due to the general lack of sanitation.

Ignorance of the origins of disease and, even more, persistence of traditional beliefs about illness are the underlying causes of many deaths among the Hmong. These ways of thinking isolate traditional Hmong society from the progress of modern medicine. The slightest illness is blamed on the spirits who "demand" sacrifices. Without exception, the village shaman is called in to try, in vain, to exorcise the illness. Not until after long ritual ceremonies have proven fruitless is the patient, by then in an extremely weakened condition, taken to the nearest dispensary, often a day's walk away. Very often all the nurse or doctor can do at that point is watch the patient die, and he can count himself lucky if his impotence does not further reinforce the deceased's family in its mistrust of modern medicine.[53]

Labor productivity is directly linked with health. In fact, in nonindustrialized countries like Laos productivity problems are often actually medical problems, such as the physical stamina of the workers and the health care available to them. There can be no increase in labor productivity without first an improvement in the people's health.

Mass public education and public health campaigns are the most effective tools available for eradicating endemic diseases. To achieve full effectiveness, health improvement actions, both medical and educational, require the participation of the population itself. They must be carried out within the framework of community development and must be an integral part of an overall development policy.

THE ECONOMIC LEVEL

The biological level just described reflects, to some degree, the economic standard of living of traditional Hmong society. A more detailed picture of the economic level can be derived from an analysis of the typical family budget, though the connections between the two are not always intuitively obvious.

THE TRADITIONAL FAMILY BUDGET

THE TRADITIONAL FAMILY BUDGET The traditional Hmong family is an almost totally self-sufficient entity. Its budget is intended to provide for all of its needs for the year, both in food and clothing and in services. In a closed economy where a monetary system is all but nonexistent, the family budget must be evaluated not in terms of cash income but rather in terms of production. The results of many field studies form the basis of the following summary of the mean annual production and consumption of a traditional Hmong family.

AVERAGE ANNUAL BUDGET OF A HMONG FAMILY OF SIX

	TOTAL PRODUCTION	DOMESTIC CONSUMPTION AND SERVICES	TRADE AND BARTER	STORES AND SAVINGS
PRIMARY PRODUCTION				
AGRICULTURE				
Rice	1,200 kg.	90%	–	10%
Corn (unshelled)	2,000 kg.	90%	–	10%
Opium	8 choj*	37%	50%	13%
Other products	Variable	90%	–	10%
LIVESTOCK				
Poultry	35 head	87%	5%	8%
Swine	10 head	80%	8%	12%
Cattle	Variable	Variable	Variable	Variable
HUNTING AND GATHERING				
Hunting	Variable	100%	–	–
Gathering	Variable	100%	–	–
HANDICRAFTS				
Weaving	Disappearing	100%	–	–
Basketry	Variable	100%	–	–

1 choj = 380 grams

COMPONENTS OF THE FAMILY BUDGET Having established the total annual budget of a Hmong household, let us now look at some of its components: household consumption, barter and the cash sector.

Household Consumption Household consumption occupies a predominant place in the traditional Hmong economic system. It includes not only food but also a number of other goods and services.

Our survey[54] showed that, on the average, a Hmong family produces 1,600 kilograms of paddy per year, or, allowing for a 25 percent loss during hulling, around 1,200 kilograms of rice. We also know that the Hmong eat three meals a day, consisting primarily of rice. Using an average daily rice consumption (before cooking) of 750 grams per adult and 350 grams per child, a family of six (the average), consisting of parents and four children, will eat about 1,060 kilograms of rice in a year. This leaves a reserve of only 140 kilograms of rice to cover unforeseen circumstances such as visits and ceremonies and to provide seed grain for the next crop. But what of the misfortune that stalks the Hmong family every moment of its life? All it takes is for death to strike one of its members and its rice reserve can disappear at one fell swoop, often forcing the family deeply into debt.

Corn, for a time the staple of the Hmong diet, is today eaten only occasionally, as a stopgap when the rice harvest has been poor. Almost all of it is fed to poultry and pigs. Since there is very little trade in either of these animals, they are generally earmarked for family and community consumption, for special occasions like weddings and traditional festivals, or for ritual sacrifice. We have already seen how the livestock sacrifices entailed by Hmong funerals can amount to real hecatombs!

Finally, hunting and gathering also contribute significantly to the diet. Hunting has always been and still is a major activity of Hmong men. They organize treks to hunt large game (wild boar, deer, bear, wild ox or gaur, tiger, etc.) using flintlock rifles. Crossbows are used to bag smaller game like squirrels and birds. The lush mountain forests surrounding Hmong villages provide an ample supply of both edible plants, such as bamboo shoots, wild tubers and various kinds of mushrooms, and those used for medicinal purposes, all of which can be had simply for the taking. The products of hunting and gathering are consumed entirely by the family itself.

Because food is the most significant component, there is a tendency, when making initial approximations of household consumption, to overlook other elements. The traditional Hmong lifestyle, however, involves the expenditure of resources for many other goods and services consumed by the household in addition to food. Among the more important of these are the building of the house, the manufacture of farm implements and household utensils, weaving and basketry, the gathering of wood for cooking and heating, the gathering of hay and banana stalks to feed livestock, and some of the domestic work done by women, such as corn grinding and rice hulling.

This brief summary illustrates the importance of household consumption in the Hmong subsistence economy; it accounts for approximately 80 percent of all primary production. The single exception is opium. Only part of its production is consumed or saved (in the form of silver ingots) where it is grown; the rest is used as a medium of exchange in all sorts of transactions. Opium is the principal, if not the only, source of cash for the traditional Hmong family. The lack of any sort of infrastructure in the mountains means that it is often the only commercially profitable product they produce. It is opium sales, for example, that make possible the purchases of cloth and salt so indispensable to the Hmong household. Let us now take a look at the importance of opium in the traditional barter economy.

Barter A holdover from earlier forms of economic organization, barter is still a relatively widespread form of exchange in the Kingdom of Lan Xang, particularly in the north. This is because rural Laotian society is, in general, still very traditional. Each village acts as its own economic unit, each ethnic group forms a world of its own, having very little contact with its neighbors. Far from urban areas and major avenues of communication, the traditional economic system is still based largely on the exchange of food and services between various social categories (e.g. farmers and blacksmiths, villagers and shamans, etc.) and between different ethnic groups.

Within the Hmong village, patterns of exchange are manifold, ranging from "lending a hand" to actual provision of goods. If he has fallen behind with his planting or harvesting, the Hmong peasant often calls upon his neighbors for help in catching up. The days they put in working in his field will be repaid by an equal number of days of his or his family's labor. This form of mutual aid is widely practiced in the mountains. It motivates the work by providing greater output and, at the same time, strengthens the solidarity of the farmers. That closeness is further demonstrated in exchanges of consumer goods. When he runs out of salt, fat or rice, the villager turns to his neighbors, usually his clan brothers. He might trade a bowl of salt for two bowls of fat or he may simply borrow food, which he will pay back sooner or later. Among the Hmong there is no such thing as lending at interest; the practice of usury is considered contrary to their moral values. The ancient tradition of generosity of the rich toward the poor contributes greatly to the cohesiveness of traditional Hmong society. Such a practice not only strengthens the bonds among members of the clan and community but, more importantly, constitutes a kind of security, an insurance against misfortune.

No Hmong village, though, however traditional it may be, can achieve total self-sufficiency. The Hmong have always had to import salt, the one thing the mountains do not produce. Periodically they go down, often in caravans, to replenish their salt supplies from the Tai in the valleys or the Lao in the plains, sometimes striking up great friendships with them. These seasonal excursions gave rise to the markets of Xieng Khouang, Sam Neua, Luang Prabang, Sayaboury and Houei Sai. The Hmong living in the mountains surrounding the Plain of Jars often traveled as far as Tha Thom and Muong Kao in Borikhane province in search of salt.

In addition, the Hmong are now increasingly dependent on the outside world for cloth. Hmong hemp cloth, which 25 years ago was woven in every Hmong household, has all but disappeared. Today it is woven by only a handful of Green Hmong women. The considerable labor it entails, beginning with the growing of the hemp, has long been the despair of the White Hmong woman, who has given up the pleated skirt of bleached hemp for the more practical black cotton trousers. Many families have abandoned weaving altogether, preferring to buy the finer Japanese textiles which are available in abundance. "In exchange for credit for cloth and other needs from the market," writes Lemoine, "the [Hmong] farmer will promise to pay in rice at harvest time. In mid-December, you can see pack horses laden with rice coming down the trails to Sayaboury. They carry the *kalong*[55] of rice promised to the merchants in the valley."[56]

During my youth, I witnessed the same phenomenon occurring, at perhaps an even brisker pace, in Xieng Khouang province. Prior to 1961, the date of resumption of hostilities in northern Laos, each year saw long caravans of merchants criss-crossing the country. Hmong farmers were going down to the lowland markets to sell, usually by barter, the products of their fields and barnyards, while Chinese, Lao and even some Hmong merchants were moving in the opposite direction to exchange their manufactured goods for opium, often covering several hundred kilometers of mountain trails up hill and down dale. Each expedition, which usually lasted a month or two, consisted of as many as 20 or 25 heavily laden pack horses and almost as many men, seldom armed. Laos was at peace then, and there was practically no brigandage.

Opium played a primary part in all these transactions. With its high value and small volume, opium lends itself wonderfully to the local economic system. Its pervasive economic and financial influence make it a universal, respected currency among the Hmong and other highland peoples as well as among the Chinese and the Lao. According to a long-established and well-known system of valuation, opium is reckoned in *choj* ("bars"), *lag* ("ounces"), *txiaj* and *fiab*. These units are related in a decimal system of weights:

1 *choj* = 10 *lag* = 100 *txiaj* = 1000 *fiab*

A "bar" of opium (so called because it is equal in weight to a bar, or ingot, of silver) weighs approximately 380 grams and a *lag* one-tenth that amount, or about 38 grams. Measurements are usually made with opium scales from China. Minor services are generally paid for directly in opium, as are certain ritual services. With opium, a farmer can buy salt from the Lao or farm tools from the village blacksmith. A bolt of black cloth can be bought for eight or ten *lag*, a rifle for 30 or 40, a horse for 100.

Opium helps give the Hmong a strong position in the hierarchy of ethnic minorities in Laos. On the one hand, it assures them of a relatively stable standard of living; on the other, its trade acts to establish a kind of economic satellization of nearby villages inhabited by other ethnic groups. Addicted to opium, these people come regularly to do odd jobs for the Hmong in exchange for a few grams of opium scrapings. Although they live at almost the same altitude as the Hmong, some of these groups do not grow opium themselves but willingly work as seasonal laborers in the opium *rai* of the Hmong.

While opium is practically ubiquitous in the mountains, its influence is gradually declining in the big cities like Vientiane, where there is a solidly established monetary system based on the *kip*, the Laotian national currency. In fact, opium is severely restricted by legal measures prohibiting its sale or use. Opium enters the cities clandestinely where it is quickly exchanged for silver bars, as in Luang Prabang, or for bank notes, as in Vientiane, before entering into various transactions.

The Cash Sector   In traditional Hmong society, the cash sector is as weak as the barter sector is thriving. The very low frequency of cash transactions is a result of the low level of cash income and of the almost total absence of a market system for either selling or buying in the mountains. There is a pervasive lack of confidence in the kip, with good reason: it has been devalued several times and is now held at an artificially high value by an international currency support fund.[57] Finally, certain structural features of the Hmong village economy tend to keep it in a near-stagnant condition. The natural environment, the very low population density spread over such a vast area, and the egregious lack of passable roads severely restrict the potential for both the production and marketing of products.

However, all indications are that the cash sector has flourished at times in the past. The large amounts of silver held by traditional Hmong families is one such indication. In every Hmong home are found 27-gram Indochinese silver piasters, the latest coinage of which dates back to 1936, as well as numerous silver coins with face values of 20, 10, and 5 centimes, valued according to their weight relative to the piaster. How can the presence of these coins, which are obviously part of an organized monetary system, be explained?

During the colonial era, the French administration required that the poll tax levied on all residents in Laos be paid in silver specie. The only way the Hmong could get silver piasters was to sell some of their crops, livestock and game. Since all the minorities, whether Tai, Mien, Lu or Hmong, tended to be suspicious of paper money, which to them had no intrinsic value, silver piasters and 5-, 10- and 20-centime coins circulated so extensively in their "country" that by 1937 they had become a universally accepted currency, functioning on a par with opium. The weekly markets in towns like Meo Vac, Dong Van and Lai Chau in North Vietnam and Sam Neua, Xieng Khouang and Nam Tha in northern Laos were beginning to abound with a multicostumed throng of people speaking all kinds of languages and dialects. Chinese was often used as a lingua franca by the various ethnic groups. As its use spread, the piaster wielded a growing influence over economic and financial affairs in the region, eventually spreading beyond the borders of Indochina into Yunnan and Guangxi provinces in China.

As the piaster established a foothold in the markets of northern Indochina, it upset the old Chinese monetary system based on the silver ingot by introducing its own valuation system:

1 piaster = 5 twenty-centime coins *or* 10 ten-centime coins *or* 20 five-centime coins

Since the weight basis of the old and new systems was different, the following mixed scale had to be established:

1 silver bar (*choj*) = 14 piasters (27 grams x 14 = 378 grams)
1 ounce (*lag*)   = 1 piaster + 4 ten-centime coins (38 grams)

For a long time the two systems coexisted, becoming ever more tightly woven into the ways of the mountain peoples of Indochina.

Nowadays, the kip, the national currency of Laos, is gradually supplanting the silver piaster, which is now used mainly for decorative purposes (necklaces, rings, and so on) and in certain traditional practices. The kip circulates in the form of 1-, 5-, 10-, 20-, 50-, 100-, 200-, 500- and 1,000-kip notes. However, a great many obstacles, both political and psychological, must be overcome before the kip currency system, relatively new to the mountain people, becomes a part of their everyday lives. Despite the fact that education has greatly encouraged the development of the cash sector in the mountain economy and that the war has completely swept away old economic structures and thus hastened this development, most Hmong remain fairly hostile toward paper money. In fact, the traditional Hmong is careful not to hold many paper kip, which may become worthless overnight. Hmong households quickly convert whatever profits they manage to make, however small, into silver, which remains relatively stable in value over time. They usually seek out Chinese jewelers to exchange their surplus kip for silver bars and coins. In 1969, an Indochinese silver piaster was worth about 600 kip, a silver bar about 9,000. A household can also sell its surplus opium at one *choj* of opium (380 grams) for a bar of silver. Opium is literally worth its weight in silver!

The Plain of Jars. Huge jars constructed in the distant past testify to the presence of man. The Plain of Jars has been the scene of fierce battles many times during the history of Laos.

A Hmong village surrounded by hills in Luang Prabang province (1972). The village is divided into two hamlets with small paths connecting the houses.

Some Hmong roofed their houses with thatch, others with wooden tiles like this house in Xieng Khouang province. Notice the millstone on the side of the house.

In many Hmong villages, a system of bamboo pipes brought mountain spring water to the door of each house.

A Hmong woman carrying water from the spring to her house in Houei Kham, south of Long Cheng (1974).

Hmong girls (wearing Lao clothes) operate a millstone to grind corn or soybeans. People of all ages socialized around the millstone in traditional Hmong villages.

Hmong women fed pigs and chickens twice a day: early in the morning before going to the fields, and in the evening after returning from work.

The blacksmith played an important role in traditional Hmong society. Among other things, he provided the tools necessary for farming.

Baskets on their backs, Hmong women chat briefly before leaving for work in their fields. Life was hard but happiness brightened their faces.

A Hmong family plants rice in a *rai*. Slash-and-burn agriculture, necessitated by the mountainous topography, is a common practice throughout Southeast Asia and in many other parts of the world.

The Hmong village of Muong Cha, with its irrigated rice fields (1974). Wherever possible, the Hmong sought out land suitable for irrigated rice growing.

Rice harvest in the mountains. Yield declines substantially with the number of years a field is cultivated, which explains the semi-nomadic traditional lifestyle of the Hmong.

Not a flower garden but a field of opium poppies in the mountains. Lacking modern medicine, the Hmong used opium for medicinal purposes as well as a medium of exchange in trade and barter.

Moua Lia, Inspector of Primary Schools in Xieng Khouang province, visiting village schools to conduct teachers' conferences, encourage students and meet with Hmong communities about educational issues (1969).

The village school of Phak Khe in the Long Cheng area (1974). Hundreds of such schools were created to educate Hmong and other minority youth in southern Xieng Khouang province.

Hmong girls embroider new finery in preparation for the New Year celebration. Everyone looks forward to this occasion to reaffirm old traditions and to make new acquaintances.

A Hmong girl and boy in traditional costumes, ready to participate in the several-day-long New Year festival.

A Hmong mouth organ player performs traditional dances. Called a *qeej* in Hmong, this instrument is also an essential component of Hmong funerals, where its sounds accompany the souls of the deceased back to the land of the ancestors.

Hmong New Year in the mountains provided many kinds of lively entertainment, including bull fights, popular with young and old.

Touby Lyfoung (center front, wearing tie) surrounded by a group of Hmong leaders in Xieng Khouang city (1946). Educated and respected, Touby Lyfoung played an important role in the history of modern Laos.

Toulia Lyfoung, half-brother of Touby Lyfoung, defended the interests of the minority ethnic groups in the Laotian Constitutional Assembly in Vientiane in 1947.

King Srisavang Vatthana (center, wearing uniform and cap), Prince Souvanna Phouma (with pipe), General Vang Pao (holding cap), General Ouane Rathikoune (in jacket), Interior Minister Pheng Phongsavanh (background, right of General Ouane), and King's Council member Touby Lyfoung (foreground, with cane) during a visit to Long Cheng (1968).

จุ่ ฉ่อยภัมฮ้าง โรมภัมนัทมา
เพิ๊ๅตมเวๅ ภัมตมเวๅ เป้มเวภาบ

The author (center, wearing tie) with the *chao muong* of Xieng Khouang province at a conference on national reconciliation and reconstruction (1973).

Laotian Constitution Day (May 11, 1974). Tougeu Lyfoung (left), General Director of the Ministry of Justice and younger half-brother of Touby Lyfoung; Touby Lyfoung (center), Deputy Minister of Telecommunication; and Yang Dao, National Political Consultative Council member, after an official ceremony in Vientiane.

A group of Hmong partisans in Laos during the First Indochina War (1953), variously equipped as irregular French guerrillas.

Long Cheng military base (1968). Constructed with assistance from the CIA, Long Cheng served as the headquarters of General Vang Pao during the conduct of the secret war.

General Vang Pao (center, 1969-70) directed major military operations in the Plain of Jars area.

One-third of the Hmong in Laos became in-country refugees, living on "rice from the sky," assistance from the U.S. Agency for International Development channeled through the Royal Lao Government.

Along with the Hmong, the Lao, Phouan, Khmou, Mien and Tai Dam came to know the desolate fate of being refugees in their own country (1969).

Prince Souvanna Phouma (fourth from left in first row) led the formation of the Provisional Government of National Union in Luang Prabang on April 5, 1974.

Prince Souphanouvong (fifth from left in first row) chaired the National Political Consultative Council, whose work resulted in a draft of a national political strategy for Laos in May 1974.

Marshal Zhu De, former commander-in-chief of Mao Zedong's Red Army and later vice-chairman of the PRC Central People's Government Council, welcomes Yang Dao to the Great Hall of the People in Beijing (April 1975).

Evacuation of Long Cheng on May 14, 1975. Thousands of people rushed to flee the country aboard the last departing U.S. transport planes.

Silver accumulated in this way is buried as surreptitiously as possible in the forest by the head of the family. Anxious about absconders and thieves, he usually does not tell his heirs where the cache is hidden until the last possible minute. If death overtakes him before he shares his secret, the savings of years, if not generations, may be lost forever. This is exactly what happened when Fay Yia Yang drowned in the flooded Nam Ngum river in 1959, leaving behind thousands of silver bars in many undisclosed locations, some of them undiscovered to this day.

Despite the great secrecy with which everyone surrounds his personal hoard, its value rarely escapes the knowledge of the Hmong, who know how to "reckon everyone's income and expenditures with a precision that would honor an economist. From there it is an easy matter to determine, within a few bars, the holdings of everybody in the village."[58] A neighbor of Fay Yia Yang could, therefore, with reasonable accuracy, estimate his buried fortune at several thousand bars, the product of years of opium trading. By searching their memories of his comings and goings, his children were later able to recover some of this wealth. In Pha Hok, a village of 90 households, Lemoine counted at least ten heads of families with accumulations of 200 to 300 bars of silver, the equivalent of 1.8 to 2.7 million kip.[59] Equally amazing was the size of the fortune left by the great leader Lo Blia Yao to his five wives and 33 sons and daughters when he died in 1935: a thousand bars of silver, two thousand silver piasters and more than a thousand head of cattle and buffalo.[60]

As remarkable as these figures are, they cannot mask the low living standard of the great majority of the Hmong, a standard which lies at the very fringe of subsistence. In normal times, the industriousness of a Hmong enables him to produce enough to feed and clothe his family. However, we know from experience that his wealth is generally not more than a few bars of silver and a few silver piasters, carefully reserved for solemn occasions and important transactions such as those surrounding wedding ceremonies.[61]

In such a setting, none of its equivalents can take the place of silver. Silver alone has the magical ability to evoke the feeling of wealth. The question facing development officials is how to mobilize this mass of unproductive, hoarded wealth and invest it rationally in a progressive, modern economy.

THE SOCIAL LEVEL

Traditional Hmong society is characterized by the persistence of archaic social and psychological structures, by a total absence of national consciousness and by a very low level of education.

PERSISTENCE OF ARCHAIC STRUCTURES
Social and psychological structures among the Hmong are perfectly adapted to the economic structure they help maintain. As we saw earlier, their traditional social organization is, like that of each of the ethnic minorities, quite distinct from that of the neighboring populations, from whom they tend to keep almost completely apart. While official administration is practically nonexistent among the Hmong, clan solidarity is strong enough to constitute a kind of guarantee against group misfortune, and the bonds of kinship through marriage stout enough to give the

Hmong a measure of security. It is these security-providing social structures which explain the attachment of a Hmong to his ethnic identity, which is his pride and strength. This concept helps one understand why the traditional Hmong is a person who looks primarily to the past, from which he draws his moral principles and to which he owes his social system and his present way of life.

Closely identifying with his ancestors, the Hmong leads a simple, rough life with few needs and little motivation to expend additional effort for the sake of improving his material well-being. If he enjoys complete freedom, if he has a family as a home base, if he has a house, no matter how wretched, if he has enough forest to hunt and land to plant, the Hmong is perfectly content and shows no desire whatever to change the course of his existence. It seems natural that a man should be satisfied with the way he lives if he knows nothing better! The traditional Hmong, isolated in his rocky mountain fastness, is far from all innovation and technical progress that might improve his standard of living. All he wants is to live the way he is accustomed to living, that is, to live like his ancestors. This is why traditional Hmong society has remained unchanged over the centuries, frozen into a standard of living and level of technology by a vicious circle: since there is no surplus available for creature comforts, desires must not exceed available resources, and since no new desires are felt, technology stagnates and no new surplus is created. It is clear, therefore, that the main reason for the traditionalism of their aspirations is the self-defensive reflex of the group, which, in order to ensure its survival, must oppose any drain of resources or energies on the part of its members. The role of psychology in all of this is anything but negligible. The indifference of some Laotian leaders and, even more, the disdain for the Hmong nurtured by certain classes in the dominant society have long reinforced a feeling of ethnic separateness among the Hmong and encouraged and strengthened the maintenance of their traditional social and psychological structures. This antipathy between mountain people and plains dwellers no doubt existed in China even before the Hmong came to Laos.

ABSENCE OF NATIONAL CONSCIOUSNESS Although the Hmong are aware of their ethnic unity (as has been demonstrated repeatedly in the past), they remain totally ignorant of the concepts of nation and country. Their "country" is the vast upthrust of mountains and forests reaching as far as their eyes can see. They cannot fathom how an artificial, invisible political boundary could cut off roads they have traveled freely for centuries, and the very idea of passports is incomprehensible to them. For the Hmong who have never left their mountains, the world has not changed since the dawn of time.

Every year hundreds of Hmong families in the border regions of northern Laos leave one political territory for another, looking for new fields or fleeing, as they are today, from war and insecurity. Knowing nothing of international law or of laws governing specific countries, their emigrations and immigrations are never recorded in any official registry, and their settling in a region is dictated only by the abundance of forests to be cleared. Since they are attracted only to the largely uninhabited mountains, their movements are accomplished fairly unobtrusively, without disturbing the local order in any way. Often local authorities merely report their presence without ever setting foot in one of their villages. They are equally uninterested in ascertaining whether these mountain people were born in the country or whether they came from across a border, that is from Vietnam, Thailand or China.

To the traditional Hmong, it matters little what nationality people assign to them, because they know that for them nationality is meaningless. They have never seen a representative of their government and often do not even know who is running the country.[62] The millions of dollars that flow into the country evaporate almost without being noticed. But no matter: the Hmong have never based their welfare on help from the outside. What the Hmong is seeking, above all else, is respect for his identity and his traditions and the justice and freedom he has always fought for. This is why, if he feels that his security is threatened or that his life is in danger, he will abandon, without looking backward, the mountain where he was born to look for a new "country" where he can once more enjoy the right to live a life of freedom.

This lack of national consciousness affects not only the Hmong and the other mountain minorities; it is characteristic of all the Laotian populations, who live deeply enfolded in their regional and ethnic singularities. The party, regional and family politics played by some Laotian leaders hardly contribute to the awakening of a patriotic sentiment strong enough to unlock a mentality so deeply rooted in its age-old ways. Thus the problem of national integration is a particularly acute one in Laos.

LOW EDUCATIONAL LEVEL   Finally, traditional Hmong society is marked by the notable absence of any formal educational system, which explains its very low level of education. The illiteracy rate is, even today, estimated at more than 99 percent in certain mountain regions of Laos.

Historically, modern Lao civilization was born and developed in the plains along the Mekong River, around the towns where trading was carried on. The back country has traditionally remained apart, isolated by mountains and forests, by terrible roads impassable for six months of the year, by its widely scattered population and, finally, by the language barrier. Besides these geographical and cultural obstacles, there is also the political factor. In order to "avoid any possible break-up of Laos," the French government, during more than half a century of domination, pursued a policy of "creating an aristocracy of peoples." It was no doubt for much the same reason that the leaders of independent Laos long hesitated to build schools in the mountains, hoping thereby to keep the minority ethnic groups in a state of intellectual inferiority.[63] The formation of a true nation implies, in our view, a community of thought and will which can never come into being as long as social or ethnic groups are being sacrificed to the advance of progress.

One must not be too hasty, however, in drawing conclusions based on the extremely large number of people in Asia who can neither read nor write. Intellectual development, even in the narrowest sense of the word, has no necessary relationship to the level of formal education, and even so-called "academic" education itself is in no way a guarantee of the ability to read and write. It has often been observed that illiterate Hmong living in the border regions of northern Laos can speak several languages fluently but that it becomes far more difficult for them to learn to do this once they have learned to read and write. Traditional Hmong society has never fallen into the trap of considering "illiterate" tantamount to "ignorant."

Although the Hmong have never had their own written language, traditional education, both practical and moral, is alive and well.[64] This traditional learning is essentially utilitarian; it does not fall prey to the absurdities encountered in some modern education in both Africa and in Asia, patterned after that of the former colonialist countries. Thus there are found among the Hmong experts in arms-making, music, traditional medicine, and so on, who hand on to the next generation their knowledge and their techniques. Along with the masters recognized as such, there are also traditional singers, who keep alive and elaborate an ever-richer oral literature, and storytellers, from whom the villagers learn history, geography, mythology, natural science and a good many other things. People remember and repeat endlessly what they have heard and draw the appropriate conclusions, moral and otherwise.

At first glance, traditional Hmong society still seems to be deep in its age-old sleep. Yet today there are perceptible indications of change. On the one hand, needs are expanding and the Hmong are able to see clearly the gap between human needs and monetary resources. Newly-perceived needs run up against the barrier of inadequate buying power. On the other hand, the areas under cultivation are shrinking with each passing year because of gradual exhaustion of the soil due to the practice of slash-and-burn agriculture, and the increasing appearance of relative overpopulation is making the Hmong aware of the problem of labor productivity. With these things in mind, we see a new economy beginning to take shape in the Hmong village, which seems ready to shake off its centuries of torpor.

FOOTNOTES:

[1] The very serious problem of soil regeneration in the mountains is discussed in Chapter Seven.

[2] René Dumont, *False Start in Africa*, Collections Esprit "Frontières Ouvertes," Seuil, Paris, 1962, pp. 14-15.

[3] The starting point in the calendar is the Hmong New Year, celebrated in late November-early December. Thus each "month" is approximately three to five weeks ahead of its corresponding month in the Western calendar.

[4] Lemoine, *Social Organization in a Green Hmong Village*, p. 56.

[5] Ivez de Beauclair, *A Miao Tribe of South-east Kweichow and Its Cultural Configuration*, Taipei, 1960.

[6] Lemoine, *Social Organization in a Green Hmong Village*, p. 64.

[7] Pierre Gourou, *Soil Use in French Indochina*, Centre d'Etudes de Politique Etrangère Publications, Hartman, Paris, 1940, p. 179.

[8] Charles Robequain, *Le Thanh Hoa*, Vol. 1.

[9] Pa Nou Thao, personal interview, Appleton, Wisconsin, October 1991.

[10] A hectare is approximately 2.5 acres.

[11] Lemoine, *Social Organization in a Green Hmong Village*, p. 68.

[12] Ibid., p. 65.

[13] Pierson helped plan and build the experimental Hmong farm at Tha Ngone near Vientiane. (Cf. Chapter Eight.)

[14] A day of labor by any of the three family members, scaled to one hectare.

[15] Lemoine, *Social Organization in a Green Hmong Village*, p. 55.

[16] René Dumont, *The Cultivation of Rice*, Société d'Editions Géographiques, Maritimes et Coloniales, Paris, 1935, p. 361.

[17] Joel M. Halpern, *Aspects of Life and Culture Change in Laos*, Council on Economic and Cultural Affairs, 1958.

[18] Georges Condominas, in Gourhan, L. and Poirier, P., *Ethnology of the French Union*, Vol. II, Presse Universitaire de France, Paris, 1953, p. 647.

[19] Pierre B. Lafont, in *Bulletin de l'Ecole Française d'Extrême-Orient*, Vol. I, Part 1, Paris, 1960, p. 168.

[20] Chao Ly, *Initiation and Agriculture in Laos*, Ecole Supérieure d'Agriculture de Purpan, Toulouse, 1969-1970, p. 71.

[21] Lemoine, *Social Organization in a Green Hmong Village*, p. 63.

[22] Laos, National Statistics Bureau.

[23] Lemoine, *Social Organization in a Green Hmong Village*, p. 99.

[24] Fridman, *Agricultural Future of Trân Ninh*, doctoral dissertation, Vol. I, Paris, 1953, p. 52.

[25] A. Pidance, "The Textiles of Trân Ninh," *Bulletin Economique de l'Indochine*, 9th Year, No. 51, 1906, pp. 412-423.

[26] Ibid.

[27] The Bank of Indochina piaster (*piastre*) was the official currency of Indochina prior to World War II. It weighed 27 grams and had a silver content of 90 percent. Its value was tied to the French franc. In December 1906, one piaster equaled 2.85 francs. (*Bulletin Administratif du Laos [1907-1908]*).

[28] Pidance, "The Textiles of Trân Ninh," pp. 412-423.

[29] R. Cresson and Robert Jeannin, "Meo Hemp Cloth," Institut Indochinois pour l'Etude de l'Homme, Vol. VI, Paris, 1943, pp. 435-447.

[30] Fridman, *Agricultural Future of Trân Ninh*, p. 52.

[31] Opium yield estimates taken from Jacques Dumarest, *Opium and Salt Monopolies in Indochina*, advanced doctoral dissertation, School of Law and Economic Sciences, University of Lyon, 1938.

[32] Lemoine, *Social Organization in a Green Hmong Village*.

[33] According to the U.S. Bureau of Narcotics and Dangerous Drugs, the total production of raw opium in Laos was approximately 50 tons in 1953 and between 100 and 150 tons in 1968. (Alfred W. McCoy, *The Politics of Heroin in Southeast Asia*, Harper and Row, New York, 1972, p. 258 [ref. p. 424]).

[34] Gabriel Garnier, Lucien Bezanger-Beauquesne and Germains Debraux, *Medical Resources of French Flora*, Vigot, Paris, 1961, p. 500.

[35] This privilege was strengthened by the order of September 3, 1948, in which the High Commissioner of France in Indochina granted to the Mien and the Hmong alone permission to grow opium.

[36] Dumarest, *Opium and Salt Monopolies in Indochina*. Figures refer to all of French Indochina.

[37] Ibid.

[38] Ibid.

[39] Ibid.

[40] Fridman, *Agricultural Future of Trân Ninh*, p. 42.

[41] Ibid.

[42] 35 piasters = US$1 (1953).

[43] Jean Bertolino, "The Land of a Thousand Pleasures," *Atlas*, No. 32, March 1969, p. 16.

[44] The kip is the official currency of Laos. It was first issued in 1955, when it was valued at 35 kip to the U.S. dollar. It was subject to extreme variations in value, falling at one point in 1976 to 14,000 kip/US$1. New kip were issued in 1979; the current official exchange rate (1991) is 700 kip/US$1.

[45] Most of the opium sold on the Sam Thong and Long Cheng markets was smuggled in from Vientiane, to which it had come secretly from the Golden Triangle area on the borders of Burma, Thailand and Laos.

[46] *Le Figaro*, September 25-26, 1971.

[47] Opium growing seems to be allowed within legal limits in the so-called "liberated zones" under Neo Lao Hak Sat control.

[48] The average Hmong family in the 1970 survey in Xieng Khouang province kept a flock of four to five hens and two or three roosters. The hens brood, on an average, 2.5 times per year, producing an average of six to ten live chicks per brood.

[49] Unlike the Hmong, many ethnic groups in Southeast Asia do not feed poultry and pigs regularly. Most of the time these animals are simply left to forage for themselves.

[50] Bernard Bourotte, "Marriages and Funerals Among the White Meo in the Nong Het (Trân Ninh) Region," Institut Indochinois pour l'Etude de l'Homme, Vol. VI, Paris, 1943, pp. 33-56.

[51] Roux and Tran, "Some Ethnic Minorities in Northern Tonkin," p. 392.

[52] Dr. Tounalom is a graduate of the College of Medicine and Pharmacology of the University of Bordeaux in France. He has worked at the Sene Souk Hospital in Sam Thong since 1966.

[53] We recognize, of course, the usefulness of shamanistic treatment as psychotherapy. One of the challenges even today (1992) is to teach the Hmong to distinguish between psychological problems and biologically induced disease.

[54] Cf. p. 13.

[55] Metal containers with a capacity of 18 kilograms of rice.

[56] Lemoine, *Social Organization in a Green Hmong Village*, p. 236.

[57] The Foreign Exchange Operations Fund (FEOF), an IMF-sponsored currency support consortium financed by the United States, France, Britain, Japan and Australia.

[58] Lemoine, *Social Organization in a Green Hmong Village*, p. 247.

[59] Ibid.

[60] Roux and Tran, "Some Ethnic Minorities in Northern Tonkin," p. 392.

[61] The Hmong brideprice must be paid in silver. Traditionally, the amount ranged from three to more than twenty bars of silver. In 1964 it was set at six silver bars in the Sam Thong-Long Cheng region, a rule which is generally respected.

[62] Most of the ethnic groups in Laos do know that there is a king, though few have ever seen him.

[63] Phimmaha Panyanouvong, "Who Comprise the Lao?" *L'Etudiant Lao* (Lao Students' Bulletin, Bordeaux Section), Paris, February 1971, p. 32.

[64] Several orthographies, including the one used in this book, have been developed recently for the Hmong language.

The Transitional Village Economy

The Hmong village economy turned a sharp corner at the end of World War II and is now undergoing a rapid transformation. Depending on the attitude the Hmong adopt toward innovation, this transformation may either be a process that leads the village economy into ever deeper impoverishment and eventually into self-destruction or an evolution that integrates the village economy into a dynamic regional economy, thereby assuring it a measure of development.

THE SELF-DESTRUCTION OF THE TRADITIONAL VILLAGE ECONOMY

We have seen that the traditional Hmong economy is having more and more difficulty feeding its people. As the Hmong population continues to grow at an ever-increasing rate, annual harvests fall farther and farther short of the need. How can the Hmong peasant cope with this new situation using traditional patterns of labor? To ensure his family's survival, he is forced to implement two solutions at the same time: first, to expand his *rai* by clearing and planting new mountain slopes and, second, to ignore the rules for fallow time and shorten the rotation cycle of his fields. Both practices impoverish the soil and hasten its erosion. In the long run it becomes barren and sterile. Inevitably, the destructive effects soon make themselves felt in the village economy. Today all of Hmong country is suffering from such practices. Many regions once covered with great forests have become vast expanses of scrub grass. The mountains of Nong Het are a particularly striking example. Chao Ly, the first Hmong agricultural engineer in Laos, estimates that 50,000 hectares of forest lands are destroyed annually in Xieng Khouang province alone.[1] It should be noted that this figure refers to the province in the 1960s and includes not only the *rai* fields of the Hmong but also those worked by the Khmou and other ethnic minorities.

It is inevitable, under these conditions, that village-scale production by means of archaic techniques will eventually suffer an irreversible decline. The entire region faces the threat of being dragged down into poverty and destruction. The traditional village risks becoming the creator of deserts! Meanwhile, the population continues its upward spiral, quickening the pace of economic regression and causing ever-accelerating exhaustion of the land and decline in subsistence levels.

At this point, the population must turn to emigration. Hmong families are leaving the mountains of Pha Thong in Luang Prabang for the heights of Phou Khao Khouai in Vientiane province. Others are departing the Xieng Khouang region for the still-virgin lands around Sayaboury, unwittingly continuing the destruction of natural capital and preparing, by the very act of settling down, to move on again to other horizons. This is the eternal migration of the Hmong, prisoners of the vicious circle that constitutes their way of life.

The Hmong, however, are becoming increasingly aware of the limits to their movements and of the social and economic consequences which stem from them. The proverb "Rolling stones gather no moss" is not unknown to them. Many would like to change their way of life. The desire for more stable productivity from their labor, the aspiration for a better life under more adequate conditions, the financial attractions of trade, and the eagerness for education in order to participate in civic and public life are all factors which are gradually changing the behavior of the traditionalist Hmong peasant.

The Hmong village economy thus finds itself under attack on two fronts: from within, because of the ever greater difficulty of ensuring the survival of its members; and from without, because of the new models of living and economic well-being propagated by towns and cities and because of ever more frequent government intervention into its closed, traditional universe. The traditional Hmong economy seems to have had its day. It is now seeking to avoid its own strangulation by integrating itself more and more into an active regional economic system.

INTEGRATING VILLAGE ECONOMIES INTO A DYNAMIC REGIONAL ECONOMY

Breaking with ancestral tradition, a growing number of Hmong villages are turning resolutely outward toward the regional economy and markets. Replacing the village microcosm, with its diminishing resources and power, is an expanded, regional-scale economy which is becoming more and more the setting for new activities of production and consumption. How did this process of economic integration get started and what are its social consequences?

STIMULATING INFLUENCES

Social and Psychological Factors   The Hmong village economy, still largely dominated by local oligarchies and ancestral customs, seems ready to shake off its apathy and awaken to the serious contradictions which make its traditional mode of existence extremely precarious. The mountain people are also becoming aware of the age-old exploitation of which they have been the victims under all regimes, and are more openly seeking reforms from which they could derive some benefit. Both endogenous and exogenous forces are at work preparing the Hmong village economy, hitherto turned inward upon itself in a kind of contemplative introversion, to accept profound economic and social change.

Economic Factors   Even as the level of satisfaction of basic needs through local production drops steadily, new needs are emerging as a result of urban contact. The traditional Hmong economy is finding it increasingly difficult to maintain its closed attitude and cling to its ancient structures without running the risk of disintegrating altogether. Today the regional economy offers it new prospects: the towns are not only sources of manufactured products such as textiles but also major outlets for its farm surpluses. Little by little the idea of economic complementarity between towns and villages is taking hold in the mind of the Hmong peasant, who has, in the process, discovered new sources of revenue and thus new ways to satisfy his increased needs.

Political Factors   The most important influences for change are political factors. The presence of Hmong leaders in the civil service and of high-ranking Hmong officers in the Laotian armed forces marks a major step toward ethnic integration in Laos. It appears that in order to exercise meaningful control over a population as diverse as that of Laos and to provide proper defense for so vast a territory, the Royal Lao Government, like the

Pathet Lao, is paying more attention to the ethnic minorities, and that the minorities, for their part, are increasingly in need of help from the government to promote their development. The nation of Laos seems to be forging its unity in the crucible of suffering that has for more than two decades beset its communities of diverse origins and cultures. The policy of integration as it appears in Laos today seems to be based on a more just and realistic foundation than in the past. Its implementation cannot be anything but beneficial to plains dwellers as well as mountain people, all of whom are being called upon to play a more active role in building the future economic and social life of Laos.

MOVING TOWARD REGIONAL ECONOMIC INTEGRATION

Integration of Hmong village economies into a progressive regional economy began in Xieng Khouang province after World War II and spread from there to other parts of the kingdom.

Xieng Khouang Province   The evolution of the Hmong village economy in this region has been a gradual process, favored by political and military events of which the northeastern part of the kingdom has always been the setting. The development has taken different forms and varies greatly from one part of the province to another.

The Period From 1946-1960   When Touby Lyfoung took office as Deputy Governor of Xieng Khouang in 1947, his departure from Nong Het was the signal for a vast migration of Hmong from the mountains to the plains. This movement led many families to settle in Xieng Khouang, Dong Dane and Lat Houang, where, beginning around 1954, the expanding economy drew a veritable avalanche of people into the region. At the same time, new Hmong villages sprang up along the roads in the mountains of Xieng Khouang province.

The proximity of the town of Xieng Khouang and of smaller settlements (Lat Houang, Phong Savanh and Ban Ban) promoted contact between the Hmong peasants and the Chinese, Indian, Pakistani and Vietnamese merchants who, by their presence, stimulated the consumption of existing products and the introduction of new ones. The availability of modern imported goods such as Japanese cloth, electric lights, household articles, and so on, created the perception of new needs and motivated the Hmong peasants to look to other sources than opium, which had become increasingly inadequate, for cash income. Where were these to be found? The solution to this problem, directly linked to contact with the modern world, seemed to lie in turning the village economy outward and adapting it to the larger economic framework of the province. To finance their new needs, the Hmong would have to increase their food crop production, expand their livestock operations and begin marketing their products.

Many Hmong families began to abandon *rai* farming in favor of irrigated rice growing, which took less work, gave a relatively stable yield and, most importantly, made it possible for them to settle down permanently. With the help of the new local government, now more representative, some of them restored the rice fields that had been abandoned when Vietnamese settlers were repatriated after World War II. This brought the lowlands of Xieng Khouang, Dong Dane and Lat Houang back into production. Other Hmong families undertook the creation of new rice paddies wherever the terrain and water supply would permit (e.g. in the uninhabited narrow valleys of the province). Those who could not find land suitable for irrigated rice growing settled around Lat Houang and established permanent farms, using animal-drawn plowing, plant and manure fertilizer, and sometimes even compost.

While agriculture was developing around the Hmong villages in the valleys and plains and flourishing in the all too short-lived atmosphere of peace, poultry and pig farming were reaching new dimensions in the surrounding hills, thanks to bumper corn crops. This budding economic boom, however, could be sustained only if there were markets to support it.

Laos had just emerged from a war (World War II) which had profoundly upset the economy of Xieng Khouang province. Roads were bad, and the larger towns in the area, such as Xieng Khouang with its population of 10,000, had a difficult time getting enough food. At the same time, the manufactured goods that continued to come into these areas by air exerted an irresistible attraction on the people of the surrounding villages. The advantages of economic cooperation were becoming increasingly clear to the Hmong, who found in the town markets an outlet for their farm surpluses and, hence, a source of cash income that could at least partially satisfy their new needs.

The first move to sell farm products was made by a handful of farmers who decided to ignore the reluctance and criticism of their neighbors, still clinging to their archaic frame of mind. Very early every morning they would go to the market nearest their village, the women carrying baskets full of whatever vegetables were in season (cucumbers, Chinese mustard, tomatoes, beans, pumpkins), the men driving pigs or carrying chickens. From time to time, caravans of two or three horses brought loads of rice into Xieng Khouang, Lat Houang or Phong Savanh for delivery to Indian, Pakistani, Chinese and Vietnamese merchants. With the money it brought the Hmong would buy cloth, kitchen utensils and the many other things they now needed.

During the transition from a subsistence to a market economy, the impact of local markets on traditional society was enormous. The reason lies in two features of such markets:

○ the counterbalance they provide to the compartmentalization of an extended family-based society living on itself — they force family and ethnic groups to communicate with one another

○ their nature as social phenomena rather than as simply places for trading — they are the centers where information is exchanged and news is spread.

At that time, two kinds of markets were operating in Xieng Khouang province: the daily markets and the periodic (weekly or monthly) markets.

DAILY MARKETS   The daily markets operated every morning from 6:30 to 10:00 AM in towns with thriving business districts or those located near military bases. In 1960 there were five markets in the province, where Phouan and Hmong farmers came every day to sell their produce: Xieng Khouang, Lat Houang, Plain of Jars, Phong Savanh and Ban Ban. With the exception of Xieng Khouang, which because of its size (pop. 15,000 in 1960) and its commercial and political importance attracted large crowds, these markets were relatively small. Only about 20 vendors and 100 customers kept them in regular operation.

The small size of these markets can be explained by the absence of a secondary economic sector (industry), the inadequacy of the tertiary sector (government and commerce), and the lack of an organized distribution system for farm products (fruits, vegetables, poultry, etc.). There was no central market where these products could be collected and shipped into the cities or abroad. To these factors must be added the long distances between the villages and the nearest market. The Phouan or Hmong farmer could obviously not afford to walk 7 to 15 kilometers every day to sell a few baskets of greens or a few cucumbers. The exceptions were those who lived close to the markets, such as the Hmong around Dong Dane, Sam Sone and Phou Khe, and the Phouan around Ban Tone, Ban Nanou, and Ban Nam Tom and its surroundings, who daily supplied the market at Lat Houang (pop. 1,500 in 1960) with the products of their fields and flocks and of their hunting and gathering.

PERIODIC MARKETS   The periodic markets were by far the more interesting in their organization, their size, and the volume of business they did. More in keeping with the rhythm of farming and with the lifestyle of the still very traditional families, these markets were held every five days according to a definite schedule. The schedule was staggered, so that, while any one village would host such a market only every five days, a market could be found nearly every day in one of the other nearby participating villages. This rotating system of market organization assured the province of what amounted to a kind of permanent itinerant fair. The Phouan, Khmou and Hmong farmers knew when and where the markets would be held so they could choose, on the basis of distance, the market to which they would take their produce.

The location of the marketplace was determined by two interrelated factors: a central position relative to the surrounding villages and ease of access (a road or track passable by vehicles) for the merchants of the towns. The periodic market was less closely linked to a center of population; it was more of a meeting place for peasants and traders. The actual site might be a small village with no more than 20 or 30 inhabitants, without any commerce of its own but having the requisite combination of characteristics for a market intended to serve the needs of villagers within a radius of 10 to 15 kilometers.

Market day was quite a sight at Lat Sene, a village of about 60 people in 1960, built at a crossroads. On foot, on horseback and by car, people of all ethnic groups would gather there regularly. Because of the distance to the market (10 to 15 kilometers), the Hmong would be the first to arise. Well before dawn they would load their horses, shoulder their baskets and come down the mountains. They timed their coming so as to reach the plain with the first light. On the way they would meet many Phouan and Khmou, all, like them, on their way to sell their families' products. As the farmers headed in from all directions, the market was also filling up with a throng of merchants, most of them Chinese, arriving from Lat Houang, Phong Savanh and even Xieng Khouang, driving Land Rovers, Jeeps and Opels laden with all manner of merchandise.

In a twinkling, Lat Sene was transformed, its usual sleepy serenity replaced by an incessant tumult of human voices mingled with the cries of chickens and pigs. On market day the tiny hamlet would burst with a thousand customers for the 400 or more vendors selling all sorts of things, from local products to imported goods. Hmong farmers were selling their Chinese mustard, cucumbers, peaches and pears, their fluffy rice, their pigs and capons as well as their opium. The Phouan would bring their fish, ducks and eggs, their *khao pun* (a rice-noodle soup) and their sticky rice. Chinese merchants offered cloth, clothing and shoes in their stalls. Everything from beef on the hoof to the finest embroidery needles was on display at the market. Many people came simply to stroll, drawn as much by the festival atmosphere of the wheeling and dealing as by the races, featuring horses covered with tiny bells, that were a regular feature of market day. Business went on until half past noon, when the farmers packed up and left the quickly-emptying marketplace. As if by magic, Lat Sene would become as deserted and somnolent as before.

In 1960 there were some ten or more of these periodic markets in Xieng Khouang province. They contributed greatly to the growth of trade in the region by pushing the village economy from the subsistence stage to that of a market economy.

The Period From 1961-1969   Beginning in 1961, political and military events destroyed these commercial structures almost completely. The mercantile spirit, however, remained very much alive in the populations of Xieng Khouang. Although the war wiped out the population centers and completely disrupted the provincial economy, the fleeing inhabitants carried with them, along with their other traditions, the practice of commercial trade. As the plains of Xieng Khouang province fell prey to the horrors of the bloody war, the Phouan, Khmou and Hmong quickly sought refuge in the mountains overlooking the southern part of the Plain of Jars. Despite their forbidding appearance, these mountains soon became the setting for renewed economic activity, stimulated both by the size of the markets in the large towns of Long Cheng, Sam Thong and Pha Khao and by the development of a cash economy, the result of the many military personnel and government officials living on wage income. This cash economy, in turn, led to the appearance of commercial and artistic professions such as dentistry, photography, tailoring and watch repair. In the space of a few short years, the traditional economy of the Xieng Khouang plateau had changed completely.

AGRICULTURE   Wherever security was adequate, the Hmong continued to practice their traditional agriculture. The mountains around Long Cheng and Sam Thong were covered with rice and corn *rai*, although the soil was too poor to grow opium poppies, a particularly demanding crop.[2] As time went on, these fields were moved farther and farther away from the settlements. By 1969 the fields of most of the Long Cheng farmers lay some three or four hours' walk from their homes.

Meanwhile, the search for land suitable for irrigated rice fields intensified. The tiniest valley in the triangular area bounded by Sam Thong, Long Cheng and Pha Khao was cleared and partitioned, yielding good annual rice harvests. Irrigable lowlands have become scarce. Many people are longingly eyeing their old villages back on the Plain of Jars, where rice fields have lain fallow for many years and where it is still possible to clear new paddy.

But while awaiting peace a man must still live and provide for his family. Since 1964 poppy growing has practically disappeared from the region, so it has become a matter of some urgency to find other sources of revenue to replace the crop that so long served as both cash source and currency. For some Hmong peasants, the problem has been partially solved: the larger towns, such as Sam Thong (pop. 15,000) and Long Cheng (pop. 30,000),[3] are eager markets for their farm products and hence good sources of cash income. Some have specialized in growing and selling rice and corn, others in raising pigs and fish.[4] Everywhere in the area secondary crops have sprung up, supplying the markets daily with seasonal produce: sweet potatoes, manioc, sugar cane, watermelons, pineapples, pumpkins, ginger, beans, Chinese mustard, tomatoes, and so on. Increasing demand is stimulating the growing of fruit trees (tangerines, peaches, Chinese pears, papayas, plums, bananas), which could be done more extensively if security were better. Traditional farming and stock-raising techniques are still used, however, preventing improvements in yield and productivity, the primary condition for rapid economic growth. The one innovation is the use of seasonal workers, which allows an increase in the size of the fields under cultivation and, thus, in the amount of farm surpluses available for sale.[5]

Responsibilities for selling farm products are divided clearly by gender. The men drive pigs, carry chickens and lead pack horses loaded with rice or corn to the local market. The women engage in the selling of fruits and vegetables. At the time of our visit in 1969, there were again three daily markets in the south part of the Plain of Jars, operating from six-thirty in the morning until about three to five o'clock in the afternoon. The largest one was in Long Cheng, which drew more than 2,000 people every day, 600 of them sellers, both men and women. Each day they slaughtered and sold

14-16 pigs, weighing 50-70 kilograms each
8-10 buffalo, weighing 250-300 kilograms each
1 or 2 oxen, weighing 200-250 kilograms each.

A flock of middlemen was needed to handle the very high volume of small transactions. Competition played only a minor role. The first vendors to arrive set their prices and the others followed suit. Sometimes prices were set beforehand by an informal buyer-seller agreement, which generally led to uniform prices throughout the market.

COMMERCE   Since 1961, control of commerce in Xieng Khouang has been passing gradually into the hands of Lao, Hmong and Khmou, largely because of the departure of the Chinese, Vietnamese, Indian and Pakistani merchants, forced by political and military events to leave the region. Little by little foreigners have been replaced by local residents taking a chance on new initiatives and getting steadily better at their new occupation as merchants, inquiring ever more knowledgeably into the tastes and needs of their customers and trying to take advantage of promising situations.

In every town and refugee center there is organized commerce, facilitated by the establishment of a new airline, Xieng Khouang Air Transport, which links the mountains of the northeast with the capital, and by a network of roads and tracks that connects Sam Thong, Long Cheng and Pha Khao with each other and with the surrounding villages. Every month, two to three hundred tons of the most varied kinds of merchandise are delivered from Vientiane to Long Cheng. Some of it is sold there by the three hundred or so Lao, Hmong and Khmou merchants. The rest goes out to Sam Thong and Pha Khao aboard a fleet of 20 Land Rovers, Jeeps and Toyotas transformed into delivery trucks. From these towns, caravans of horses laden with cloth, household articles and manufactured goods regularly plod along the many trails leading to the most remote mountain villages.

Judging by our observations in October 1969, trade is particularly brisk at Long Cheng. Many stores and shops compete for wholesale and retail business. The crowds in the marketplace, the feverish activity of the merchants, and the quantities of goods ware-housed for future sale all give the impression of peace and prosperity in a region particularly hard hit by more than ten years of deadly conflict. Almost anything can be found in the shops of Long Cheng: Lao skirts lie side by side with cloth from England and Hong Kong, Hmong silver bracelets gleam next to Swiss watches and Japanese transistor radios. Merchants also sup-ply the needs of the residents for consumables such as medicine, soap, writing paper, etc.

Prices vary markedly among shops and localities, increasing with the distance from Long Cheng and the other large towns, especially near the ends of roads. The same goods that can be bought for 500 kip in Long Cheng cost 650 kip at Pha Khao and 800 kip at Muong Cha, an area about 30 kilometers east of Long Cheng with no road connections. Bargaining is the rule in both buying and selling. However, the practice of free competition acts to maintain some limits on prices. In this short period of time experience has made the sharp Hmong peasant men and women into veteran merchants.

Along with stores and shops, Long Cheng boasts of an ice cream factory and some ten or so restaurants. Here one can partake of Lao- or Hmong-made *pho* and *mi*, those famous Vietnamese and Chinese specialties, and get refreshments ranging from beer to Coca-Cola, Green Spot and iced coffee. All restaurant prices are fixed, no bargaining is allowed. Along with the Lao, the Hmong also engage in several commercial professions in Long Cheng. There are four photographers, five dentists, two watch and radio repair shops, three shoemak-ers, a tailor and four bakers. Most of these people have studied for up to a year with Chinese teachers in Vientiane. The plentiful supply of customers assures them a very adequate living.

The cost of living is much higher in Long Cheng and the surrounding area than in Vientiane. There are two main reasons for this: first, traditional agriculture, constantly disturbed by pervasive insecurity and stripped of its best workers by military recruitment, can no longer feed the region's population. Second, all manufactured products must reach the mountains of the northeast by air, an extremely expensive mode of transportation, the cost of which has an immediate and universal effect on the prices of all goods brought in.[6] However, some food products, such as locally grown vegetables and pork and buffalo meat, are actually cheaper in Long Cheng than in Vientiane since they are sold directly, without the numerous middlemen who often make scandalous profits.

Other Northern Provinces   Having lived for so long on the fringes of the dominant society, Hmong in the other provinces of northern Laos have not experienced as rapid an economic evolution as the Hmong on the Xieng Khouang plateau. Nevertheless, events since 1961 have upset their peaceful existence and brought about profound changes in their attitudes toward innovation and progress. The expansion of the war resulted in a decrease in the areas under cultivation. Opium production, their one source of cash income, was cut back sharply. Often it had to be imported clandestinely from Burma for consumption. To meet their needs for cloth, Hmong families had to bring their farm products to the mar-kets of Luang Prabang, Houei Sai, Sayaboury and Vientiane. Contact with urban life further hastened the process of economic opening-up.

The mountains of Phou Khao Khouai, 60 kilometers north of Vientiane, are the most typical example. Jolted suddenly from their age-old torpor, the Hmong of this region began, in 1962, not only to develop their ginger crop but also to raise capons and fatted hogs for sale to the huge market of the capital. When military regulations imposed two years later banned all livestock trade between the mountains and the plain of Vientiane, the Hmong switched to the manufacture of reed brooms. A thriving broom industry soon developed up in the Buffalo Horn Mountains, providing leisure-time work for some two hundred Hmong families. Vientiane residents buy an estimated several tens of thousands of Hmong brooms each year. Such a family or cottage industry is not very profitable, however, and suffers from the problem of marketing. All sales are made on a door-to-door basis. The price of brooms dropped from 100 kip in 1964 to 70 kip in 1969, despite massive inflation of the national currency during that time.

Even more remarkable have been the agricultural achievements of the Hmong in Sayaboury province, a region little affected by the current war. With the help of the Royal Lao Government and the United States Agency for International Development (USAID), almost 200 Hmong families got started in flooded rice growing in 1963. A huge irrigable area, capable of producing two harvests per year, was set aside in the Muong Phieng valley for resettlement of refugees. It was intended to bring under cultivation some 3,500 hectares during the rainy season and 2,200 hectares in the dry season.[7] An average of 1.5 to 2.5 hectares of land was distributed free to each of the Hmong families in the villages of Ban Nam Hia, Ban Phone Ngam and Ban Nam Pang. Since 1969 these villages have enjoyed a modern irrigation system made possible by the construction of a reinforced concrete dam on the Nam Tan river.

With an eye toward encouraging farm production, the Royal Lao Government has, with American aid, set up an Agricultural Development Organization (ADO). The Agricultural Development Organization sells seed for IR-8 and IR-5 rice[8] as well as new high-yield varieties (e.g. Samphathong), fertilizer, pumps, hand tools, and the like to the growers for cash or on credit. The ADO also makes loans for the purchase of buffalo to work the irrigated rice fields and buys any surplus rice the farmers are not able to sell on the local market. This rice is then sent as aid to refugee centers throughout the country.

For their part, the Hmong growers are attempting to organize in order to cut their production costs. The 49 Hmong families of Phone Ngam, for example, have formed a cooperative in their village. In 1969 they bought their first tractor with the dues they collected. In 1970 they harvested 630 tons of paddy and made a net profit of 5.987 million kip. They are already considering ordering two more tractors; 140 silver bars (1.26 million kip) have been set aside for these potential purchases, and they may seek an ADO loan for the difference. The progress of this Hmong refugee village has evoked the admiration of Lao officials, who say that "the Hmong of Muong Phieng have become better farmers than the Lao." However, there remains a problem that will have to be solved sooner or later: that of marketing the rice. In practical terms this means a rational organization of marketing channels for the mutual benefit of growers and consumers.

Under the direction of Yves Bertrais,[9] a French Oblate missionary, and Charles Pierson, Senior Rural Development Officer with the United Nations Food and Agriculture Organization, the catechists of the Vientiane Center for the Hmong Apostolate began working a 7.5-hectare farm in Tha Ngone, 25 kilometers north of the capital. After three years of trial and error, they decided that the farm would concentrate on hogs and laying hens. By the end of June 1971 the farm had a fairly respectable stock:

HOGS (LARGE WHITE)		LAYING HENS (RHODE ISLAND RED)	
Boars, 8 months to 2 years	3	Roosters	10
Sows, 7 months to 1.5 years	10	Hens, laying	1,120
Suckling pigs, 1 month	44	Chicks, 10 day	850
Piglets, 3 months	25	Chicks, 2 months	570
Hogs, 6 to 7 months	12	Pullets, 4 to 6 months	1,120

The hogs are sold live at about seven or eight months to a hog raisers' association of which the Hmong farm is a member. This organization, originally set up by Lao farmers, resells the hogs to Chinese and Vietnamese butchers in the markets of Vientiane. Between January 1970 and January 1971 the Tha Ngone farm sold 15 Large White hogs, which yielded a net profit of K157,000. It hopes to sell even more in the years ahead. During the same period, 273,000 eggs were sold to the morning market in Vientiane, bringing a gross return of K4,653,750. To meet increasing demand, the farm plans to enlarge its laying flock and produce even more eggs for sale in Houei Sai, Luang Prabang and Long Cheng.

Making money, however, is not the primary purpose of the Tha Ngone farm. It was established to support the Hmong catechists in their role as promoters of development and to "serve as an initiation and training center for farmers who want practical instruction, in exchange for their direct participation in the production process."[10] Another project using this same approach is now under way to raise beef and dairy cattle in the Na Pheng region at the foot of the Buffalo Horn Mountains. The forage crops (Guatemala grass) planted in 1971 should be ready for the first cattle in the spring of 1972.

Relatively sheltered from the war, the Muong Phieng and Thong Pheng-Tha Ngone areas seem to offer good prospects for sound and balanced development. Upon their success may rest the economic future of the Hmong populations in all of Laos.

MOVING TOWARD SOCIAL INTEGRATION OF THE HMONG

Social integration, at once the cause and the effect of economic integration, is characterized by the extension of education to all strata of the population, by development of administrative and technical expertise, and by the awakening of national consciousness.

EXPANSION OF EDUCATION   The tyrannies, harassments and injustices of all kinds experienced by the Hmong in the past finally brought them to the realization that some education would be necessary in order to defend their interests more effectively. At first, entire families contributed to send their most gifted children to be educated in the plains, the only places where there were any schools. By the time these children returned home they had gained enough knowledge to help their people in securing their rights and to lend the Laotian nation their collaboration in building its multiethnic structures.

At the urging of Hmong leaders, the first school was set up in the Hmong highlands at Nong Het (Xieng Khouang) in 1939. Once the school began operating, school attendance quickly became widespread in the Xieng Khouang mountains. From only nine in this single school in 1939, the number of Hmong students rose to 1,500 in 20 village schools in 1960. By 1969 the figure had reached 10,000 in more than 100 village schools and seven complete elementary schools, staffed by 450 male and female teachers, mostly Hmong. According to Moua Lia, Superintendent of Elementary Schools for Xieng Khouang province, in October 1969, 50 percent of the school-age Hmong children in the southern part of the Plain of Jars were attending village and elementary schools.[11] Elementary education is gradually spreading to other mountain regions of Laos as well.

Secondary education is also expanding. In 1971, 340 Hmong students were enrolled in public and private secondary schools in Vientiane, and 37 more were matriculated at universities in France, the United States, Canada, Australia, Italy, Japan and the Soviet Union. Some of these students are already completing their studies. No doubt they will return to Laos to do their part in furthering their country's development. The bonds that unite them to their families, as well as their awareness of belonging to a nation, are strong enough to rule out, at least for the present, any "brain drain" among the Hmong.

Hmong educational development could, however, be even more rapid if educational programs and methods more closely matched their social and economic needs and were better suited to their cultural environment. All teaching, for example, is done in Lao, the official language of the country but one which the ethnic minorities speak inadequately or not at all. The vast majority of Hmong students encounter a serious language barrier, which renders their intellectual development and acquisition of new knowledge haphazard at best. This explains the very high dropout rate, the relatively advanced age of students in the lower grades,[12] and the widespread relapse into illiteracy, all typical of education among the Hmong.

In the process of communicating knowledge and ideas that is education, language is the basic foundation. No educator would deny that the ideal vehicle for instruction is the child's native tongue. In the words of the United Nations Educational, Scientific and Cultural Organization (UNESCO):

> From the psychological point of view, it [the native language] represents a system of symbols which works automatically in his mind when he wants to express himself or understand. From the sociological point of view, it binds him intimately with the collectivity of which he is a part. From the pedagogical point of view, it enables him to learn more quickly than he would in another language unfamiliar to him.[13]

The Laotian government, concerned with making education "serve the whole of the Laotian community," is not insensitive to the problem of language. In the ethnic minority regions, Lao cannot be learned properly nor can it take on the function of a cultural element since it is not used outside the classroom or in the home and since, for the vast majority of mountain children, the school years comprise only a very small portion of their lives. Not

HMONG STUDENTS WORLD-WIDE, 1971[§]

FIELD OF STUDY	AUSTRALIA	CANADA	FRANCE	ITALY	JAPAN	USSR	USA
Agronomy	—	—	1	—	—	—	—
Economic and Social Development	—	—	2	—	—	—	—
Economics	—	—	4	—	—	1	2
Education	—	—	2	—	—	—	—
Electronics	—	1	—	—	1	—	—
Engineering and Applied Sciences	—	1	2	—	—	—	—
Law	—	—	4	—	—	—	—
Letters*	—	2	2	1	—	—	1
Medicine	—	—	3	—	—	—	1
Military**	—	—	1	—	—	—	—
Sciences***	—	—	3	—	—	—	—
Sociology	1	—	1	—	—	—	—
TOTAL: 37	**1**	**4**	**25**	**1**	**1**	**1**	**4**

[§]These statistics reflect only the number of Hmong students sent abroad for study by the Royal Lao Government. No information could be obtained on the number of Hmong students from the so-called "liberated zones" who may have been sent to study abroad (in communist countries).

*Modern French, English, Chinese, Vietnamese
**St. Cyr (French Army Officers' Training School)
***Mathematics, physics, chemistry

only does the present overly-academic educational system fail to prepare young highlanders for their working lives, it actually engenders feelings of alienation from their own culture and runs the risk of creating uprooted individuals with no true cultural home. The Royal Lao Government stipulated, therefore, in the Educational Reform Act of 1962, that

> in every possible case, ethnic groups will be given their primary education in their native language along with instruction in the national language.... Lao education will aim at producing citizens who are physically healthy, morally balanced, with a sense of what it means to live in society, capable of practicing their vocations competently, people attached to their village, happy in their village, all of them endowed, each at his own level, with genuine culture, however modest, and with true wisdom.[14]

Actual practice, however, falls far short of the promise of the Reform Act, which, if fully implemented, could not help but benefit all Laotian citizens.

This raises an interesting question: Does the fact that an ethnic group continues to speak its own language, has its own alphabet and develops its own culture constitute a threat to Laotian unity?[15] Acceptance of such a hypothesis would, by logical extension, mean that Switzerland as well as many nations in Asia and other parts of the world would long since have toppled. In fact, the strength of these renowned multiethnic states lies precisely in an awareness of a shared destiny, awareness that cannot be gained without realistic, fair and adequate education. National unity does not require ethnic, cultural, religious or ideological homogeneity. Such purely idealistic unity does not exist anywhere in the world. Rather, national unity is the fruit of a community of thought which makes all citizens of the country, regardless of their social or ethnic origins, equal before the law, aware and responsible, in solidarity with each other and strengthened with patriotic fervor. It is no accident that the Neo Lao Hak Sat has granted the Hmong the use of their own written language, which, in turn, has become an effective weapon in the party's social, economic and political revolution.[16] Providing to all citizens a suitable, sound education that will truly help them, with full awareness, achieve their own development and take charge of their own destiny: this is the aim which alone can justify the tremendous educational efforts going on in Laos today.

FROM PROFESSIONAL TRAINING TO AWAKENING NATIONAL CONSCIOUSNESS

Despite schooling ill-suited to the mountain environment, a small number of Hmong are managing to get some education, enough to enable them to climb the first few rungs of the social ladder open to ethnic minorities. In 1969, more than 300 male and female Hmong nurses were working in the 200-bed Sene Souk Hospital at Sam Thong, in the 50-bed infirmary at Long Cheng and in 48 dispensaries scattered throughout the refugee settlements in the southern part of the Plain of Jars. Two nurses' training schools, offering courses of six months to two years, have been established in the Sam Thong-Long Cheng area. Administrators, lawyers, engineers and agricultural technicians have graduated from various colleges and universities in Laos and abroad. More and more Hmong are beginning to hold official positions in the provincial services of northern Laos.

As more Hmong professionals are trained, administration in the mountains is improving, making it easier for the Royal Lao Government and the Pathet Lao to exert control over the country's populations. At the same time, a gradual awakening of national consciousness is taking place among the Hmong as they begin to consider more seriously the role they will be called upon to play in a modern Laotian state. Evidence of this is shown by their active participation on both sides of the conflict between the princes of the kingdom. It is not unusual to see Hmong leaders held up as examples by opposing factions for the service they have rendered to the Laotian nation.

The presence of educated Hmong, both civilian and military, is having a marked impact on the psychology and attitudes of the Hmong people. Neither must the role of radio be underestimated. At present there are five radio stations broadcasting in Hmong. Two of these are in Laos: Lao Patriotic Front Radio, based in Sam Neua, and Unity of Laotian Ethnic Groups Radio, based in Long Cheng. For several hours a day, the Hmong in Laos can listen to national news and follow world events in their own language.[17] This is made possible by the spread throughout the mountains of thousands of small Japanese-made transistor radios, a rarity only a decade ago. The news they hear, though, is often contradictory: the Hmong announcer on Lao Patriotic Front Radio will vehemently denounce "American aggression in Laos," while the one on Unity of Laotian Ethnic Groups Radio will inveigh against the "invasion of Laotian territory by North Vietnamese forces." The one thing they have in common, however, is their call "on all Hmong to join closely with their Lao and Khmou brothers to fight foreign imperialism."

The political commitment of the Hmong in a divided Laos seems to stem from a sense of national consciousness which has been forged slowly over the past 25 years. But what good has it done them? The next chapter will examine this question.

FOOTNOTES:

[1] Ly, *Initiative and Agriculture in Laos*, p. 63.

[2] Contrary to the claims of Frank Bowming and Banning Garrett that "[i]n 1964, the population of Long Cheng had risen to close to 50,000, who were set to work growing opium poppies in the hills surrounding the base." (*Temps Modernes*, No. 298, Paris, May 1971, p. 2004 ff.)

[3] In 1969.

[4] There were a score of fish ponds in Long Cheng in 1969.

[5] Ly, *Initiative and Agriculture in Laos*, p. 64.

[6] Freight charges from Vientiane to Long Cheng were 50 kip per kilogram in 1969.

[7] Laos, Department of Planning, *1969-74 Master Plan*, p. 77.

[8] Special high-yield varieties of rice developed by the Ford and Rockefeller foundation-financed International Rice Research Institute at Los Banos, near Manila in the Philippines.

[9] Father Bertrais carried out missionary and economic development work among the Hmong in Luang Prabang, Houa Phanh and Vientiane provinces from 1949 to 1975. In 1978, he began a project in Jahovey, French Guyana, in which, together with a companion project located in Cacao, some 1,500 Hmong, originally refugees from Laos, make their living by raising rice, vegetables, prawns and lychee and marketing them in French Guyana and Surinam.

[10] Charles Pierson and Yves Bertrais, *Rural Extension Project Among the Hmong Highlanders*, Catholic Mission of Laos, Center for the Hmong Apostolate, Vientiane, January 1969, p. 5.

[11] This figure is well above the national average of 35 percent, due primarily to the establishment of many military-supported schools in villages where there are no government schools. Where civilian teachers are unavailable, military personnel are assigned to teach in these schools.

[12] The average age of Hmong children in the seventh year of school in 1969 was 14-15 years, compared to an expected age of 12.

[13] United Nations Educational, Scientific and Cultural Organization, *Use of Vernacular Languages in Teaching*, Basic Education Monograph No. VIII, Paris, 1963, p. 15.

[14] Laos, Ministry of Education, "Educational Reform in Laos," *Education*, No. 20, Vientiane, August 1962, p. 53.

[15] Cf. Bounsong Phanekham, "The Education Ministry's Bet," *L'Etudiant Lao* (Lao Students' Bulletin, Bordeaux Section), Paris, 1971, p. 44.

[16] Author unknown, *The Lao Revolution at Twenty*, Laos?, December 1965, p. 7.

[17] Unity of Laotian Ethnic Groups Radio broadcasts in six languages: Lao, Hmong, Khmou, Tai Dam, Mien and Vietnamese.

CHAPTER SIX

The Wartime Economy

Ten years of violent war have made Laos into an immense refugee camp which stretches from the north to the south of the Kingdom of a Million Elephants. More than 600,000 people, a fifth of the Laotian population, have been uprooted by the expanding Indochina war. This tragic situation compels reflection on the social and economic problems posed by these massive exoduses. The Hmong in the northeastern part of the country, the region hardest hit by the war, provide an ideal case for examination.

POPULATION DISPLACEMENTS

The guerrilla war has found in Laos, the mountain country, its favorite kind of battleground. The expansion of the war has sown death and misery among the Hmong and the other mountain peoples, and its curse has spread steadily to the valley and plains peoples as well. In Laos today it is estimated that one Hmong in three is a refugee.

In Houa Phanh and Xieng Khouang provinces, the war has reached into every home and forced every individual, down to the very youngest, to make the agonizing choice of flight or death. War has become the lot of all, of those who make it as well as those who simply endure it. Virtually the entire population of the northeastern part of the country has seen the framework of their lives upset, bringing changes in location, livelihood and concerns.

Since 1961, fierce battles have taken place regularly on the Plain of Jars, the prize of every war fought in northern Laos. Tens of thousands of men and women of all ethnic groups have fled in waves under bombs and rocket fire, their homes and lands devastated in turn by Pathet Lao and North Vietnamese troops and by Vientiane government forces. They have taken refuge in temporary settlements to the south, where there is little to eat, where schools are nonexistent, where sanitary conditions are deplorable, and where hopelessness and despair are constant companions.

During these troubled times, total disorder prevailed; what government there was intervened only to attend to the most pressing situations. The heat and the rains, compounded by the lack of hygiene among people accustomed to living in relative isolation, quickly led to the spread of disease and epidemics, ravaging the teeming refugee population, particularly the children.

In the space of only a few years the southwest part of the Plain of Jars, once a lush green forest where tigers roamed, has been "urbanized" under the pressure of a continuing exodus that has no relationship whatsoever to the normal sort of economic development linked to industrialization. Today more than 200,000 people live in settlements and military bases ranging from 500 to 30,000 inhabitants, confined to a mountainous strip only 50 by 90 kilometers in area. The rest of the province is total desolation. Because of the massive numbers of the displacees and the presence and requirements of the army, each of these encampments has become an important center for social change.

Since the fall of Na Khang (the last advance post of the government forces) in 1968, life in this region has been, except for brief periods and in varying degrees, a daily struggle for physical safety and a bitter search for respite. Each dry season may well mean another move; the last one took place in 1971. Threatened with encirclement by a pincers movement of Pathet Lao and North Vietnamese troops, more than 30,000 Lao, Phouan, Khmou and Hmong, mostly women and children, left the Sam Thong-Long Cheng area to settle temporarily further to the south at Phak Khe and Ban Sone, under the most deplorable conditions. A few actually moved as far south as Vientiane.

Some families who managed to survive this debilitating life have been displaced ten or more times in the space of ten years, suffering the all too familiar physical and mental consequences. Few are the families which have not been broken up by so many years of tribulation. The upheavals of the peoples of Xieng Khouang are a measure of the material destruction wrought over a decade. A look at the human geography of the country makes it plain that the Hmong are not the only ones to "just go on running and dying, dying and running."[1] The whole of the Laotian people are suffering through this calvary, the bitterest of the century.

THE WARTIME ECONOMY

The continuing hostilities have brought about, in addition to the social consequences just described, the gradual establishment of a wartime economy. One indication of this is the inability of the Phouan plateau of Xieng Khouang province to feed its own population and its increasing dependence on outside assistance. Abandoned rice fields and decimated cattle herds are almost all that remain of a once-thriving economy. It will take a long time to rebuild the economy of this region, now more than 80 percent destroyed. Its reconstruction is severely hampered by continuing insecurity and by military recruitment, which robs it of most of its working population. The population density in this area, where more than 200,000 people are crammed together, reaches the unheard-of number of 44 people per square kilometer (114/sq. mi.).[2] In some places, Hmong refugees can find neither poultry nor pigs for their ritual needs so they are forced to make do with plain stones in their stead! This simple example speaks volumes about the economic state of the repeatedly devastated province.

At the height of the war, efforts were made to ease the province's economic situation. So far these efforts have come to naught due to lack of adequate technical and political leadership. Today the majority of the more than 200,000 Lao, Hmong and Khmou refugees are still living on governmental assistance, chiefly from the United States. Most of the aid goes to satisfy the basic needs of the displacees: food, cooking utensils, medicine, seed grain, farm implements, etc. Some is also used to assist those people who wish to settle in new permanent sites such as the Muong Phieng area in Sayaboury province. Others, who intend to return home as soon as the shooting stops, are temporarily installed at places like Long Cheng or Ban Sone, where they try, insofar as possible, to grow their own food.

The juxtaposition of the three types of socioeconomic systems we have just studied reflects accurately the uneven evolution of the Hmong economy. In general, the mountain regions, scarcely touched by currents of modernity because of their extreme isolation, are still basically traditionalist in their social and economic organization. The valleys and plateaus, which have been opened up somewhat by roads and landing strips to the market economy, are hampered by the lack of rational, planned organization of either production or marketing.

Finally, the combat zones are doomed to insecurity, poverty and misery as long as the present conflict goes on; its prolongation only accelerates the economic deterioration of all of Laos.

The growing unreliability of a declining traditional economy, the uncertainty of a transitional economy and the anxiety of a wartime economy are all forcing the Hmong into changing their ancient social and technological systems, into accepting major changes and innovations, and into adapting as quickly as they can to a modern economy. Little by little we are witnessing the spread through the mountains of the idea that economic progress is not only possible but that it is one of the necessary conditions for the realization of other objectives as well: individual improvement, mutual interests, more solid national integration, and better living conditions for future generations. These sociological and psychological changes lie at the very heart of the creation of the requisite conditions for any economic takeoff. It remains to be seen how the Hmong and the other mountain peoples will be included in an integrated strategy for national development and how the considerable potential of the mountains of Laos will be tapped.

FOOTNOTES:

[1] Jean-Claude Pomonti, "The Calvary of the Meo People," *Le Monde*, Paris, May 12, 1971.

[2] Population density averages 12 per square kilometer for the country as a whole.

Prospects for Economic and Social Development

THE PLAINS AND THE MOUNTAINS

Laos has two quite distinct regions: the plains along the Mekong River, and the mountains, the so-called "back country." The plains enjoy large amounts of foreign aid, and the area is steadily modernizing. The mountains, left mostly to their own devices, are turning increasingly inward upon themselves. This paradoxical situation largely explains the country's economic imbalance, an imbalance further aggravated by the continuing political instability. If this imbalance is not corrected soon, it will not only retard severely the economic expansion of Laos but may well widen the already considerable gap between ethnic groups, which certain politicians, who make no secret of their scorn for the mountain "savages," attempt to maintain.

These economic and political considerations raise some important questions: How can Laos solve its economic and ethnic problems? What resources do the mountains hold? To what degree will the people of these regions be able to take part in the political and economic reconstruction of Laos? Without claiming to offer fully-formed solutions to these critical problems, Part Three presents a brief survey of some of the development opportunities afforded by the mountain regions of the Kingdom of Lan Xang.

Developing the Mountain Regions

For the present and for some time to come, Laos will need to base its economy on agriculture. Its geographic situation compels it to look for high value-low bulk raw materials which can be exported or products which can be processed domestically, sending finished or semi-finished goods onto the market. From these requirements stems the necessity to create both upstream and downstream agricultural and processing industries.

The number of producers of ordinary commodities such as food products is far too high for the number of consumers (ninety percent of the Laotian people make a living by farming). It is important, therefore, to channel some of the manpower from this primary sector into other economic activities, particularly in the secondary and tertiary sectors. This will, in turn, broaden the domestic market for farm products.

Orographic and climatic conditions dictate that, for the present, the plains of Laos must be devoted essentially to the growing of rice. It is necessary, therefore, to consider other regions for the development of industrial or semi-industrial crops, whose producers will provide the direct and stable market the rice growers need.

The climate in the mountain areas is particularly favorable for intensive farming at a relatively high level of productivity and with greater profitability than in the plains. This is especially true for:

○ all kinds of livestock

○ coffee and tea

○ medicinal and essential oil plants

○ fruits (oranges, lemons, avocados, apples, pears, strawberries)

○ potatoes and other truck garden crops (for direct consumption and preservation)

○ certain grain crops (barley, Mexican wheat).

Livestock products, herbal medicines and essential oils could easily find buyers on the markets of Southeast Asia. All that would be required is an in-depth study of existing markets and a commitment by the country of Laos to provide products of commercial quality at competitive prices. This could be accomplished either through joining existing international trade agreements or by creating new bilateral agreements. The products listed above fit nicely into the structure of intensive, strongly-integrated family agriculture. This system, supported by a temperate climate which permits people to work harder and longer than is physically possible in the plains, is the only one which will succeed in the mountains.

It is generally and quite mistakenly assumed that agricultural yields in the mountains are lower than those in the plains. This error tends to divert the attention of most Lao leaders, who feel that, it being the case, the major thrust of development should be toward improving the lowlands and, hence, toward increasing rice production. It turns out that Laos would have an extremely difficult time competing in this commodity with its neighbors (Thailand, Cambodia, Vietnam and Burma), which are better suited topographically and geographically for rice production than are the Laotian plains. Laos would be better advised to take its time and analyze its own situation carefully rather than simply following the example of neighboring countries where conditions differ significantly.

One of the main factors in Laos's favor is the diversity of its climate, which creates a natural economic complementarity between the plains and the mountains. Carefully planned, systematic improvement of both regions will enable Laos to achieve rapid economic expansion even as it creates domestic commercial outlets for its rice production. This perspective underlies the discussion of the development of the mountain regions of northern Laos.

GENERAL PRINCIPLES FOR DEVELOPMENT OF THE MOUNTAINS

The aim of development of the mountain regions is two-fold: first, to develop Laos's resources and to increase the production and hence the incomes of the mountain peoples, and, second, to bring about economic, and thereby ethnic, integration of the country. To achieve this two-fold objective, it will be necessary to mount intensive human as well as technical action.

TECHNICAL ACTION
THE PRIMARY SECTOR

Agriculture Development of the primary agricultural sector must simultaneously pursue individual, regional and national objectives. It must seek to

○ increase the income of the farmers significantly

○ diversify production and, consequently, the sources of income of the mountain peoples

○ add to the country's resources by increasing its exports.

Food Crops To diversify food crop production, it will be necessary to

○ begin a program of local seed selection and improve existing cultivation methods

○ introduce high-yield varieties of rice (IR-5, IR-8, etc.) along with improved cultivation techniques perfected in other regions or countries.

Industrial Crops Increase in income and diversification of income sources require a search for crops with a high economic yield (tea, coffee, pyrethrum, etc.) to replace the opium poppy now banned in Laos.

Livestock If it is to meet domestic demand and even begin to contemplate exports, Laos will have to improve and increase its livestock production as quickly as possible through

○ better protection of livestock against disease

○ modification of traditional stock-raising practices

○ introduction and popularization of livestock with the lowest possible transformation coefficient[1]

○ association of livestock operations with agriculture, particularly forage crops, as much as possible

○ popularization of high-quality feed at affordable prices.

Forests Because of the poverty of some of the mountain soils, economic development of the forests must be based on labor investment in reforestation. Adequate forest resources must be built up to ensure future supplies of lumber and firewood not only for the mountain peoples but for the plains and cities as well. The Department of Forests and Water Resources will have an expanding role to play in the national economy.

THE SECONDARY SECTOR Development of the primary sector will necessitate, as a consequence of some of its activities, the establishment of processing industries to upgrade and add value, sometimes considerable, to its products. The secondary sector will provide jobs for cash wages and, through purchases of the food produced by the primary sector, give farmers a regular income. It should also enable the national government to increase its fiscal resources through the growth of exports and the increase in tax revenues generated by this new economic activity.

Agriculture

Food Crops The overall aim of secondary-sector food crop development is to achieve maximum productivity so that each farmer can feed the greatest number of people. Plans must be made for the creation of processing industries, the utilization of storage techniques, and combinations of the two. The main objective is to assure non-farmers of regular, year-round food supplies at reasonable prices.

Industrial Crops Non-food crops serve two economic functions: some strengthen the domestic market by reducing imports of non-durable consumer goods, others are destined primarily for export. Much more research must be done into the domestic and foreign market potential of industrial crops which could be grown in Laos. Such research has barely begun, and what little there is concerns mainly products of the plains.

Processing adds value to these products, increasing their specific value by reducing their tonnage, thus achieving considerable economies in freight costs. Exports of processed products, by their nature, produce greater foreign currency returns per unit of raw material than those of unprocessed products. National revenue will, as a necessary consequence, be increased both by wages and taxes and by an improvement in the balance of payments, which currently runs deeply in the red.[2]

Livestock A rising standard of living will have as a direct result an increase in annual per capita meat consumption. This, in turn, will stimulate the growth of livestock raising. Secondary economic activities in the area of livestock might include

○ operation of slaughterhouses judiciously distributed in the region

○ creation of processing industries to handle inputs to and by-products of livestock production (animal feed, glue for paper and plywood, leather goods, etc.)

○ production of dairy products (which presupposes new patterns of consumption and would require nutritional education).

Forestry   Building up forest resources could lead, in the future, to major secondary economic activity through

○ construction of semi-mobile sawmills to cut logs into beams and boards

○ development of craft industries for making finished wood products such as furniture, etc.

○ systematic exploitation of precious woods for export either as raw wood or, preferably, after processing or fabrication.

THE TERTIARY SECTOR   The result of developing the secondary economic sector will, necessarily, be the emergence of the tertiary sector needed to store, transport and sell its products. The people engaged in these service occupations will become additional consumers of the region's food products. An ideal situation could emerge in which there would be a natural development of the market economy which already involves a large portion of Laos's population, although not always accompanied by the necessary increases in production to support it.

HUMAN ACTION

More important than any technical action is the human action upon which will depend its success or failure. This human action consists of giving the people the skills and attitudes they need to implement the principles of development. More intensive agricultural methods, ever-closer association of farming with livestock production, and the emergence and growth of new activities in the secondary and tertiary sectors will require the government to make a concerted effort to provide leadership, education and training, as well as to develop a rural cooperative system.

Leadership   The role of leadership is to work through persuasion, "by arousing enthusiasm for the goals proposed so that everybody thoroughly understands that he is working for himself and his children."[3] Leadership must be provided in many arenas simultaneously: cultural, medical, agricultural, social and political. Providing leadership and guidance to farmers will lead to higher production in the primary sector and will contribute in large measure to the development of secondary and tertiary activities. It could lead, for example, to the establishment of Rural Development Assistance Centers.

Education and Training   The task here is to provide "a general education with accelerated technical training"[4] for all concerned. Educators must be trained and agricultural teaching methods adapted to make them more effective motivators of the social action contemplated.

The Cooperative System   The establishment of cooperatives has as a precondition the success of rural leadership. The cooperative system that is to form the basic economic framework cannot be imposed from the outside. It must be perceived as a need by those who consciously decide to promote their own economic and social development. This calls for a gradual "raising of consciousness," which could be made part of a functional literacy program.

Setting up cooperatives will require the training of staff and specialists to ensure that the organizations are properly run, and the provision of a minimum level of education to at least some of their members so that they will be able to supervise the operation of the cooperatives.

Labor Investment Rural leadership must also have as one of its goals the popular acceptance of the idea of working for the community in the form of labor investment. This will lessen the need to use government funds or foreign loans for economic development, which would only increase the public indebtedness. An additional result of such collective undertakings will be to raise the civic consciousness of the people.

The general principles set forth here are the *sine qua non* for the integrated development so highly extolled by the Royal Lao Government. Compliance with these basic principles will constitute the foundation of the nation's social and economic future. Let us now examine how these principles might be applied to some specific possibilities for economic and social development offered by the mountain regions of northern Laos.

ECONOMIC DEVELOPMENT

Land is generally underused in the mountain regions. Despite the difficulties it may entail, it is certain that the mountain population could be increased and the productivity of the land raised significantly by improvements in agriculture, animal husbandry and forest culture.

AGRICULTURE

Agriculture in the mountain regions of Laos has not been developed to its fullest extent. The low population density and the vast expanse of uncultivated land support the contention that it would be relatively easy to expand the area of farmland by opening up unoccupied valleys and hollows and by making use of sufficiently thick soils on slopes of less than 25 percent.[5]

GENERAL OBJECTIVES Agricultural development in the mountains should pursue a three-fold objective:

Rapid Increase in Production Expansion of farm production should be as diversified as possible. This will allow both an improvement in the nutrition of the people and the production of a substantial surplus for other uses. To bring about this rapid expansion will require

○ increased efficiency, such as better utilization of labor and working time, which will allow improved yields

○ continual improvement of farming methods, such as the introduction of draft animals, crop and field rotation, the use of natural fertilizers, crop protection, and so on

○ a search for high-yield, fast-growing rice varieties with early ripening and the possibility of double harvests

○ public works projects, such as construction of roads and bridges, irrigation canals, water purification plants and grain storage facilities

○ education of the farmers, who will have to display ambitious, innovative determination, a quality in short supply among them at present.

Development of Animal Husbandry   Among the Hmong, livestock-raising is traditionally linked with agriculture. The spread of the latter, therefore, will necessarily contribute to the development of the former. This contribution will come about through

○ grain production (corn and paddy)

○ growing of hay and storage of rice straw

○ growing of forage (legumes and cereals)

○ production of oil cake (from peanuts and soybeans).

Generation of Cash Income   Within the framework of the market economy which is gradually replacing village self-sufficiency, agriculture can become a major source of cash income through

○ the sale of farm surpluses (rice, corn, etc.)

○ commercialization of fruit, truck, and industrial crops (tea, coffee, medicinal and aromatic plants).

All of this will require a transportation infrastructure adequate to shatter the isolation of the mountain regions of northern Laos, as well as the organization of national and regional markets beginning with Southeast Asia.

POSSIBILITIES FOR DIVERSIFIED CROPS IN THE MOUNTAINS

FOOD CROPS

There are four categories of food crops which thrive in the climate of the mountain regions and whose expansion could mean steady improvement in the nutritional levels of the people as well as of their livestock: cereal crops, truck crops, fruit trees and tuberous plants.

Cereal Crops

Rice   As the staple of the diet, rice is and will remain the chief cereal crop of the Hmong in Laos. Mountain rice is of better quality than that grown in the plains, some varieties of which are fairly flat-tasting. Much sought-after by Chinese and Vietnamese dealers, mountain rice could form the basis of a profitable domestic trade.

Its method of cultivation, however, in swidden *rai*, is already posing problems in maintaining current production, to say nothing of expansion. The distressing fact is that every year thousands of hectares of forest are burned over, whole regions rendered unfit for crops as a result of human action. The national wealth is gradually being depleted without any opportunity for normal, timely replenishment.

Faced with this situation, which threatens the country's economic future, the Laotian government sees itself as having few other choices than to ban the practice of slash-and-burn agriculture and bring the mountain people, willingly or not, down onto the plains

— where they will be faced immediately with acclimatization problems.[6] This measure has reportedly already been put into effect in the mountain region of Phou Khao Khouai (Vientiane province), where all forest cutting is said to have been prohibited.[7] Such actions run up against the obvious problem of land availability: the land which could be allotted to the displaced mountain people is generally the poorest, since the better land is already occupied. Yet another difficulty can be expected in that once the assigned lands have been cleared and planted, they will likely be claimed instantly by their alleged owners.

It is necessary, indeed urgent, to protect the forest resources and the heritage of land which form the base of the Laotian economy. This requires that the mountain people give up completely the practice of swidden agriculture in favor of permanent farming, the only kind of agriculture which will preserve the fertility of the soil. Such a shift would bring their nomadic habits to an end and would be the beginning of substantial social and economic changes. But does this mean that the mountain people will all have to come down to the lowlands in order to get a taste of progress?

We have already seen that, in general, the Hmong standard of living in peacetime is not significantly lower than that of lowland farmers. Orographic conditions impose considerable limitations on the amount of land available for irrigated rice cultivation in the highlands. The valleys are much too small and narrow, and the water supply, which must often be provided under extremely difficult conditions, is insufficient in many places to allow for rice terraces on the slopes. Furthermore, the amount of labor required to construct and work terraces is unreasonably large. However, thanks to processes and technologies made available by modern science, the mountains can look forward to a better lot. It is possible nowadays to grow mountain rice with no more water than that provided by the rains and to do so without robbing the soil of its fertility. This is accomplished through the regular application of fertilizer and the use of erosion prevention measures.

Corn   The future of corn-growing in the mountain country is tied directly to that of animal husbandry as it is practiced there. The skills of the Hmong farmers and the favorable climatic conditions suggest the possibility of rapid medium- to long-term growth of animal husbandry in these regions. This growth will necessitate a proportionate increase in the growing of corn, the staple feed for small livestock such as hogs and poultry. Like mountain rice, corn, given modern methods and techniques, can become a permanent crop of increasing importance. On-site corn processing is recommended. In addition to local consumption there is the possibility of export to other areas of Laos as well as to the entire Southeast Asian market.

Sorghum and Millet   Known to the Hmong since ancient times, production of sorghum and millet appears to have declined in Laos. This is apparently due to the recent introduction of rain-fed rice to the highlands. These crops should be encouraged, since they can serve as a base for enriched cattle feed.

Barley and Wheat   According to Pierson,[8] barley is a cereal which could readily adapt to the ecological conditions of the mountains of northern Laos. Wheat is also not an impossibility for the Hmong highlands. Certain test-selected strains of Mexican wheat should adapt and thrive in the climatic conditions of the northern Laotian mountains.[9] During the French protectorate, experiments were made, with some success, at growing wheat at an elevation of 1,200 meters on the Phouan plateau of Xieng Khouang. The testing was interrupted during World War II, and the research results were not adequate to determine which varieties would be best suited to the area. These studies should be resumed as soon as the political situation allows. It is certain that wheat growing, if successful, would help improve the Laotian economy by reducing imports of wheat flour for use in the large cities (Vientiane, Pakse, Savannakhet, Luang Prabang and Long Cheng).

Truck Crops   Every year, the plains regions of Laos must import large quantities of vegetables from Thailand, even though such foods can easily be grown domestically. The climate in some of the high-elevation regions (Pak Song in the south, Xieng Khouang in the north, etc.) is particularly well suited to the raising of temperate-zone truck crops.

In the past, the towns of Xieng Khouang, Lat Houang and Phong Savanh got most of their fresh vegetables from Hmong peasants. With the attainment of peace and the development of an adequate infrastructure, the Hmong in Phou Khao Khouai (only 60 kilometers from Vientiane) would certainly be able to supply a good share of the capital's steadily growing demand for fresh produce.[10] The same holds true for Hmong in other provinces. All that would be required is the development of a domestic marketing system and a commitment on the part of the Hmong to provide produce of commercial quality. They would first need to raise high-yield varieties already introduced and adapted to Laos. Some Western-style vegetables would also adapt quite well to the ecological conditions of the highlands. Markets for these crops could easily be found in the cities, particularly Vientiane, where there are many foreigners (professors, technicians, international officials, embassy staff, tourists, and the like) as well as many Laotians who have adopted Western eating habits.

Fruit Crops   Another possible mountain contribution to the national economy are fruit crops. The climate is very conducive to the growing of both tropical and Mediterranean fruits. These products would easily find markets both in Laos and abroad.

Fruit consumption in Laos is growing at a faster rate than the average standard of living. The large quantities of fruit imported annually from Thailand confirm this increase, which domestic production is unable to supply. Furthermore, the large cities in areas bordering on Laos (Vinh, Hanoi-Haiphong, Bangkok, Phnom Penh and Saigon) could, once the war is over, become major markets for fruit from northern Laos.

This prospect should motivate the Department of Agriculture to undertake, as soon as politically practicable, exploratory surveys in the mountain regions to identify fruits which could be marketed domestically and exported — either fresh or processed into juice, concentrates, canned fruits or preserves — to neighboring countries. Possibilities include high-quality varieties of apples, citrus fruits and one or more varieties of peaches selected for their ability to ship well. In addition, tests of fruit trees should be started so as to acclimatize some Mediterranean species (e.g. apples, pears, plums, cherries and grapes) to the high Hmong country.

The development of fruit-growing in the mountain areas and the establishment of accompanying processing plants should encourage the mountain people to settle on permanent farms, as some Hmong villages in the Chiang Mai area in Thailand have done.[11]

An assured market and a reasonable, steady income would be enough of an incentive to persuade them to give up poppy cultivation. The effect of such a change would be better living conditions for the mountain people and rapid recovery of the national economy.

Root Crops   Among the tuberous plants already grown in the mountains are sweet potatoes, yams, manioc and taro. These plants traditionally round out the range of garden produce in the Hmong diet. Their expansion would allow the intensification of hog raising which, in turn, would provide more fertilizer for the crops.

Several areas in Laos produce potatoes: the Pak Song plateau in the south and the foothills of the Phou Bia (Xieng Khouang) and Pha Thong (Luang Prabang) mountains in the north. Besides its potential for export, potato production could find a ready domestic market, particularly in Vientiane.[12] Fridman suggests the following varieties for the Xieng Khouang region, all of which give fairly high yields: Bintje, Ideal, Saskia, Esterlingea, Early Rose and Royal Kidney. Testing should be resumed on varieties selected for tropical countries.

Other Food Crops   At least a brief mention must be made of crops such as pineapple, strawberries and, above all, sugar cane, which plays an important part in the Hmong diet. Sugar production should be encouraged, especially since consumption of it is increasing rapidly. Enough sugar cane should be able to be grown to supply local needs. However, the small, handmade processing equipment, in which two wooden cylinders are used to crush the cane, must be upgraded. Improved family-scale techniques, developed by the National Sugar Institute of Uttar Pradesh in India, in which the wooden cylinders are replaced with metal rollers driven by motors or water power, would suit the socioeconomic conditions of the Hmong and other Laotian peoples.

NON-FOOD CROPS

In Chapter Four we saw that the two principal non-food crops traditionally grown by the Hmong were opium poppies and hemp, the latter a distant second. Hemp is disappearing and opium was banned in September 1971 by a law against growing or selling the drug in Laos. If this law is enforced in the mountains, it will cause serious economic hardships throughout Hmong country, where opium has long been the principal source of cash revenue. The Laotian government ought to be more aware of this than anyone. It would, in fact, be possible to devise a carefully regulated and closely supervised system of opium growing and marketing to supply international medicinal needs. Such a system would bring in more than a negligible amount of foreign currency to augment the nation's finances.

Even if controlled opium growing were to be permitted, it would still be necessary to plan for crop diversification in the mountains. The problem is, what crops will replace opium? What industrial crops could both adapt to ecological conditions in the highlands of Laos and at the same time meet the economic needs of the nation's mountain peoples?

Annual Crops   Promising annual crops include soybeans and peanuts, which have among the highest protein content of any plants on earth. Both of these products, on occasion, make a contribution to the Hmong diet. Limited in production thus far by the home-consumption practices of the Hmong, soybean and peanut crops could be expanded in the future into a flourishing domestic market. Consumption of soybeans and their derivatives is growing rapidly in Laos, where vegetable oil is gradually replacing animal fat. At present, the supply is lagging far behind the steadily growing demand, hence the need for Laos to import these products from abroad. According to government statistics, imports of vegetable seeds and oils amount to at least 3,600 tons annually. These imports create a considerable drain on the national economy and further contribute to the worsening balance of payments, already seriously negative. Development of soybean and peanut growing in the mountains could help reduce, if not completely eliminate, such imports. This would require, on the part of the Departments of Agriculture, Commerce and Industry

- widespread education about and popularization of oil-bearing crops

- organized collection of the harvests

- establishment of crushing plants and facilities for processing the by-products into soy and peanut cakes and similar products

- establishment of an extensive marketing system.

Close coordination among several economic sectors and the cooperation of the government would be required in order for this effort to have any chance of success.

Perennial Crops   Because of their elevation and climate, the mountain regions of northern Laos seem particularly suitable for the growing of tea and coffee.

Tea   As we have seen, the tea plant flourishes on the Phouan plateau in Xieng Khouang province, where a fair amount of it still grows wild. These so-called "Shan" bushes produce a fine tea which is very much in demand. It is said that in the old days Chinese caravans would come all the way from the Northern Capital to gather the wild tea. The bushes were cut down and the tender shoots gathered and processed on site, producing the famous Imperial Tea for the court of Peking.

Until quite recently, Shan tea dominated the important markets of Hanoi and Haiphong, where the Chinese paid 100 to 200 piasters per kilogram for it, while ordinary tea brought no more than 70 piasters.[13] Today it has all but been forgotten, since the fighting on the Plain of Jars makes it impossible to get to the groves to gather it.

Once the war is over, the growing of tea should be encouraged among the Hmong, who seem made to order for the patient gathering it requires. Anyone who has tried to milk poppies knows the precision and delicacy with which these people can work. Tea, along with arabica coffee and the fruit crops discussed earlier, might well be the solution to the development of medium-elevation slopes.

Coffee   Past attempts have demonstrated that coffee adapts readily to high elevations. On the advice of Yves Bertrais, Za Nao Yang, a Hmong farmer living in Kiu Kacham (Mountain of the Wild Gaurs) in Luang Prabang province, gave up the growing of poppies and switched to coffee. In 1960 he had a plantation of several thousand trees, which earned him an annual income greater than he had ever received from his poppy fields. The resumption of hostilities forced Za Nao Yang to abandon his thriving young plantation and flee to Sayaboury.[14] His example, however, should provide food for thought to the economic policy-makers in Laos.

Arabica coffee is particularly well suited for developing the mid-level elevations of northern Laos. In addition, it would be worthwhile to try the new Brazilian varieties (*Cattura novo mundo*) and those which are resistant to the *Hemileia vastatrix* fungus, which wiped out the coffee plantations of Sri Lanka.

Shan tea and arabica coffee have a good chance of establishing themselves on the domestic and international markets provided they can be supplied in commercial quantities.[15] To this end, it would be advisable to set up tea and coffee processing plants in areas specializing in the growing of these products. Clustering of plantations would make harvesting easier, and processing would result in a final product with greater specific value.

Other Industrial Crops As the world's top producer of benzoin, northern Laos could also supply other essences much in demand on the world market, specifically pyrethrum and rose geranium, both of which grow well at high altitudes. Pyrethrum (an insecticide) and geranium (a scent) are increasingly sought after for their rare essences by industries throughout the world. Rose geranium, introduced by French missionaries to the Hmong in the Phou Khao Khouai area north of Vientiane, is still in the experimental stage. Until further results are in it would be premature to venture an opinion as to the advisability of encouraging its cultivation in the Laotian mountains.

Finally, the wide variety of medicinal plants found in the mountains constitutes a valuable potential resource for the economic future of Laos.[16] It has been found that traditional Hmong medicines are able to cure wounds and diseases which Western medicine is powerless to treat. Collaboration between traditional and modern practitioners will be required in order to identify and develop these plants, still little known in the West. This kind of cooperation is common in the People's Republic of China.

SOIL CONSERVATION While bringing lowlands and valleys under cultivation does not pose much of a soil conservation problem, the same is not true for the mountains. There every clearing or improvement of a slope must be accompanied by compulsory measures to prevent erosion, the major cause of soil impoverishment in many regions of northern Laos. This erosion is due primarily to the practice of swidden agriculture, compounded by the pounding monsoon rains, whose swift runoff carries away vital components of the unprotected soil. The steeper the slope and the more violent the rains, the faster cultivated soils are depleted. Thus it is critical that the soil be protected against erosion in order to ensure its future availability and steady crop yields.

Soil conservation can be accomplished through both biological and mechanical methods. To achieve the best results, the two methods should be used together; their careful combination is the key to fighting erosion.

Mechanical Methods Mechanical soil conservation consists of simple systems set up on slopes, which prevent erosion by containing runoff and channeling it toward areas where the danger of erosion is less. The design of these devices varies widely with the slope and the nature of the soil. Two of the most common types are contour cultivation and embankment.[17]

Contour cultivation can prevent soil erosion on grades of less than about 12 percent. Isohypses (contour lines) are mapped, dividing the slope into sections of equal elevation, and the land is plowed parallel to the contour lines. For additional protection, tall hedges of elephant grass (*Pennisetum purpureum* or *Setaria sphaceleata*) can be planted along the contour lines. This method will lead to a gradual reduction of the average inclination and to the formation of terraces. To protect the soil on slopes steeper than 12 percent, an embankment system is preferable. In this method, a series of parallel, equidistant embankments is constructed roughly horizontally, allowing for topographical variation, across the slope from top to bottom.

Biological Methods Mechanical methods alone are not sufficient to preserve or restore soil fertility. Biological techniques such as crop rotation, organic fertilization and soil covering must also be used.

Crop Rotation Farmers must be encouraged to adopt conservation-based crop rotation practices which maintain and improve the fertility of the soil. Before that can be done, however, scientific research and practical experiments must be carried out to determine the optimum patterns of crop rotation.

Organic Fertilizer On soils with steep grades, organic fertilizer (manure, crop residue, compost, etc.) is one of the few effective means of increasing soil fertility. The use of manure, however, implies the practice of confined livestock raising, as yet relatively uncommon in Laos, where, as we have seen, animals are usually left to roam freely. Without the aid of organic fertilizers, crop yields decline rapidly after two or three years of cultivation.

Chemical fertilizers should be used with discretion and only after thorough experimental testing. The relatively high cost of purchasing and transporting mineral fertilizers (which would most likely require farmers' borrowing money) and ignorance of the proper methods of applying them are serious barriers to their widespread adoption. For the foreseeable future, Laotian farmers will have to confine themselves to the use of organic fertilizers, which can be obtained readily by simply modifying traditional animal husbandry practices.

Soil Cover Finally, there is the need to protect the soil against rapid destruction of its organic matter by the sun. "To do this, [one] must maintain the thickest possible cover of trees, ground cover or weeds that have been cut down, chopped and hoed under. Cutting down plants like weeds puts organic matter into the soil without any transportation cost."[18]

If carried out properly, and with the advice and assistance of competent experts, the soil conservation methods described here will prove reliable and effective in mountain country. The effect of the fight against erosion will be to hasten the transition from slash-and-burn agriculture to the farming of plowed, fertilized fields; in other words, the transition from a semi-nomadic life to a sedentary one for the Hmong and the other mountain peoples. Introduction of the plow will allow increased productivity, and constant replenishing of soil fertility will maintain high crop yields. Agricultural progress will also benefit livestock raising, already strongly integrated into the overall production system, by supplying forage crops and in turn deriving both fertilizer and mechanical power.

LIVESTOCK RAISING

As we have seen, the Hmong engage in archaic animal husbandry practices, the products of which are destined primarily for ritual and funeral sacrifices. With the exception of swine and poultry, livestock are left mostly to their own devices. Domestic animals breed deep in the forest; no attempts are made to improve the stock through selective breeding or crossbreeding.

From a economic point of view, development of stock-raising in the mountains must move in the direction of greater added value. This will ensure the maximum possible return on labor and capital. The expansion of livestock raising could be part of a program of development for very steep slopes which cannot be plowed safely but which could be converted to natural and artificial pasture land.

GENERAL OBJECTIVES Development of livestock raising in the mountains must satisfy three principal objectives:

Protein Production The detrimental effects of a lack of protein in the diet have been documented thoroughly in the literature. Protein deficiency threatens not only the present but also future generations. It is particularly harmful to pregnant women, nursing mothers and children. "The effects of such deficiencies on small children have only recently been discovered: they impede normal development of the brain and thus affect intellectual capacity."[19]

The dietary protein deficiency so acute in the Hmong mountains is primarily the result of a lack of animal protein. This situation has been further aggravated by the widespread fighting, which decimates livestock and hampers its normal reproduction. It will only be alleviated, and finally remedied, by extensive use of the products of stock-raising and by rapid expansion of stock breeding — all of which assumes an end to the hostilities in the country.

Land and Crop Improvement Expansion of livestock raising will contribute to the overall agricultural development of the mountain areas of northern Laos through

○ animal-powered plowing and cultivation

○ manure production

○ improved fallow practices based on forage, pasture and silage crops.

Cash Income Generation The development of livestock raising must be tied in with the generation of cash income through both domestic and international marketing of its products.[20] This marketing can also be a powerful factor in the modernization of agricultural techniques. It will not be possible, let alone efficient, however, until the coming of peace allows the development of a transportation infrastructure, the basis for all economic development in Laos.

With these objectives in mind, let us now look at the possibilities offered by various kinds of livestock raising and identify those most likely to contribute to the economic development of the mountain regions.

POSSIBILITIES FOR LIVESTOCK RAISING IN THE MOUNTAINS

Cattle   By cattle are meant water buffalo and, primarily, zebu, both of which are livestock traditionally raised by the Hmong. The temperate climate, vegetation less affected by the droughts on the plains, and the absence of infectious diseases make the Hmong highlands a natural choice for the raising of cattle.[21] American experts estimate that the province of Xieng Khouang alone could support more than a million cattle.[22] Three methods of large stock-raising are possible in the mountain areas: extensive, semi-intensive and intensive.

Extensive Raising   Extensive cattle raising predominates in the Hmong countryside and, considering the region's socioeconomic conditions, will probably continue to do so for some time. Development of the extensive method requires better use of natural pasture areas: forest floors, forested savannas, grassy savannas and pseudo-steppes.[23] A great variety of grasses are found there all year round: *ncaug, muas txhov, pum khab*,[24] Imperata grass, several kinds of reeds and legumes, and a wide range of browse vegetation, particularly the bamboos.

In extensive livestock raising, seasonal changes of pasture best suit the monsoon climate, with its dry and rainy seasons. The following pattern is suggested:

○ March to May (height of the dry season) — the best pasturage is found on forest floors, where dampness sustains a variety of grasses and legumes. Around mid-May the rains begin.

○ June to September (height of the rainy season) — there is pasturage on the grassy savannas, where young shoots of all kinds, which constitute the main source of nitrogen- and energy-rich forage, are appearing.

○ October and November (end of the rainy season) — pasturage may be found on the grassy pseudo-steppes, where the ground cover has been freshly renewed by the rains.

○ December to February (damp winter season) — animals can feed on pasturage found on the forested savannas, where the fine drizzle, continuous in northeastern Laos at the onset of winter, and the morning fogs of winter keep the vegetation green.

Seasonal change of grazing lands could become a cooperative venture between Hmong and Lao stock-raisers. Lao living in the lowlands could, for example, turn their herds over to Hmong during the dry season to be driven to mountain pastures; when the rainy season came, the process could be reversed. This kind of cooperation would not only help in the recovery of the national economy, it would also encourage a rapprochement between the plains and mountain peoples and thus strengthen national integration.

Semi-Intensive and Intensive Raising   Creation of natural and artificial pasturelands on the steep slopes would make it possible to engage in intensive or semi-intensive stock-raising in the mountains. Such methods would require carefully planned rotation of grazing lands as well as networks of enclosures (thorn hedges or other, more costly, barriers) to allow the livestock to develop and reproduce satisfactorily. Besides these enclosed meadows, cattle might also be let into fields to consume crop residues: leaves, stalks and shoots of grain; tops of leguminous plants such as peanuts, dolichos (hyacinth beans) and soybeans; and weeds and grasses, which grow very rapidly once the crops crowding them out have been harvested. During the dry season, herd nutrition could be supplemented with rice straw and stored forage. Every evening throughout the year the animals would be brought into a stable where they would provide the manure essential for field and crop improvement.

More intensive cattle raising may also make dairy farming profitable, using a crossbreed of the zebu with a selected imported breed.[25] The Sahiwal dairy strain that has shown very good results in Kenya may be a good choice for introduction into Laos. Dairy production would make it possible to more effectively combat protein deficiency, which is particularly acute among children. However, the marketing of dairy products raises the problems of preservation and transportation, problems not likely to find easy solutions given present conditions.

The trend toward intensification of agriculture will create a growing need for animal manure for fertilizer. This will likely give rise to a new practice of families buying an ox or two during the dry season when prices are lowest and keeping them in a feed lot for fattening on farm residues and forage crops. Rations would include green grass during the rainy season and, following that, rice shoots, rice straw, sweet potato vines, and so on. These could be supplemented with high-yield forage crops such as *Pueraria phaselodes* (tropical kudzu), forage cabbage, forage corn, *Pennisetum clandestinum* (at high altitudes) and many others.[26] These forage crops would find very favorable climatic conditions in the mountain areas of northern Laos. The rainy season is the normally the longest season (May to October) and even during the winter (November to February) steady drizzle and morning fog are very common. This favorable climate would reduce considerably the labor required for, and hence the cost of, such an undertaking.

Intensive cattle raising methods, which will surely prove adaptable to Hmong farming practices, will find in the mountains an excellent breed of cattle: the zebu. Well fed, it can reach a startling size — the Hmong fighting zebu, which is always given the best of care, can weigh as much as 600 kilograms! A much smaller breed of zebu, originally a cross between the Hmong zebu and Lao beef cattle, also exists. In the future, it should certainly be feasible to produce higher performance animals by crossing the highland zebu with Pakistani and Indian breeds such as the Brahma, Sahiwal and Sindhi.

Small Livestock While cattle raising is of great importance to the economic future of northern Laos, small livestock should not be overlooked. Two animals, swine and poultry, appear to offer the best solution to the problem of rapidly increasing the level of meat consumption in Laos, particularly among the Hmong. The advantages of production of these animals throughout northern Laos derive from that facts that

- they are the two most commonly-eaten meats in Laos, as they are in all Asian countries

- their husbandry is the kind that fits most readily into a family subsistence economy, where the peasant is more of a farmer than a livestock raiser

- they represent the quickest and most economical way to transform vegetable protein into animal protein, a very important consideration in a country where malnutrition is typical of the general diet.

Increasing hog and poultry production among the Hmong will require, in addition to constant technical improvement, the introduction of modern medicine to reduce the incidence of human diseases and thus the need for ritual animal sacrifices. It is estimated that an average of four to eight pigs and 10 to 30 chickens are sacrificed annually by a Hmong family to propitiate evil spirits, ward off illness or avert danger. Archaic husbandry techniques and religious beliefs together constitute a serious limitation on the increase of poultry flocks and swine herds among the Hmong. Assuming that the religious issue will eventually be solved by the spread of education, discussed later, let us outline very briefly some technical innovations that should be introduced to bring about rapid development of small stock-raising in the mountain regions.

Swine   The following measures are recommended for the improvement of hog raising:

○ introduction of improved breeding stock

○ establishment of breeding and tending stations

○ intensification of vaccination and veterinary practices

○ organization of the market and improvements in transportation.

Poultry   For poultry, there is general agreement on the need for

○ selective breeding of local varieties

○ introduction of improved stock

○ improved hygiene and disease prevention

○ organization of a marketing system.

Modernizing small livestock raising in the mountains necessarily poses the problem of feed, a problem common to the entire country. Currently all enriched animal feed used in Laos is obtained from Thailand. The Laotian government is attempting to address this situation with the planned construction of an enriched-feed production plant in Vientiane. However, in view of the relatively high price of industrial products and the often exorbitant cost of transport, construction of such a plant will not automatically solve the problem of feed for livestock in the highlands.

Current conditions offer no basis for predicting any rapid or radical change in traditional Hmong patterns of animal husbandry. Intensified cultivation of permanent fields, which will tend (provided soil conservation methods are adopted) to be as close as possible to dwelling places, will make some modifications necessary. It will no longer be possible, for example, to allow livestock to wander at will without endangering crops. Hence the need will arise to build sties and enclosed runs for raising hogs and poultry. The transition from traditional stock-raising methods to more modern practices will occur naturally under these conditions.

Fish   Another rapid and economical way to combat protein deficiency in the mountain diet would be the development of fish farming. As we have seen, these populations have already begun to practice fish farming (witness the many fish ponds in the areas around Sam Thong, Long Cheng, Pha Khao and Nam Mo). The presence in the mountains of numerous permanent streams favors the construction of small dams and the creation of ponds necessary for the development of fish farming. Tests have shown that carp do well in such ponds; their raising should be encouraged. Other species, such as tilapia, could also be introduced into the mountain areas.

Goats Finally, goat raising should also be kept in mind when planning for development in the mountains. Cattle could browse on the gentler slopes while the more agile goats could graze on the steeper ones. The spread of goat raising would help enhance the mountain diet not only with meat but also with a particularly nutritious milk.

FORESTRY

The development of agriculture and livestock raising would in no way diminish the traditional role of the forest in so vast and sparsely populated a country as Laos. Estimated at 15 million hectares,[27] forests, along with tin, provide most of Laos's exported products. In 1967 exports of wood brought in 285,512 million kip out of a total of 881,235 million in exports.[28]

Long subject to abusive exploitation, the Laotian forests are gradually being depleted of their most valuable trees (teak, rosewood), which are being replaced by worthless species. This forest deterioration is a common sight near towns and along major transportation routes. It occurs much more rapidly, however, in areas where *rai* agriculture is practiced. Vast regions of northern Laos, once covered by primary forest, have, under the hand of man, become immense reaches of scrub grass. If Laos is to have an abundant and suitable supply of firewood and lumber and also retain its export capacity, adequate measures must be taken to protect existing trees, and a reforestation program implemented to provide stands of valuable forest species along major transportation arteries, where they will be easy and inexpensive to grow and harvest.

FOREST CONSERVATION   In the mountain regions, protection of forest vegetation can take three forms:

Elimination of Slash-and-Burn Farming   As we have already seen, the solution to this problem lies in establishing permanent fields. Such a transformation can be made much more easily today because of the tremendous intellectual and psychological changes which the past 25 years have brought to the Hmong and the other mountain peoples.

Enforcement of Forest Use Regulations   Some fairly detailed forest use regulations, having the force of law, are already in place: requirements to cut trees at ground level and to clear trees broken by felling, and, most importantly, a ban on the cutting of trees of less than a minimum diameter set for each species. It is the responsibility of the Forest Service to inform the people of these regulations and to see to it that they are followed. There must be much stricter compliance with these regulations; far too much leeway is allowed at present.

Building Up of Forest Reserves   The goal here is to reduce human activity to a level which allows forest vegetation to reconstitute itself naturally.

REFORESTATION Reforestation programs should be concentrated on steep slopes unsuitable for farming or livestock raising. Their purpose should be to establish new forests or to restore forests that have been destroyed.

Bamboo Bamboo forests play a triple role: they provide raw materials for building and local crafts, food (bamboo shoots) for people, and forage for cattle. Several local species of bamboo supply all three of these needs. Replanting and expanding the bamboo groves around villages would not only be desirable for reforestation but would also supply a product indispensable to the traditional way of life of these peoples.

Firewood While, generally speaking, there is no real reason to be concerned about the supply of firewood, its high price is causing a growing awareness among urban populations of the problem of forest restoration. The high prices of firewood in Xieng Khouang, Lat Houang and Phong Savanh (prior to 1961) and in Sam Thong and Long Cheng at the time of our visit in 1969 are excellent indicators of this trend. Two relatively undemanding species, *Cassia siamea* and *Peltophorum dasyrachis*, are recommended for firewood reforestation. Their rapid growth rate permits harvesting after only about ten years.

Timber Excessive and uncontrolled exploitation and especially slash-and-burn agriculture are gradually causing the disappearance of desirable timber species. Shortages of timber, already quite scarce in certain areas such as Xieng Khouang, the Plain of Jars, Sam Thong and Long Cheng, will become even more acute as the mountain people adopt a sedentary way of life. This change of lifestyle will have an impact on their standard of living and thus on the kind of building they do. The demand for lumber will grow at an ever-increasing rate.

The most promising species for timber reforestation appear to be *Tectona grandi* (teak), *Pterocarpus pedatus*, *Pterocarpus macrocarpus*, *Dalbergia cochinchinensis* and *Hopea odorata*.[29] Such reforestation would not only meet future domestic demand for building but would make it possible to export wood as a finished or semi-finished product. The restored forests would also have the indirect benefits of climatic and hydrological improvement.

SOCIAL DEVELOPMENT

Having completed our very brief survey of the possibilities for economic development in the mountain regions of northern Laos, let us now turn to the considerable social problems involved in any development in the Hmong highlands.

CHOICE OF AN IDEAL SETTING

Adoption of permanent agriculture and entry into the market economy will automatically lead the Hmong to leave their mountain fastnesses. Despite their nature as an inviolable refuge, the mountain heights, which have for centuries helped to preserve intact the identity of the Hmong, are, unfortunately, not a suitable base for development. The mountain people need to look elsewhere for economically and socially viable areas in which to settle. Considered most promising are the medium-elevation plateaus (1,000 to 1,200 meters), where the climate is admirably suited to the Hmong physiology. This is one of the reasons they have fought so hard and so long in such an extremely painful and deadly war to retain at least part of the Xieng Khouang plateau, which has always been their location of choice in Laos.

A definitive decision remains to be made about where Hmong settlements should be established. From the point of view of development, three major criteria determine this choice:

- ○ the proximity of a stream or spring capable of supplying the site with a year-round water supply

- ○ the availability of enough arable land suitable for irrigated rice growing (valleys and hills), permanent fields and secondary crops like tea, coffee and fruit trees (gentle slopes), and pastures (medium slopes)

- ○ the proximity of roads or the possibility of their construction without too much difficulty.

Such should be the new setting for Hmong people's lives as they are called upon to make the profound changes in their traditional society necessary to adapt it to present-day conditions. The sketch below is a plan for an "ideal" settlement which we would offer to the mountain peoples for consideration. Obviously this configuration is not universally applicable. It will vary considerably with local topography and with the possibilities for agriculture and livestock raising.

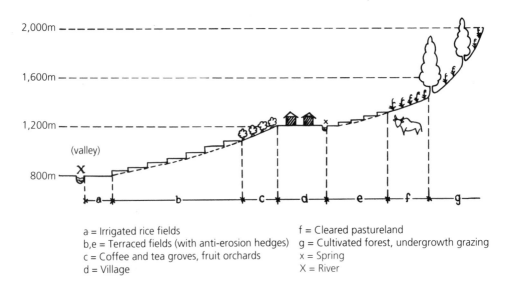

a = Irrigated rice fields
b,e = Terraced fields (with anti-erosion hedges)
c = Coffee and tea groves, fruit orchards
d = Village
f = Cleared pastureland
g = Cultivated forest, undergrowth grazing
x = Spring
X = River

MOTIVATING PERMANENT RESETTLEMENT

Once suitable farmlands have been located and the best sites for villages determined, widespread information and motivation campaigns will need to be conducted in the home areas of prospective settlers, explaining the new farming operations and helping the people prepare psychologically for the move. These campaigns would be most effective either in especially rugged mountain areas or among the concentrations of refugees that grew up haphazardly during the war. However, it must be kept in mind that such relocation, at least in the beginning, must be strictly voluntary.

The war and the mental and physical suffering which have accompanied it will make the work of education and motivation much easier. The upsets of war have laid the psychological groundwork for even more major changes. Profoundly disturbed by eleven years of unrelenting conflict, many Hmong no longer feel deep ties to the past. Their homes, their fields and their livestock have disappeared under the deluge of fire which the warring camps have rained down upon their homelands. Exhausted and enraged, they are simply attempting to survive until the "enemy" princes arrive at a political settlement.

Given these conditions, vast human migration throughout northern Laos can be expected the moment a peace agreement is signed. Phouan, Hmong and Khmou will move en masse to occupy new areas which can promise them a better life and a secure future. During this difficult period of adaptation it will be important for local authorities and the Laotian government to give them moral support and material assistance in establishing themselves in their new environment and in getting their lives started again. The entire future of Laos will depend, in no small measure, on their success.

SETTLING THE POPULATIONS

It would be advisable to create in each of the new settlements a village center to promote contact among families and to serve as a general meeting place. Within this center of trade, cultural and spiritual exchange would also be set up schools, a dispensary, various local and national government offices, a community meeting hall, playing fields, and so on. The exact location of the village center would be determined by the distribution of houses. It is essential that a village plan be developed and followed both during and after the initial resettlement period. House location, for example, would have to be approved by the village council. The plan must also provide for community development for ten or twenty years into the future.

The settlements envisioned here are much more concentrated than the villages these rural people were accustomed to prior to their moves to the refugee centers. This change will be the more pronounced in that the villages will not only be home to farmers but also to people making their living from secondary and tertiary economic activities. Many of these activities are already familiar to the mountain people. They are likely to flourish provided they can be assured of a market.

Obviously, the size of these settlements will depend on the amount of arable land available. A detailed land survey will be needed in order to determine the number of people to be settled at a given site. Two types of Hmong villages might emerge:

○ medium-sized villages with populations of 200-500

○ towns with populations of 500-1,000.

Two or three medium-sized villages might, for example, cluster around a larger town which, because of its location, would play a dominant economic and political role. Another pattern, that of large numbers of fairly widely separated hamlets of four to five houses, may, because of the dictates of the mountainous terrain, turn out to be more common in the narrow upland valleys typical of northern Laos.

Since the settlers will be coming from long distances, they must be given assistance with transportation and food. The need for food assistance will continue until they have harvested their first crops. In addition, farm implements, seed, insecticides, and so on must be provided free of charge to these people, who have been rendered destitute by the war. Such assistance, no matter how generous, must under no circumstances appear to be paternalism or charity. On the contrary, it should reflect both justice and solidarity, the new cement which will bind the Laotian nation into a unified whole.

COMMUNITY DEVELOPMENT

Community development cannot stop with resettlement. Its efforts must continue long after the people are settled into their new villages. Community development must pursue a two-fold aim:

○ to assist individuals

○ to establish relationships among members of the community.

To these ends, it will be necessary to provide community facilities and the staffs to operate them.

RURAL DEVELOPMENT ASSISTANCE CENTERS Creation of Rural Development Assistance Centers (RDACs) is an essential part of community action programs. These organizations are of critical importance in achieving community development objectives. The staff of a Rural Development Assistance Center should include

○ a director with a multidisciplinary background

○ a public health practitioner/instructor

○ a trained agro-economics instructor

○ other instructors as needed.

Initially, the RDACs should combine their social and technical development activities. Only later, when the people have been successfully motivated, can these two areas be separated. Technical activities can then become part of the cooperative system (discussed later) and be handled by the appropriate technical services.

Because of the shortage of trained staff, it will not be feasible any time in the near future for each settlement to have its own Development Assistance Center. Furthermore, the investment required by such a commitment would be prohibitive, especially in light of the nation's current financial situation. It would be desirable, however, that, at a minimum, each area have a Center to serve the villages within it. The location of the area RDAC would be determined by the distribution of settlements, which should be connected as much as possible by a network of roads. This arrangement would greatly facilitate the difficult job of the development teams responsible for providing technical, economic, administrative and political training.

COMMUNITY EDUCATION   A genuine development policy requires raising the educational level of the population. It is perfectly possible, of course, to increase agricultural production through popularization of modern farming techniques, introduction of high-yield seed grains and widespread use of fertilizers. In the long term, however, the results of this approach would not reflect the amount of effort it would require. Constant retraining of the farmers would be necessary to keep up with technological advances, which continually render current practices obsolete. Furthermore, the people themselves would not be enriched either technically or intellectually by such an approach. There can be no development without education, the very foundation of progress.

Progress is, first and foremost, the product of human effort. Consequently, if one is to get the best results from people, one must first develop them by giving them the tools to increase their knowledge, skills and capacities. Education and development go hand in hand. The development of a country cannot proceed without an adequate educational system capable of transforming the mental set of its people. Education must be able to make minds which are often prisoners of age-old traditions and turned deeply inward upon themselves receptive to new and innovative ideas. The future of Laotian, and particularly Hmong, society and its progress in such essential areas as economic growth, technology and health depend entirely on its level of educational development.

Functional Literacy   Education based solely on academic learning is coming under greater and greater criticism. The failure of mass literacy efforts and the gradual relapse into illiteracy among people whose unchanged life and work environments do not require reading or writing are instructive in this regard.[30] "All education or transmission of knowledge," writes Albert Meister of UNESCO,

> performs a social function. The most backward of societies contain a wealth of knowledge, technology and life patterns transmitted in the "deskless school" of daily contact with adults. That some of these societies have not invented writing is because it would have filled no felt need in the transmission of knowledge. Under such conditions, viewing illiteracy in these societies as a scourge is reminiscent of cultural imperialism and recalls the missionary attitude of the last century.[31]

Without a doubt, a tremendous amount of money and effort has been wasted in many countries on literacy campaigns. This is certainly the case in Laos, where the school curriculum has remained highly academic. Today literacy has ceased to be considered an end in itself and has become but one of many aspects of the technical training required for successful development.

Gradually replacing efforts at mass literacy is a new approach known as functional literacy, which "resolutely turns its back on encyclopedic knowledge and writes its textbooks with the help of [agronomic and industrial] technicians."[32] Roger Couvert describes this new kind of education as

> a technique that enables us to instill in a group or an individual a favorable attitude toward development, to bring about a genuine transformation in their minds, which will so modify their behavior and personalities as to ensure that their adaptation to modern and constantly developing society takes place in a harmonious way. [It does so] without profound psycho-

logical shocks, by short-circuiting certain negative attitudes and by preparing them for a succession of new learning experiences which will make modern men of them in their homes, their villages and their fields. To achieve this, they must master a complicated tool: writing.[33]

In other words, functional literacy aims first of all at the transformation of the individual through technical and intellectual enrichment, which, by expanding his mental capabilities, will enable him to act upon his environment by himself, based on the oral or written advice he has become capable of understanding and adapting to his personal situation.

Native-Language Education   If the Laotian government chooses to implement such an educational approach, without discrimination, throughout the country, it cannot, without risk of total failure, neglect the provision of education in at least the major vernacular tongues. We saw earlier the disastrous consequences of a policy of forced assimilation and the advantages to be derived from education delivered, at least in the early years, in the native language. Development experts insist that, because of the need to deal as quickly as possible with the growing gap between economic development and population growth, education geared to the work at hand is much more important than acquiring facility in a second language. It could also be added that the choice of a language vehicle for literacy also indicates a commitment, or lack of it, to social integration.

Orthographies for the Hmong language were developed in Laos in 1953, in China in 1956 and in North Vietnam around 1960. The Romanized Popular Alphabet (RPA) is by far the most widely-used system in the mountain regions of northern Laos.[34] Regardless of claims to the contrary by certain Lao intellectuals, it hardly seems possible that this romanized writing system, used as a tool for functional literacy, could be regarded as any kind of threat to national unity.[35] It has already demonstrated its effectiveness: thousands of young people and adults use it to communicate with each other and as a working tool of unquestionable utility in the translation of official texts, news for radio broadcasts, medical instructions and so forth. Learning the RPA (a relatively easy process requiring only a few hours for those who have attended Franco-Lao schools and well under three months for those with no previous literacy or schooling) has enabled many Hmong to become literate in the Lao language much more quickly.

Alphabets and languages do not in themselves constitute obstacles to nation-building. The important thing is what is in the hearts of the people. Injustice and oppression are at the root of the social and political ills which today trouble many areas of the globe. Only adequate education can protect the ethnic groups in Laos from this scourge by creating a community of thought and will which is the true foundation of a modern nation.

COOPERATIVE ORGANIZATION   One result of the activities of the Rural Development Assistance Centers will be the creation of a spirit of cooperation in their participants and, as a consequence, an initiative among them toward the establishment of working cooperatives. Many different kinds of cooperatives are possible:

○ service cooperatives — through which farmers could jointly purchase and use production equipment

○ sales cooperatives — which would enable them to command higher prices for their produce

○ consumer cooperatives — through which they could purchase basic necessities at lower cost.

At least in the beginning, these new cooperative ventures should be multifunctional. The more numerous and concrete the services they provide, the more obvious the advantages of cooperation will seem to the members. The distinctions among different kinds of cooperatives will emerge gradually as the movement gains in scope and strength. At the same time, markets must be set up to accommodate the growth of the cooperative system, which should be integrated as tightly as possible into economic and social development efforts.

‡

Having very briefly sketched the possibilities for economic and social development of the Hmong highlands, we must again emphasize the essential role of the people themselves in the execution of the plan. Progress is inseparable from human development, and progress must occur in all areas: technological, cultural and social. The transition to intensive agriculture in combination with livestock raising will change profoundly the techniques employed by the Hmong farmer and his concept of himself as a part of a larger community. Like the change in physical environment, the formation of more concentrated settlements will cause him to question certain traditional values and thus hasten the emergence of a new style of life. The process of change will occur more rapidly if, along with economic development of the mountain regions, an effort is made to alleviate their geographic isolation. The establishment of a transportation network is essential for the dissemination of new ideas and for the development of cultural exchanges and trade.

The difficulties which must be surmounted and the resistance that must be overcome in order for economic and social development to proceed cannot be ignored. One major criticism of the plan outlined here will surely be its failure to address the cost of its implementation. It is our firm conviction that these development efforts will pay for themselves in the long run, both for the highlanders and for the country as a whole. We deeply regret having been unable to submit the plan to the Hmong people and to our national leaders for discussion. Its importance, however, lies in its function as a possible nucleus and framework for development efforts among the mountain minorities of Laos.

Solving so difficult and complex a problem calls for comprehensive and coordinated action directed toward the leadership, education and support of the producers. In these endeavors, outside assistance should be relied upon only in the forms of advice and training. The principal role, that of human contact and persuasion, must be played by the responsible local, regional and national authorities. To the degree to which these people are aware of the tremendous distance to be traveled and to which they take an interest in the development of their own country, there will be a chance that meaningful change may see the light in the Kingdom of a Million Elephants.

CONCLUSION

This study has succeeded in giving only an imperfect presentation of Hmong society. All issues have not been examined in equal depth, nor have all the difficulties, both endogenous and exogenous, with which these people have had to cope in their struggle for change and their efforts to protect their cultural identity been explained clearly. To this must be added the limited nature of my own direct experience. Years of study have required me to be absent for long periods of time from my home and my native environment. As a result, some useful information may well have escaped my attention entirely. Finally, the armed conflict which has divided the Hmong, along with all Laotians, into two warring camps severely limited the field research upon which this study is based, confining the area of investigation to a few provinces, primarily Xieng Khouang.

I should like to have filled these gaps with published information available at the time of the research. However, with the exception of a few serious studies, such as those of Lemoine, these sources were of limited value and could be used only with great caution. Reporters and writers have long exploited the "Meo" and their opium simply because they could not defend themselves. Whether for commercial, political or personal reasons, many have engaged in shameless exaggeration, speculation and outright fabrication about these supposed "ignorant savages." Few voices, least of all those of their "uncivilized" subjects, have been raised to challenge these writings. Respect for persons and even simple justice seem to have been lost in the pursuit.

Superficial though it may be, it is my hope that this analysis will help others to better understand the Hmong people, in their traditional environment as well as on the national and international scenes. I have shown that the Hmong people are a people like any other, with a unique culture, social structure and philosophy of life. Like Soviet, American or French citizens before them, they are sharing, at the price of their blood, in the building of their nation. The pace of their integration into Laotian society will accelerate, urged on by historical realities which those in power cannot afford to ignore any longer, save at the peril of their country's future. As destructive as the war has been, it has done much to create a Laotian national consciousness. Adversity has brought ethnic groups closer together and cemented their solidarity. Many understand for the first time that they are bound to a common destiny and that their success from now on will depend upon their determination to achieve unity in diversity.

Even as they remain faithful to the memory of their ancestors, the Hmong can play an important role in the building of the Laos of tomorrow. On the political level, the Hmong can contribute actively to the strengthening of the national foundation by moving into positions of ever-increasing importance and by collaborating more and more closely in all areas. Their integration into Laotian society will bring with it that of other ethnic minorities, enlarging national consciousness through a broader base of participation in the service of the nation as a whole. A more realistic attitude on the part of the Lao leaders will be required. Exclusion of ethnic minorities from the country's leadership jeopardizes their integration and, with it, the future of Laos as a nation. "Esteeming each other in mutual respect, supporting one another in collaboration, and strengthening unity in diversity should be the political watchword for a multiethnic Laos."[1]

These political measures, taken in the interest of achieving true national integration, will, on the social level, have the effect of reducing, if not eliminating, discrimination against ethnic minorities. Only under conditions of complete equality will the Hmong, working in close cooperation with their majority and minority countrymen, be able to play a significant role in the creation of a new and more harmonious Laotian society, based on social justice, individual liberty, mutual respect and national solidarity.

Finally, on the economic level, the Hmong will be able, in the new atmosphere of cooperation, to contribute to the expansion of national development, enabling the country to move rapidly toward economic independence, a necessary prerequisite to true political independence. The development of the mountain regions must be planned from this perspective. Its implementation will set off a process of integration that will inevitably lead to the formation of a true Laotian nation. Diversity of production will encourage the growth of trade between plains and mountains, creating economic interdependence and weaving bonds which will further strengthen national unity. Development will lead to economic integration, which will, in turn, bring about ethnic integration and, hence, the birth of a national consciousness.

Development of the mountain regions will also contribute to the improvement of national security. Laos is more than the narrow strip of land along the Mekong River. It comprises a vast territory of plains, valleys and mountains. The highland positions of the Hmong and other ethnic minorities are critical to the nation's defense. These peoples, who make up half, if not more, of the total population, must not be sacrificed to the march of progress.

May this modest work play a small part in helping to make Laos a true nation, unified, free and prosperous in its diversity.

PARIS
1972

EPILOGUE (FIRST EDITION)

A year after the completion of this study, all of Laos was jubilant. The Agreement on Restoration of Peace and Achievement of National Reconciliation in Laos, signed in Vientiane on February 21, 1973, by the Royal Lao Government and the Neo Lao Hak Sat, had finally ended almost three decades of war. National reconciliation was formalized on April 5, 1974, with the formation of the Provisional Government of National Union and the National Political Consultative Council.

The National Political Consultative Council is an independent advisory body to the Provisional Government of National Union.[1] Presided over by Prince Souphanouvong, it comprises 42 members: 16 representing the Vientiane government, 16 from the Neo Lao Hak Sat and 10 neutral members acceptable to both sides. The ethnic minorities are represented by five members, three from the Neo Lao Hak Sat (La Soukan [Phou Noi[2]], Lo Foung Lobliayao [Hmong] and Visit Santivong [Ching[3]]) and two from the Vientiane government (Bounthan Heuangpraseut [Khmou] and the author [Hmong]). The mission of the National Political Consultative Council is to study matters of national and international significance and to lend its support to implementation of resolutions of the Provisional Government of National Union.

Henceforth, the future of Laos will depend primarily on the perspicacity and practicality of its leaders whom, enemies only yesterday, destiny has united once more. The new politics they create together will consign the country to salvation or perdition. Nationally, it is imperative to achieve unity from diversity as quickly as possible. That unity, a synthesis of ethnic, cultural and religious riches, constitutes the foundation of a successful and prosperous Laos. A willingness on the part of both sides to set aside personal interests and ideological allegiances for the good of the national interest will be required. Only by showing a common determination to forget the quarrels of the past, to preserve democratic rights and liberties, and to guarantee equality and justice to all will it be possible to consolidate a multi-ethnic structure under the crown of Laos. Internationally, the policy mapped out by Prince Souvanna Phouma appears realistic. Laos's geographical situation, its rather small population, comprised of diverse ethnic groups many of whom also live in neighboring countries, and the prospects for its development mandate a policy of strict neutrality, which, guaranteed by the superpowers, will, in the end, ensure its domestic prosperity and international respect.

This respect is due, first of all, to King Srisavang Vatthana, who, over long and wearisome years of trial and testing, has steadfastly maintained the ideal of Laotian unity and who is still today its ultimate guarantor. The efforts of Prince Souvanna Phouma, who, regardless of the circumstances, has never failed in the struggle for a peaceful and neutral Laos, must be honored. The spirit of abnegation and determination, inspired by a deep patriotism, shown by Prince Souphanouvong, must be praised. The whole of the Laotian people owe an immeasurable debt of gratitude to these statesmen for the peace they have restored to the country, that peace in which it places its hopes for the new era now dawning.

VIENTIANE
October 30, 1974

FOOTNOTES:

[1] The quantity of feed required to produce one kilogram of product.

[2] Laos's trade deficit was over 11 billion kip in 1968. This means that imports were ten times as large as exports, a situation that has been the case since 1960.

[3] René Dumont, *Development and Socialism*, collab. Mazoyer, Collections Esprit "Frontières Ouvertes," Seuil, Paris, 1969, pp. 109-110.

[4] Ibid.

[5] According to the Ministry of Economy and Planning of Laos, only 22 percent of Laotian land is unsuitable for agriculture. Only eight percent is actually under cultivation at the present time (1969).

[6] This is a very serious problem. We observed 47 deaths due to malaria in the space of only a few months among a group of 1,100 Hmong who had been moved from the Phou Khao Khouai plateau to the Na Nhao valley in Vientiane province.

[7] These government regulations were in fact put into effect in late 1972 and early 1973.

[8] Former director of the Xieng Khouang Agricultural Station.

[9] Dumont, *Development and Socialism*, pp. 109-110.

[10] At the very least, the eventual return of the Hmong who are living in temporary settlements in the Plain of Jars would provide an excellent opportunity for a program of integrated development.

[11] Lemoine, *Social Organization in a Green Hmong Village*, p. 249.

[12] In the past Laos exported potatoes to Vietnam, Cambodia and Thailand.

[13] In 1953-54.

[14] Za Nao Yang is currently (1992) living in French Guyana.

[15] The People's Republic of China could be a major potential market for arabica coffee.

[16] Cf. J. E. Vidal and Jacques Lemoine, "Contribution to the Ethnobotany of the Hmong in Laos," *Journal d'Agriculture Tropicale et de Botanique Appliquée*, Vol. XVII, Nos. 1-4, January-April 1970.

[17] A considerable body of literature exists on the subject of erosion control. Selected sources are listed in the bibliography.

[18] René Dumont, "Additional Notes on Developing the Medium and High Regions (People's Republic of Vietnam)," *Traditions of Revolution in Vietnam*, Anthropos, Paris, 1971, p. 404.

[19] Gunnar Myrdal, *The Challenge of the Poor World*, Gallimard, Paris, 1971, p. 94.

[20] Prior to World War II, for example, Laos, particularly the Xieng Khouang plateau, exported cattle to Vietnam, Cambodia and Thailand.

[21] In recent years, however, epizootics have apparently penetrated even the mountains.

[22] Brossollet and Joyaux, "Laos," p. 25.

[23] The Plain of Jars is a typical example of a pseudo-steppe.

[24] Hmong names for the most common varieties of grasses.

[25] The non-selected Hmong or Lao cow gives very little milk.

[26] The Peradenya Central Agricultural Station in Sri Lanka has extensive information on high-altitude forage crops.

[27] Phay Sirisombath, "The Traditional World of Laos," *Reflets*, No. 2, Centre International des Stages, Toulouse, 1971, p. 18.

[28] Laos, Department of Commerce.

[29] J. E. Vidal, "Vegetation of Laos, Part II," *Work of the Forestry Laboratory of Toulouse*, School of Science, University of Toulouse, 1934-1960, p. 424 ff.

[30] In Africa alone, over four million people revert to illiteracy every year.

[31] Albert Meister, *Functional Literacy and Economic Development*, United Nations Educational, Scientific and Cultural Organization, Paris, 1971, p. 15.

[32] Ibid., p. 13.

[33] Roger Couvert, *Functional Literacy, Laos*, United Nations Educational, Scientific and Cultural Organization, Paris, November 1968, p. 49.

[34] The Romanized Popular Alphabet is sometimes called the Barney-Smalley system after two of its inventors: G. Linwood Barney, an American anthropologist and former Christian and Missionary Alliance missionary in Laos, and William A. Smalley, an American linguist. The third co-inventor of the RPA orthography was Yves Bertrais, a French Catholic missionary. Today (1992) the RPA, or minor local variations thereof, is the most commonly used orthography by Hmong throughout the world.

[35] Cf. Lysao Lyfoung, "Let Us Keep Using the Latin Alphabet for Hmong Writing and Being Ardent in Learning the Laotian Language According to the Constitution," *Vientiane News* (English), Vol. 4, No. 121, January 20, 1974.

CONCLUSION

[1] Dao Yang, "Multiethnic Laos," *L'Etudiant Lao* (Lao Students' Bulletin), Paris, April 1970.

EPILOGUE (First Edition)

[1] The NPCC is also provisional in nature. Its mission will be accomplished with the legislative elections scheduled for 1976.

[2] An ethnic group living mainly in Phong Saly province.

[3] A minority ethnic group in southern Laos.

PART FOUR

Hmong in a Shattered Nation

A DREAM DESTROYED

Seventeen years after the takeover of Laos by the Pathet Lao, memories are still clear and painful of the political events, beginning in February 1973, which were so brutally to change popular euphoria into national tragedy. This last part offers a few examples of the promising beginnings of post-war reconstruction and of Hmong participation in this long-awaited effort. It also presents an eyewitness view of the course of events which brought political revolution, social chaos and economic disaster to the Hmong as well as to the entire nation of Laos.

CHAPTER EIGHT

Post-War Reconstruction

HMONG AND THE PEACE PROCESS

On February 21, 1972, at the height of the secret war in Laos, U.S. President Richard M. Nixon made a historic trip to Beijing where he met with Premier Zhou Enlai and other high-ranking officials of the People's Republic of China. The Sino-American discussions covered not only renewal of diplomatic ties and economic and social cooperation but also the withdrawal of American troops from Indochina. The PRC considered the presence of American troops in Southeast Asia one of the main obstacles to normalization of relations between the two countries, severed since the communist victory in China in 1949. Washington and Beijing ended their hostilities with a "handshake ... over the vastest ocean in the world — twenty-five years of no communication."[1]

In the diplomatic wake of this reconciliation, U.S. National Security Adviser Henry Kissinger accelerated his negotiations with North Vietnamese Politburo member Le Duc Tho, begun secretly in Paris a year earlier. The purpose of these negotiations was to define the conditions of settlement of the war in Indochina: among other issues, the withdrawal of both U.S. and North Vietnamese troops from South Vietnam, Cambodia and Laos and assurance by both governments of the integrity, sovereignty and neutrality of Cambodia and Laos.

As the negotiations between the United States and the Democratic Republic of Vietnam developed the details of a military cease-fire and a political settlement in Vietnam, the Pathet Lao pressed for a similar settlement in Laos. In October 1972 they began unconditional negotiations with the Royal Lao Government in Vientiane. The two parties quickly differed on issues such as the suspension of the Laotian constitution, dissolution of the National Assembly, and neutralization of Vientiane and Luang Prabang, all demanded by the Pathet Lao.

On January 28, 1973, a cease-fire agreement was signed in Paris by the United States, North and South Vietnam. Two weeks later, Kissinger arrived in Vientiane to speed up the stalled negotiations on a Laotian cease-fire, which the North Vietnamese had assured him at Paris would take place within 30 days. When asked by Kissinger about the reasons for the delay in signing a reconciliation agreement with the Pathet Lao, Ngone Sananikone, former Minister of Economy and Planning and leader of the Vientiane delegation to the negotiations, replied,

> I then ... let him know my grave reservations which had not yet been agreed to by the Pathet Lao delegation. Mr. Kissinger told me, "There is nothing important in your reservations. You have been called upon to form a government of national union with them [the Pathet Lao] and to live with them in [a] unified country. Give up all your reservations and sign the Vientiane agreement in February...."[2]

Following Kissinger's visit, Sananikone continues, Prince Souvanna Phouma convened a meeting of members of his government and top-ranking military officers at which he threatened to resign if the negotiations did not proceed. Finally, under pressure from right-wing politicians and military leaders, the Royal Lao Government signed the Vientiane Agreement with the Neo Lao Hak Sat on February 21, 1973, ending the war in Laos and calling for peace and national reconciliation.

In July, the Hmong General Vang Pao, who had supported the negotiations with the Neo Lao Hak Sat and the resulting Vientiane peace agreement, explained the situation with great confidence to a group of Laotian leaders, including the author, gathered at his residence in Vientiane.

> The Pathet Lao are Laotians themselves. They eat *khao nio* [sticky rice] and *padeck* [fermented fish] like us. We have fought each other for decades for nothing. Now the time has come when we must sit down together, discuss our differences, settle our quarrels and bring peace to our country.[3]

On April 3, 1974, Prince Souphanouvong, leader of the Neo Lao Hak Sat, arrived from his secret headquarters in Vieng Say (Sam Neua) at the Vientiane international airport aboard a twin-engine, high-winged *Ilyushin* piloted by Soviets but struck with the Neo Lao Hak Sat colors (a white circle on a blue and red background) and bearing, in Lao characters, the inscription, "Air Liaison Group of the Neo Lao Hak Sat." Tens of thousands of people lined the three kilometers from the airport to the palace to welcome the Red Prince as a national hero. After twelve years of fierce fighting, the Vientiane Agreement had finally brought about a cease-fire, to the joy and relief of all Laotians, especially the Hmong who had suffered so much during the secret war.

With the assent of King Srisavang Vatthana and to a delighted welcome by the population of the royal city, the Provisional Government of National Union (PGNU) and the National Political Consultative Council (NPCC) were formed in Luang Prabang on April 5, 1974, a little more than a year after the initial Vientiane Agreement. They were headed respectively by Prince Souvanna Phouma, leader of the Royal Lao Government, and Prince Souphanouvong, leader of the Neo Lao Hak Sat. The interim national governing institution and its companion advisory body consisted of both communist and non-communist politicians, who shared equal rank and comparable positions and responsibilities. On the Royal Lao Government side, the Hmong were represented in the Provisional Government by Touby Lyfoung, who became Deputy Minister of Telecommunication, and on the Consultative Council by the author, who was elected Vice Chair of its Economy and Finance Committee. Surprisingly, the Neo Lao Hak Sat appointed no Hmong representative to the PGNU. On the NPCC, however, Lo Foung Lobliayao, a younger brother of Faydang Lobliayao, held the position of Vice Chair of its Education and Culture Committee.

Prince Souphanouvong convened the first meeting of the National Political Consultative Council in Luang Prabang on International Labor Day, 1974. Before the assembled NPCC members, the diplomatic corps and dignitaries of the kingdom, the prince delivered an impassioned speech, broadcast nationwide, on national unification.

> Two previous attempts at Laotian reconciliation have failed.[4] Today I officially urge all the belligerent factions to forget the remains of the past and join with us in the effort to bring about national reconciliation. This third attempt should be the last one, it must succeed. We must put our strengths together to build a new Laotian nation, unified in its ethnic diversity, based on social justice and economic progress, independent and neutral in the community of nations.[5]

His statements were received enthusiastically by all the peoples of Laos.

On May 24, after nearly a month of individual studies, intense consultations, hard-hitting discussions and official meetings, the NPCC concluded its work with a draft of a national political strategy which was ratified by the Provisional Government in July and signed into law by Princes Souphanouvong and Souvanna Phouma the following December.[6] The Eighteen Point Political Program, as it came to be called, aspired to

> build a peaceful, independent, neutral, democratic, unified and prosperous Laotian king-
> dom in conformance with the supreme interest of the fatherland and in order to satisfy the
> ardent yearnings of the Laotian people of all ethnic backgrounds and the august wishes of
> His Majesty the King.[7]

To reach this goal, the domestic strategies of the Eighteen Point Program were

- to unify all people from various ethnic backgrounds and at all levels of Laotian society

- to bring about equality of all Laotian ethnic groups in the political, economic, cultural and social areas

- to fully assure democratic freedoms

- to organize free and democratic elections at all levels

- to guarantee the freedom of religion

- to provide equal rights and protection for women

- to develop a prosperous economy, free of political conditions

- to preserve the traditions and customs of all ethnic groups

- to develop a progressive educational system to enhance the solidarity among ethnic groups and gradually improve their cultural, scientific and technical levels

- to develop a public health system that would reach the most remote villages of the country

- to assure employment and improve living conditions in both the cities and the countryside

- to eliminate the social consequences of the war and assist war victims and demobilized military to return to economic productivity.[8]

PLANNING FOR POST-WAR RECOVERY

The peace talks begun in October 1972 between the Royal Lao Government and the Neo Lao Hak Sat were watched with special interest at the Ministry of Planning. As Chief of the Human Resources Division, I was invited to join a task force charged with planning for post-war Laos. The team, chaired by RLG Commissioner of Planning Pane Rassavong, comprised economists, agricultural and forestry technicians, and other technical experts. Its first job was to collect background information. Joint workshops were organized with other Ministries:

- the Ministry of Defense — to plan for military demobilization and for the rehabilitation and reintegration into civilian life of the tens of thousands of war veterans, widows and orphans

- the Ministry of Social Welfare — to plan for the resettlement to their original villages of the more than one-half million in-country refugees, 100,000 of them Hmong, whom the war had driven from their now-destroyed homes

- the Ministry of Health — to examine the medical conditions of the population in general and of the refugees in particular

- the Ministry of Education — to plan for the education of the thousands of refugee children who would accompany their families to their former home areas or to new resettlement sites

- the Ministry of Finance — to study the financing and technical support of reconstruction projects — and many others.

The entire mechanism of government was mobilized toward peace and development. With high spirits and intense motivation, ministries, divisions, departments and services resounded with the themes of national reconciliation, family reunification, peace and progress.

As soon as the cease-fire which followed the Vientiane Agreement in February 1973 allowed the task force to travel safely inside the country, a series of development seminars were organized for *chao muong* (district chiefs) across the kingdom, from Luang Prabang in the north to Khong Sedone in the south. Wherever the team went it was welcomed by the local population, which expressed its joy and confidence about the future. Not war but peace, the people said with one voice, after suffering for so many years in the deadly conflict. After first explaining its mission to the *chao khoueng* (governor) of the province and his staff, the task force met in special session with all the *chao muong* in the province to discuss local social and economic problems, to plan for future development of the province, to assess local labor, land and financial resources, to analyze available government technical and financial assistance, and to prioritize short-term development actions.

Differences in geography, ethnic composition and the extent of war-inflicted damage presented unique development problems in each area. Lao *chao muong* from lowland areas along the Mekong River, largely spared by the war, asked for more schools and teachers, for hospitals and dispensaries, for dams and irrigation systems, and for road and bridge construction. Phouan, Khmou and Hmong *chao muong*, whose populations had been driven from bombed villages and devastated farmlands, sought, for their mountains and plateaus, an effective resettlement program to help their people rebuild dignified and prosperous lives. Their priorities consisted of immediate needs: secure arable land, temporary shelters, food assistance until they could again become self-sufficient (expected to be no more than two years), appropriate agricultural and technical assistance, health care, and basic education for their youth.

The task force was, unfortunately, denied access to the almost two-thirds of the country still controlled by the Pathet Lao, particularly the forest and mountain areas along the border with North Vietnam. "Lack of security" was the constant response to the team's request for access. Under such restrictions, it was impossible to find out what was happening behind the Pathet Lao "bamboo wall." How many people were living there and, of those, how many were in need of resettlement? What were the social, economic and health conditions? What was the status and what were the needs of education? To all of these questions, the Neo Lao Hak Sat in Vientiane replied only that it already had its plan and that, when the time was right, it would be revealed. Meanwhile, Lao Patriotic Front Radio, broadcasting from Vieng Say, said nothing about national reconciliation but continued to harangue military and civilian populations alike to push toward "final victory." Such messages created doubts among some rightist politicians, who accused the Neo Lao Hak Sat of preparing for war while speaking of peace. In the face of the Pathet Lao's categorical refusal of access, the task force had to be content with gathering information from farmers, merchants, nurses and teachers who had fled these areas during the war. Using studies done during the French protectorate, augmented by more recent maps furnished to the Royal Lao Army by the U.S. military, the team strove to construct a meaningful development plan for this part of post-war Laos.

In this complex context, the Ministry of Planning task force was assigned the job of studying the situation of the Laotian highlanders. With the cooperation of the Xieng Khouang governor's office, the team organized a series of workshops in Long Cheng in the summer of 1973, the first of their kind in the 150-year history of the Hmong in Laos. The purpose of these workshops was to educate Hmong *nai kong* about the Laotian constitution; the national defense, economic, judicial, education and public health systems; and the country's international trade and diplomatic policies. Four hundred Hmong *nai kong* from six provinces of northern Laos participated, in groups of one hundred. Each workshop lasted one month and included a one-week visit to Vientiane, where the *nai kong*, many of whom had never left their home provinces and few of whom could speak Lao fluently, let alone read or write it, visited the Ministries of Defense, Finance, Education and Interior and met with representatives of key economic and industrial sectors. The workshops were an overwhelming success; Hmong *nai kong* felt they had learned more in one month than they had in their entire lives.

As part of their planning, some of the task force toured agricultural development projects in northern Laos. In the Hmong village of Phou Pha Deng, located in the Golden Triangle area of extreme northwestern Laos, team members visited a two-year-old experimental nursery staffed by a U.S. Agency for International Development agricultural expert and Lao and Hmong agricultural technicians. There they saw growing the coffee, ginseng, cardamom and mushrooms being promoted as substitutes for opium in northern Laos. Discussions with village leaders went on far into the night as they expressed their concerns about the future of the newly-signed Vientiane Agreement and their needs for arable land, schools, medicine, technical assistance and infrastructure improvement in order to bring about the profound changes necessary to develop and prosper in peacetime.

RE-OCCUPATION OF THE MOUNTAINS

It was with an explosion of joy that the 100,000 Hmong refugees in Xieng Khouang province learned of the Vientiane peace agreement. Driven from their homes by the fierce fighting, many had eventually migrated to crowded temporary settlements scattered throughout the southern Plain of Jars.[9] Unable to farm, most of them subsisted solely on food relief from the U.S. Agency for International Development (USAID). At the time of the Vientiane Agreement, the bulk of the refugee population was living along the main road between Long Cheng-Houei Kham-Muong Cha and Houei Kham-Ban Sone. In late 1973, with the cooperation of the Ministry of Planning and the help of USAID technicians, who used aerial surveillance to locate villages, ground teams from Long Cheng conducted a census in that area. The results showed a concentration of the population in mountainous areas, interspersed with deep, unoccupied valleys.

Encouraged by the cease-fire, respected for a time by both sides, the Hmong began to plan their post-war lives. Early in 1974 thousands of Hmong left the Long Cheng area, which was too mountainous for farming. With nothing to return to in their obliterated villages, these migrants once again took up the southward direction which the Hmong have followed throughout their history. Kia Pao Kue and Chia Koua Kha, both former *nai kong*, were among the first to leave the mountains in the southern Plain of Jars. Taking two hundred people with them, they moved to the Ban Done valley at the edge of the plain of Vientiane, where they established two villages. Following time-honored tradition, the villagers cleared forests for *rai* and, at the coming of the first rains, planted rice, corn and a variety of vegetables. They also planned to raise chickens, pigs and cattle. Their hope was that after a few years of hard work they would regain their economic independence.

Another much larger group of refugees left Long Cheng under the leadership of Xiong Pao Ly, a well-known Hmong *nai kong*. These 3,000 Hmong and 1,000 Khmou moved to the Muong Kassy area south of Sala Phou Khoune, near the intersection of Vientiane, Luang Prabang and Xieng Khouang provinces. They made their way in a convoy of heavily-laden trucks to the valley of Pha Lak-Pha Khouai, a few kilometers west of RN 13, the principal north-south artery of the country. Unpopulated and still covered with virgin forest, Pha Lak-Pha Khouai offered the necessary conditions — arable land and adequate water supply — for permanent settlements. According to Ly, the 600 families created six new villages and transformed the valley into agricultural fields by cutting down the trees and burning the land. Each family had two to three hectares of *rai* on which they grew rice, corn, sugar cane, banana trees and many kinds of vegetables including tomatoes, Chinese mustard, cucumbers, pumpkins, green beans and watermelons. They planned to set up an irrigation system from the many springs in the valley to bring water into the *rai* and to make them into flooded rice fields over the next few years. They considered pooling their silver bars and other savings to buy tractors and trucks needed for development of the villages. In the beginning, each family raised 100 to 400 chickens and two or three sows with 12 to 20 piglets. Only a few people had cows, horses or buffalo. Their goal was to be able to feed themselves within one year in the new settlement. They also built three schools so the children would not have to sacrifice their education.[10]

The largest refugee movement occurred into the area between Ban Sone and the Nam Ngum dam on the Nam Ngum River, about 70 kilometers north of Vientiane. Boua Fue Yang, former *chao muong* of Muong Sone, recalls that in early May 1975 there were about 20,000 people in that area, about two-thirds of them Hmong and the rest Lao, Phouan and

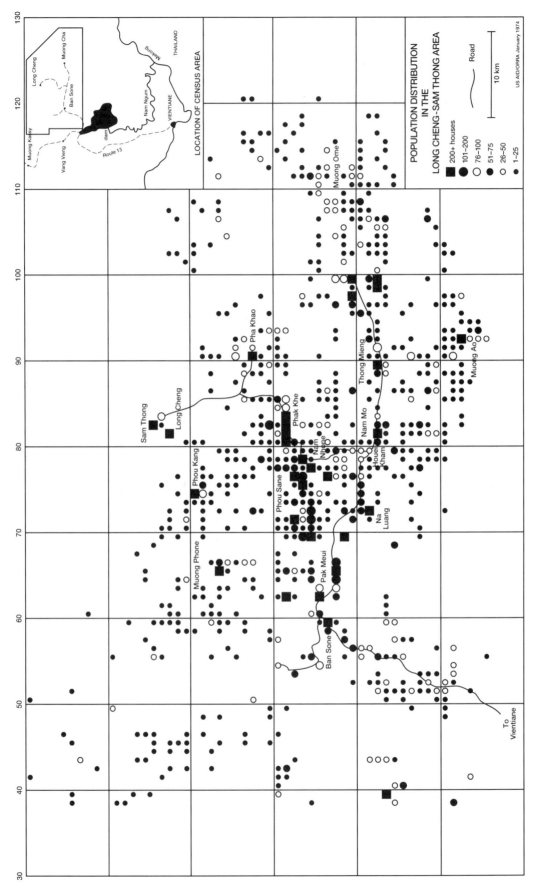

POPULATION DISTRIBUTION
IN THE
LONG CHENG–SAM THONG AREA

LOCATION OF CENSUS AREA

200+ houses
101–200
76–100
51–75
26–50
1–25

Road

10 km

US AID/ORRA January 1974

Muong Ome

Pha Khao

Muong Ao

Thong Mieng

Sam Thong
Long Cheng

Phak Khe

Nam Mo

Phou Kang

Nam Nhope

Houei Kham

Phou Sane

Na Luang

Muong Phone

Pak Meui

Ban Sone

To Vientiane

Long Cheng
Muong Cha
Muong Kassy
Ban Sone
Vang Vieng
Route 13
dam
Nam Ngum
Nam Song
Mekong
THAILAND
VIENTIANE

Khmou. They built their villages along the road connecting the Second Military Region to Vientiane. The first group of Hmong refugees settled in Ban Nam Sone, a few kilometers south of Ban Sone. A second group of Hmong from Phou Koum moved further south and settled in "Kilometer 23," named for its distance from RN 13 at Ban Houei Mo. A third group of Hmong from Phou Fa created the village of "Kilometer 22," and a fourth group of about 200 Hmong and 6,000 Lao and Khmou went to establish themselves about three kilometers north of the Nam Ngum dam in the Nam Phau valley, which was unoccupied and still forested. Many other smaller groups also settled in the area. It was their plan to transform the Nam Phau valley into irrigated rice fields as quickly as possible. But before their dreams could come true, political pressures forced them to leave the country.[11,12]

Some Hmong chose to join the 3,000 refugees already permanently resettled in the new village of "Kilometer 52," so called for its distance from Vientiane on RN 13. There they grew dry rice, corn, sugar cane, pineapples and papaya trees and tried their hands at silkworm raising.

In early 1975, about 200 Lao families and about 50 Hmong families were living and working in the village of Tha Din Deng, a combination agricultural-cattle raising pilot project. Located on the south side of the Nam Ngum River about 18 kilometers north of Vientiane, at the foot of the Buffalo Horn Mountains, the project consisted of about 3,500 hectares of land, enough to support 1,500 families. The plan was to convert 600 to 700 hectares to irrigated rice fields capable of producing two crops a year and to devote the remainder of the land to cattle pasture. Financed by USAID and supervised by the Royal and Provisional Governments, this pilot project was an attempt to train Lao and Hmong farmers in the techniques of crop rotation (rice with corn, soybeans, etc.) and selective animal breeding (local cattle with Australian bulls, local sows with Yorkshire hogs, etc.). The Tha Din Deng project was abandoned in 1976 because of the political situation.[13]

Still other Hmong families moved to Muong Phieng in Sayaboury province, where some 1,000 families were already benefiting from the five-million-dollar USAID Nam Tan irrigation project.[14] As early as 1970 the Hmong there had already adapted well to lowland life: they grew two crops of rice annually, raised large flocks of ducks and increasing numbers of water buffalo, developed commercial fish ponds, built substantial houses, and, in general, enjoyed a vastly improved standard of living. But in 1975, as if struck by a plague, they, along with thousands of others, abandoned everything and fled to Thailand in search of freedom.

Despite these movements, many Hmong continued to live on or near former military bases, having grown accustomed to the commercial, educational and medical benefits these areas provided. Some of these were Royal Lao Army and special forces personnel and their families, some served in various regional offices and administrations, others taught in schools, and still others operated small businesses. By far the largest group were farmers, who found ready markets for their agricultural products in these population centers. Despite a massive reduction in American military and economic assistance following the Vientiane peace agreement, these people believed that the status quo would endure at least for a while.

THE AGRICULTURAL DEVELOPMENT ORGANIZATION

In 1973, shortly after the signing of the Vientiane Agreement, which called for the disbanding of the special forces, USAID created a branch of the Agricultural Development Organization (ADO) in Long Cheng. The mission of the Long Cheng ADO was to assist demobilized RLA troops and special forces to return to civilian life. It intended to pursue a three-pronged strategy of domestic animal distribution, job creation and economic development.[15]

Animal Distribution   The objective of animal distribution was to buy bulls and water buffalo from Lao and Hmong civilians and distribute them as war compensation to demobilized officers, from captains to colonels. The animals would provide an economic base for the transition of these soldiers into civilian agricultural occupations. The ADO set up animal distribution centers in Long Cheng, Muong Cha, and Muong Phone. By May 1975 more than 300 bulls and 200 water buffalo had been distributed, one animal per person.

Pig Farms   The ADO created four large pig farms to create jobs for war veterans, to raise animals for distribution, and to provide meat to the local population at competitive prices. The Long Cheng fattening center consisted of a large, modern pigsty with a cement floor, a corrugated aluminum roof, and a running water system. Designed to accommodate 500 animals, it reached about 200 head by May 1975, when it was abandoned. The Nam Nhone farm, built in the same style, was a breeding center. By late 1974, the farm had 50-60 Yorkshire breeding sows. Its manager, Nyia Her Lo, regularly visited refugee settlements to distribute this new variety of hogs to Phouan, Hmong and Khmou farmers for crossbreeding and herd development. The large Lo family also grew many kinds of fruits and vegetables, including a pineapple grove atop a small hill near their homes, and raised chickens and ducks for family consumption.[16] The Pha Deng center, consisting of two modern pigsties each capable of sheltering 1,000 animals, was intended to supply pork to regional markets. It never became operational. Construction of the Nam Pha farm, also a pork supply center, had just been completed at the time of the communist takeover in 1975 and, like the others, failed due to political events.

Chicken Farms   Three large ADO chicken farms were set up in the southern Plain of Jars. The farms provided income for the demobilized soldiers hired as employees, attempted to raise the level of local protein consumption by providing competitively priced meat, and promoted agricultural development by purchasing corn and other crops from local farmers for processing into chicken feed. The Long Cheng farm, created shortly after the Vientiane Agreement, comprised two long wooden buildings with cement floors and corrugated roofs, each with a capacity of 20,000 chickens. Bought as chicks in Thailand, the chickens were sold three or four months later in local and regional markets. Between June 1973 and January 1975, the farm sold approximately 120,000 chickens for around 100 kip apiece. Pha Deng, built after Long Cheng, had just produced its first flock of 20,000 chickens at the time of the May 1975 upheavals. Both it and the Muong Cha center, which had not yet become operational, were abandoned.

These examples of the promising beginnings of economic development, as well as many others which could be cited, illustrate the effort and motivation of the Hmong in the reconstruction of post-war Laos. How eloquently they contradict statements by some United Nations officials that the Hmong who fled to Thailand were not political but economic refugees, continuing, as they had during the war, to follow the CIA in search of free food.[17] The truth is that the entire population of Laos benefited greatly from the Vientiane peace agreement and, at least in Royal Lao Government-controlled areas, strove, in a mighty national effort, to rise from the ashes of the long and devastating war.

As much as the Hmong had suffered and fought during the war, so strong then was their determination to rebuild their lives in peace and prosperity. In southern Xieng Khouang province, the increase in land under cultivation (made possible by increased security and the large number of demobilized troops freed up for work on the farms), the introduction of new techniques in domestic animal raising, and the improvement of the transportation infrastructure all contributed to the recovery of the Hmong economy. In a short span of two years of peace, half the Hmong refugee population again became self-sufficient.

Economic trends in the Hmong mountains in the spring of 1975 were especially encouraging. Rice surplus from the previous year was sufficient to feed most Hmong families until the 1975 harvest without difficulty. Meat production was increasing rapidly, making meat prices in the Long Cheng area among the lowest in the country. One kilogram of pork, for example, cost only 650 kip there, compared to 1,500 kip in Vientiane. The Hmong hoped that by 1980 they would be able to flood the markets of Luang Prabang, Sayaboury and Vientiane with their vegetables, temperate-climate fruits and domestic animals. They also planned to develop schools and health care centers in the mountains to provide their children with adequate education and to improve the health of their people. But this dream was short-lived. The winds of the communist Pathet Lao revolution would soon sweep aside all that lay in their path, creating a monumental human tragedy in the Kingdom of a Million Elephants.

FOOTNOTES:

[1] Richard M. Nixon, *RN: The Memoirs of Richard Nixon*, Simon and Schuster, New York, 1990, p. 560.

[2] Ngone Sananikone, "Comments on the Negotiations Between the Government and the Pathet Lao With a View Toward Peace and National Reconciliation," unpublished speech, Paris, 1984?, p. 6.

[3] Personal recollection, Vientiane, July 1973.

[4] 1957 and 1962.

[5] Personal recollection, Luang Prabang, May 1, 1974.

[6] The strategy was officially entitled, "National Political Program for the Building of Peace, Independence, Neutrality, Democracy, Unity and Prosperity in the Kingdom of Laos."

[7] Khamla Kinsada (Adjoint du Chef de Bureau), "National Political Program for the Building of Peace, Independence, Neutrality, Democracy, Unity and Prosperity in the Kingdom of Laos," Le Bureau du Conseil Politique National de Coalition, Luang Prabang, February 5, 1975.

[8] Ibid.

[9] Cf. Chapter Six.

[10] Xiong Pao Ly, personal interview, Saint Paul, Minnesota, December 1991. In 1978, because of political pressure, Ly and 1,400 others left Pha Lak-Pha Khouai and fled to Thailand.

[11] Boua Fue Yang, personal interview, Saint Paul, Minnesota, December 1991.

[12] (Author's note) On May 14, 1975, driving back to Vientiane from a meeting two days before with General Vang Pao at Long Cheng on what was to be my last night in Laos, I looked with sadness on the hundreds of hectares of sown fields stretching out on both sides of the road between Ban Nam Sone and Nam Phau. Tender rice and corn plants, only a foot or two high, blanketed the fields like a green carpet. How tragic and unnecessary the group of armed Pathet Lao soldiers looked positioned on the "Tiger Rocks" near the road. I knew that I would never see the rice and corn harvests myself but I had no idea that the fields would be abandoned so soon by their hard-working owners.

[13] Vong Souvannarath, personal interview, Saint Paul, Minnesota, December 1991. Souvannarath was the director of the Tha Ngone development project (which included Tha Din Deng) and is now (1992) an agronomy researcher in Minneapolis, Minnesota.

[14] W. E. Garrett, "No Place to Run," *National Geographic*, Vol. 145, No. 1, January 1974, p. 108.

[15] Geu Vang, personal interview, Saint Paul, Minnesota, December 1991. Vang, a former lieutenant colonel, was assigned by General Vang Pao to head the Second Military Region Development Office.

[16] Nyia Her Lo, personal interview, Saint Paul, Minnesota, December 1991. In 1975 Lo was forced to abandon Nam Nhone and flee with his family to Thailand. At present (1992) he lives in Saint Paul, Minnesota.

[17] Robert Cooper, personal communication, Minneapolis, Minnesota, November 1983.

CHAPTER NINE

The Tragedy

Isolated in the mountains, the Hmong largely ignored the political intrigues that were brewing on the national and international scenes. They celebrated the 1974 New Year in traditional fashion in an atmosphere of peace. In villages throughout northern Laos they dressed in splendid finery, killed new year pigs, and invited relatives and friends to family celebrations to bid the old year farewell and welcome in the new. In Long Cheng, General Vang Pao received foreign guests from Vientiane and expressed his confidence in the advent of a new era. The political situation in Indochina, changing by the minute, had seemingly been forgotten in the long-overdue festivities.

Meanwhile, the fighting in Cambodia and South Vietnam was at its peak, despite the 1973 Paris Agreement in which both the United States and the Democratic Republic of Vietnam had committed to withdraw their troops from South Vietnam, Cambodia and Laos. In the spring of 1975, the communist Khmer Rouge began a siege of the Cambodian capital of Phnom Penh, which fell on April 17. Hanoi then launched a massive offensive against Saigon, which, in turn, succumbed on April 30.

Encouraged by communist victories in the neighboring countries, the Pathet Lao hardened its attitude toward right-wing leaders, now abandoned by their American allies, who were completing their military withdrawal from Indochina. In fact, the Laotian communists had never been content to share political power with the Royal Lao Government, which they accused of being "corrupt and pledged to foreign imperialism." Knowing they could not hope for a political, much less a military victory so long as their right-wing opponents enjoyed massive American military and economic assistance, the Pathet Lao used the 1973 Vientiane Agreement as a Trojan horse to infiltrate their operatives into all levels of the country's military, police, and public administration, as well as into student and civilian organizations. Pathet Lao leaders expected that the Provisional Government, set up under the Vientiane Agreement, would last the few years necessary for Hanoi and its Viet Cong allies to "liberate" South Vietnam. Their intention was to use this time to increase their popularity among Vientiane loyalists through an intense campaign of political education and popular organization, making ready for the time when conditions would be right for a take-over of power.

Pathet Lao obduracy was evident from the time of the formation of the Provisional Government of National Union and the National Political Consultative Council. Discussions between representatives of Vientiane and the Neo Lao Hak Sat, tense from the beginning, grew more heated as time went on. Remaining faithful to the NPCC mission of national reconciliation, the Vientiane representatives threw their energies into fighting for an equitable and durable political solution. On many occasions they contested Pathet Lao positions which they considered contrary to the provisions of the Vientiane Agreement and put forth counterproposals aimed at creating a working agreement between the two factions. After weeks of confrontation, the Eighteen Point Political Program was born, quite different and much more conciliatory than the original program propounded in a nationally-broadcast diatribe against "American imperialism and its lackeys" by Prince Souphanouvong in Luang Prabang on May 16, 1974. This was the same prince who, just two weeks before, at the first meeting of the NPCC, had spoken so impassionedly for national reconciliation!

Pathet Lao politics were suspected of being part of a global strategy aimed at the international spread of communism. In late April 1975, the German Democratic Republic, in recognition of the neutral status of Laos, invited an NPCC delegation to visit East Berlin for the purpose of developing a cooperative friendship between Laos and the GDR. Shockingly, and completely against diplomatic protocol, a member of the Presidium of the GDR People's Chamber stood up during a banquet for the NPCC delegation in Leipzig and accused the "damn Meo" of being responsible for communism taking so long to be victorious in Laos. An eloquent reply by the author, emphasizing the unity of Laos, the participation of the Hmong on both sides of the war, and the resolve of all parties to work together for peace and national reconciliation completely silenced the heckler and thoroughly embarrassed the German hosts. From East Germany the delegation traveled to the USSR, where they were welcomed at the May Day celebrations by Nikolai Podgorny, chairman of the Presidium of the Supreme Soviet. Speaking through an interpreter, he declared that "if the right-wing reactionaries resist the course of history..." and made a gesture clearly indicating decapitation! The intransigent attitude of the Soviet leader shocked the NPCC delegation and caused deep concern over the future of the Laotian coalition.

As the United States was withdrawing the last of its military aid from the "Vientiane party," including the once-powerful General Vang Pao, the Pathet Lao was strengthened by continuing Soviet support and by the presence of 60,000 North Vietnamese troops remaining illegally in Laotian territory. After the communist victories in Cambodia and South Vietnam, the Pathet Lao proceeded to ignore the Vientiane Agreement and the Eighteen Point Political Program. On May 1, the Union of 21 Organizations and the National Student Federation, both thoroughly infiltrated and controlled by Pathet Lao agents, organized large demonstrations in Vientiane, Thakhek, Savannakhet, Pakse and Luang Prabang to denounce right-wing government officials, military and police officers, and to condemn American imperialism in Laos. On May 9, fearing for their personal safety, five ministers of the Provisional Government, including the Minister of Defense, resigned their positions and, together with a number of leading Army officers, secretly crossed the Mekong River into Thailand.

Beginning in May 1975, Pathet Lao troops harassed RLA military positions at many points along the cease-fire line established by the Vientiane Agreement. In Sala Phou Khoune, about 130 kilometers north of Vientiane at the junctions of RN 7 and RN 13, Pathet Lao troops provoked a critical cease-fire incident. On the night of May 3-4, under cover of darkness, their soldiers crossed the cease-fire line and penetrated 11 kilometers into territory held by General Vang Pao. The general responded by sending a squad of T-28 fighter planes from Long Cheng to attack the enemy and was, according to plan, immediately accused by the Pathet Lao of violating the cease-fire. On May 4 and 5, the Pathet Lao launched a general offensive, supported by tanks and artillery, forcing Vang Pao's soldiers to retreat. On May 6, General Vang Pao met with Prince Souvanna Phouma at his residence in Vientiane. The Laotian prime minister accused the Hmong general of being too hot-headed, ordered him to withdraw his troops from Sala Phou Khoune, and offered him a position at the Royal Lao Army headquarters in Vientiane. Highly insulted, General Vang Pao refused the offer, resigned his commission as commander of the Second Military Region, tore off his three general's stars, handed them back to Prince Souvanna Phouma, and returned to his base at Long Cheng.

In the capital, Pathet Lao agents began a propaganda campaign accusing the Hmong of being mercenaries of the American CIA. On May 8, Khaosan Pathet Lao, the Lao People's Party newspaper, wrote, "We must eradicate the Meo minority completely." Late in the evening of May 10, word reached Vientiane that communist Pathet Lao and North Vietnamese troops were massing in the southern Plain of Jars, Vang Vieng and Tha Thom in preparation for a pincers attack on General Vang Pao's headquarters, considered the last stronghold against complete communist victory. Strong personal pleas, delivered the next morning, persuaded Prince Souvanna Phouma, in his capacity as head of the Provisional Government, to call off the attack on Long Cheng. When a nonfunctioning telephone prevented direct communication of this decision to Phoumi Vongvichit, vice prime minister and one of the communist representatives in the coalition government, the prince sent a personal emissary (the author) to convey the message. In response to the news of Prince Souvanna Phouma's decision, as well as to requests for withdrawal of communist troops from the Long Cheng area and a search for a political solution in the Second Military Region, the vice prime minister accused General Vang Pao of having violated the terms of the Vientiane Agreement. Completely unmoved by explanations that the general had, in fact, complied with every clause in the agreement and that the Hmong people, along with all the Laotian people, aspired to peace and supported national reconciliation, Vongvichit demanded that Vang Pao "cooperate" with Pathet Lao military leaders and "comply with the Vientiane peace agreement" as officers in the First, Third, Fourth and Fifth Military Regions had already done.

Isolated in his headquarters and completely surrounded by North Vietnamese and Pathet Lao troops, General Vang Pao attempted to organize a final resistance. On May 12, in a gesture of despair, he made a fateful decision: to attack Vientiane before the enemy launched its final assault on Long Cheng. Only after frantic, eloquent pleading was the general persuaded of the suicidal nature of his plan not only for himself and his army but for all the Hmong in Laos. Two days later, along with thousands of his closest collaborators, he abandoned Long Cheng and crossed into Thailand.

News of the departure of the Hmong military and political leaders spread like wildfire. Within days, thousands of Hmong, fearing for their lives, began to leave the mountains. Families joined other families, forming convoys that stretched for miles. Carrying what little they could on their backs, they followed tortuous trails ever deeper into the forests, always heading in the direction of the setting sun. Many would die of hunger and disease, others would be killed in communist ambushes or be swept away in the swift waters of the Mekong River. Only the lucky ones would eventually reach the safety of Thailand.

On December 2, 1975, the Pathet Lao officially took over the country of Laos, abolishing the six-century-old monarchy, dissolving the Provisional Government of National Union and the National Political Consultative Council, proclaiming the birth of the Lao People's Democratic Republic, and establishing political institutions patterned after other communist states. Tens of thousands of Lao, Tai Dam, Khmou, Mien and Hmong civil servants and military officers, as well as the majority of ordinary citizens of all ethnic groups, still holding out hopes for a peaceful, democratic Laos as outlined in the Eighteen Point Political Program, decided to try to live under the new regime. The Pathet Lao, however, viewed these former enemies as a threat to the security of the new socialist government. Beginning in June 1975, even before the official Pathet Lao take-over, former Vientiane-allied PGNU and NPCC members were subjected to political "re-education." Thousands of former public officials and military officers were forced to follow them, being held in some 68 re-education camps along the Laos-Vietnam border. Many would never return.

By early 1976 the political situation in Laos had deteriorated to the point that intellectuals, business people, educators, technicians, students and peasants were leaving the country in waves. Between 1975 and 1990, almost 400,000 Laotians of all ethnic backgrounds, well over 10 percent of the country's entire population, voted with their feet and became international refugees, scattered throughout the world. Approximately one-third of the Hmong population left Laos during this time. Thousands of the Lao, Hmong, Khmou and Mien who remained organized resistance movements in the mountains and the jungles. The flight of its best and brightest and much of its labor force, as well as the lack of security for those who remain, have made the once prosperous Kingdom of a Million Elephants into one of the five poorest countries on the face of the earth.

EPILOGUE (SECOND EDITION)

Since the fall of Laos, the world has changed profoundly. People have claimed rights, freedom and democracy in all parts of the globe. From Nicaragua to Russia, from eastern Europe to Southeast Asia, dictatorships of all kinds have been overthrown, making room for more humane societies seeking social justice and economic progress. In this climate of cooperation among nations, it is time for Laos, too, to seize its chance. Laotian leaders everywhere must reconsider their political positions. Intolerance, intransigence and ideological narrow-mindedness caused the failure of three attempts at national reconciliation, unimaginable human suffering, the jeopardy of the nation's future, and the condemnation of the world community. Now that capitalism and communism have reconciled, creating new strategies of national development and international cooperation, and nationalist and socialist partisans have ended their fratricidal struggles in neighboring Kampuchea, the time has come for Laotian leaders both inside and outside the country to seek a true reconciliation founded on liberty, democracy and national solidarity. Only this fourth, durable Laotian unification can offer a permanent solution to the fate of the nearly one-half million Laotian refugees scattered throughout the world. In a spirit of peace, cooperation and unity, many may choose to return to their homeland, bringing new knowledge and skills acquired during their exile abroad to contribute to the social, economic and political development of Laos, which will, at last, take its rightful place in the comity of nations.

MINNEAPOLIS
May 14, 1992

BIBLIOGRAPHY

Abadie, Maurice, *Ethnic Groups in Northern Tonkin from Phong Tho to Lang Son*, Société d'Editions Géographiques, Maritimes et Coloniales, LOAG I:117, Paris, 1924.

Amiot, Joseph, "Repression of the Miao-tsu in 1775," letter, *Mémoires Concernant l'Histoire, les Sciences, les Arts, les Moeurs, les Usages, etc. des Chinois par les Missionnaires de Pékin*, Vol. 3, Nyon, Paris, 1778.

Anonymous, "Another Account of the Conquest of Miao-tsee Country," *Mémoires Concernant l'Histoire, les Sciences, les Arts, les Moeurs, les Usages, etc. des Chinois par les Missionnaires de Pékin*, Vol. 3, Nyon, Paris, 1778. pp. 412-422.

Archaimbault, Charles, "Annals of the Kingdom of Xieng Khouang," *Bulletin de l'Ecole Française d'Extrême-Orient* (BEFEO), Book LIII, Part 2, Paris, 1967.

Asian Development Bank, *Program of Integrated Agricultural Development on the Plain of Vientiane (Laos)*, September 1969.

Ayrolles, L. H., *Indochina No Longer Responds*, Armand Prudhomme, Saint Brience, 1948.

Balandier, Georges, "Traditional Social Structures and Economic Changes," *Cahiers d'Etudes Africaines*, Paris, January 1960.

Barthélémy, R., "Comments on Administrative Decentralization and a Racial Policy for Laos," in *Comptes Rendus et Rapports du Congrès de l'Organisation Coloniale*, Vol. I, 1922, pp. 139-140.

Bernatzik, Hugo, *Spirits of the Yellow Leaf*, Plon, Paris, 1955.

Bertolino, Jean, "The Land of a Thousand Pleasures," *Atlas*, No. 32, March 1969.

Bertrais, Yves, *Hmong-French Dictionary*, Catholic Mission of Laos, Vientiane, 1962.
— *Ntawv kho mob* (Nursing Manual), Catholic Mission of Laos, Vientiane, 1965.

Bourotte, Bernard, "Marriages and Funerals Among the White Meo in the Nong Het (Trân Ninh) Region," Institut Indochinois pour l'Etude de l'Homme, Vol. VI, Paris, 1943, pp. 33-56.

Burchett, Wilfred, *The Second Indochina War: Cambodia and Laos*, International Publishers Co., Inc., New York, 1970.

Burnot, *The Meo Minority of Tran Ninh*, Report No. 7, Institut International d'Administration Publique (IIAP), Paris, 1952-53.

Caply, Michel, *Guerilla in Laos*, Presses de la Cité, Paris, 1966.

Chesnaux, Jean and Marianne Bastid, "China 1: From the Opium Wars to the Franco-Chinese War, 1840-1855," *Collection d'Histoire Contemporaine*, Hatier Université, Paris, 1969, p. 100.

Clair, L., "United Nations Experience in Integrated Rural Development in Laos," General Scientific and Technical Delegation, SEDES, Paris, 1965.

Coèdes, Georges, *The Peoples of the Indochinese Peninsula*, Paris, 1965.

Condominas, Georges, *We Have Eaten the Forest*, Paris, 1957.

Condominas, Georges and Gaudillot, *The Plain of Vientiane*, study report, BDPA, Paris, 1960.

Couvert, Roger, *Functional Literacy, Laos*, United Nations Educational, Scientific and Cultural Organization, Paris, November 1968.

Cresson, R. and Jeannin, Robert, "Meo Hemp Cloth," Institut Indochinois pour l'Etude de l'Homme, Vol. VI, Paris, 1943, pp. 435-447.

Cucherousset, Henri, "The Habits and Customs of the Meo," *Eveil Economique de l'Indochine*, No. 377, 1924.

Diguet, E., *The Highlanders of Tonkin*, Paris, 1908.

Dumarest, Jacques, *Opium and Salt Monopolies in Indochina*, advanced doctoral dissertation, School of Law and Economic Sciences, University of Lyon, 1938.

Dumont, René, *False Start in Africa*, Collections Esprit "Frontières Ouvertes," Seuil, Paris, 1962.

——, *The Cultivation of Rice*, Société d'Editions Géographiques, Maritimes et Coloniales, Paris, 1935.

Dumont, R. and Mazoyer, *Development and Socialism*, Collections Esprit "Frontières Ouvertes," Seuil, Paris, 1969.

Ester, B., *Agrarian Evolution and Population Pressure*, Flammarion, Paris, 1970.

Fall, Bernard, *Indochina 1946-1962*, Lafont, Paris.

——, "The Problem of Governing Ethnic Minorities in Cambodia, Laos, and Both Zones of Vietnam," in *Political Problems of Poly-ethnic States*, P/PR/12, p. 28 ff.

——, "The Viet Minh (1945-1960)," *Cahiers de la Fondation Nationale des Sciences Politiques*, Paris, 1960.

France, Department of Foreign Affairs, "Soil Conservation in the Southern Sahara," *Techniques Rurales en Afrique*, No. 12, Centre Technique Forestier Tropical, Paris, 1969.

Fridman, *Agricultural Future of Trân Ninh*, doctoral dissertation, Vols. I-III, Paris, 1953.

Fromaget, Jacques, "Geological Studies in the Northern Part of Central Indochina," *Bulletin du Service Géographique de l'Indochine*, Vol. XV, Part 2, Hanoi, 1927.

Garnier, G., Bezanger-Beauquesne, L. and Debraux, G., *Medical Resources of French Flora*, Vigot, Paris, 1961.

Geddes, W. R., "The Human Background," *Symposium on the Impact of Man on Vegetation of the Humid Tropics*, Goroka (Territory of Papua and New Guinea), September 1960.

Girard, H., "Comments on the Meo of Northern Tonkin," *Association Française pour l'Avancement des Sciences*, 30th session, Ajaccio, 1901, pp. 165-166.

Gourhan, Leroi and Poirier, P., *Ethnology of the French Union*, Vol. II, Presse Universitaire de France, Paris, 1953, p. 647.

Gourou, Pierre, *Soil Use in French Indochina*, Centre d'Etudes de Politique Etrangère Publications, Hartman, Paris, 1940.

Halpern, Joel M., *Aspects of Life and Culture Change in Laos*, Council on Economic and Cultural Affairs, 1958.

Hamada, H., "Lao and Miao farming on the Plateau of Xieng Khouang, Laos," *Mingkou Gaku-Kenkyu*, XXIII:1, 1959.

Harbison, F. and Myers, C. A., "Training: The Key to Development," Collection *Développement et Civilisation*, Editions Ouvrières, Paris, 1967.

Haudricourt, André-Georges, "Introduction to the Historical Phonology of the Miao-Yao Languages," *Bulletin de l'Ecole Française d'Extrême-Orient* (BEFEO), Book XLIV, Part 2, Paris, 1951.

Haudricourt, André-Georges and Hedin, L., *Man and Cultivated Plants*, Gallimard, Paris, 1943.

Herbert, J., *Introduction to Asia*, Albin Michel, Paris, 1960.

Hirshman, A. O., *Strategy of Economic Development*, Editions Ouvrières, Paris, 1964.

Izikowitz, Karl Gustav, *Lamet, Hill Peasants in French Indochina*, Goteborg, 1951.

Joukov, E., Delioussine, L., Iskenderov, A. and Stepanov, L., *The Third World, Problems and Perspectives*, Editions du Progrès, Moscow, 1970.

Kao, L., *Wars of National Liberation and Social Revolution*, doctoral dissertation, Institute for the Study of Economic and Social Development, University of Paris, June 1967.

Labarthe, C., *Some Aspects of Urban Development in Laos*, master's thesis, College of Liberal Arts, Institute of Geography, University of Bordeaux, October 1969.

Lacoste, Y., *Geography of Under-Development*, Presse Universitaire de France, Paris, 1965.

Lafont, Pierre B., *Swidden Agriculture Among the Proto-Indochinese in the Central Highlands of Vietnam*, Paris, 1967.

Laos, Department of Planning, "Laos in 1969: A Geographical and Historical Presentation; Economic and Financial Situation," *1969-1974 Master Plan*, Vientiane, July 1969.

—, Ministry of Education, "Educational Reform in Laos," *Education*, No. 20, Vientiane, August 1962.

—, *The Laotian Constitutional Assembly (March 15-May 10, 1947)*, Imprimerie Française d'Outre-Mer, Saigon, 1949.

—, *Laotian Constitutional Assembly (March 15-May 10, 1947)*, Staff Communique No. 9, Vientiane, April 8, 1947.

Lartéguy, Jean, *The Fabulous Adventure of the Opium People*, collab. Yang Dao, Presses de la Cité, Paris, 1979.

Latouche, Serge, "The Fragmentation of the Economy and National Accounting: The Experience of Laos," *Développement et Civilisation*, No. 33, March 1968, pp. 60-73.

Lauj, Tsab (Cha Lao) and Yaj, Diav (Dia Yang), *Kwv Txhiaj Hmoob* (Collection of 99 Courting Songs), Vientiane, 1967.

Lebel de Chateauvieux, *Commentary on the Laotian Constitution*, Report No. 11, Institut International d'Administration Publique (IIAP), Paris, 1948.

Le Boulanger, Paul, *History of French Laos*, Plon, Paris, 1931.

Lemoine, Jacques, *Social Organization in a Green Hmong Village*, doctoral dissertation, College of Liberal Arts and Humanities, University of Paris, 1968.

Le Thanh Khoi, *The Education Industry*, Editions de Minuit, Paris, 1967.

Lombard-Salmon, C., *An Example of Chinese Acculturation: The Province of Gui Zhou in the Eighteenth Century*, advanced doctoral dissertation, Paris, 1970.

Lunet de la Jonquière, *Ethnography of Southern Tonkin*, Leroux, Paris, 1906.

Ly, Chao, *Initiation and Agriculture in Laos*, Ecole Supérieure d'Agriculture de Purpan, Toulouse, 1969-1970.

Lyfoung, Touxoua, "An Opinion on the Problem of Ethnic Groups in Laos," *L'Etudiant Lao* (Lao Students' Bulletin, Bordeaux Section), 1971.

Meister, Albert, *Functional Literacy and Economic Development*, United Nations Educational, Scientific and Cultural Organization, Paris, 1971.

Mieville, R., "The Wild Apple Trees of Trân Ninh," *Bulletin Agronomique de l'Institut Scientifique de Saigon*, Vol. VII, Saigon, 1920, pp. 204-207.

—, "The Cultivation of Hemp in Trân Ninh," *Bulletin Agronomique de l'Institut Scientifique de Saigon*, Vol. V, Saigon, 1920, pp. 157-159.

—, "The Cultivation of European Fruit Trees in Laos and Tonkin," *Bulletin Agronomique de l'Institut Scientifique de Saigon*, Vol. III, Saigon, 1920, pp. 86-90.

Moréchand, Guy, "Hmong Shamanism," *Bulletin de l'Ecole Française d'Extrême-Orient*, Volume 16, Paris, 1968.

Moréchand, Guy; Yaj, Txhim (See Yang); Yaj, Zoov Ntxheb (Zong Say Yang) and Yaj, Vam (Vang Yang), *Kab Ke Pam Tuag* (Funeral Chants), Vientiane, 1967.

Myrdal, Gunnar, *The Challenge of the Poor World*, Gallimard, Paris, 1971.

Ngaosyvathn, Pheuiphanh, *Movements and Use of Foreign Capital in Laos*, master's thesis (economics), College of Law and Economic Sciences, University of Paris, February-March 1971.

Osborn, G.M.T., *Government and the Hill Tribes of Laos*, Princeton University Studies, Princeton, New Jersey, May 11-14, 1965.

Panyanouvong, Phimmaha, "Who Comprise the Lao?" *L'Etudiant Lao* (Lao Students' Bulletin, Bordeaux Section), Paris, February 1971.

Pearson, Lester B., *Toward a Common Action for the Development of the Third World* (Pearson Report), Editions de Noël, Paris, 1969.

Pidance, A., "The Textiles of Trân Ninh," *Bulletin Economique de l'Indochine*, 9th Year, No. 51, 1906, pp. 412-423.

Pierre, George, *Panorama of the Present-Day World*, Presse Universitaire de France, Paris, 1965.

Pierson, Charles L. and Bertrais, Yves, *Rural Extension Project Among the Hmong Highlanders*, Catholic Mission of Laos, Center for the Hmong Apostolate, Vientiane, January 1969.

Raquez, A., "Among the Meo of Trân Ninh," *Rev. Ind.*, September 9, 1910, pp. 924-927.

Rassavong, Pan, "Economic Outlook for Laos," *La Revue Française*, No. 203, Paris, October 1967, p. 77.

Riviere, "Notes on the Meo and the Trade in the Mekong River," *Ann. Geograph.* 3, 1893-1894, pp. 105-107.

Robequain, Charles, *Le Thanh Hoa*, Vol. 1.

Rocher, *Yunnan Province (Revolt of the Miao)*, Paris, 1879.

Rochet, Charles, *Laos in the Storm 1939-1945*, Vigneau, Paris, 1945.

Rooj Ntawv Hmoob, *Xov Xwm Ntawv Hmoob* (Cultural Magazine in Hmong), Nos. 1-41.

Rostow, W. W., *The Stages of Economic Growth*, Seuil, Paris, 1960.

Roux, Henri and Chu Van Tran, "Some Ethnic Minorities in Northern Tonkin," *France-Asie*, Nos. 92-93, Saigon, January-February 1954.

Savina, F. M., *History of the Miao*, Imprimerie de la Société des Missions Etrangères de Paris, Hong Kong, 1930.

—, "Miao Tsu-French Dictionary," *Bulletin de l'Ecole Française d'Extrême-Orient* (BEFEO), XVI:2 and XXII:246, 1916.

Sion, G., *Geography of Laos*, Catholic Mission of Laos, Vientiane, 1961.

Sirisombath, Phay, "The Traditional World of Laos," *Reflets*, No. 2, Centre International des Stages, Toulouse, 1971.

Suryadhay, Inpeng, "The Rural Lao Community," *Revue Juridique Politique*, 22:2, April-June 1968, pp. 627-634.

United Nations Educational, Scientific and Cultural Organization, *Use of Vernacular Languages in Teaching*, Basic Education Monograph No. VIII, Paris, 1963.

Vaucel, G. F., *Zootechnical and Economic Considerations of Some Domestic Animals in Laos*, Vigot, Paris, 1930.

Veopradith, Khounkham, *The Human Factor in the Laotian Economy*, master's thesis, College of Law and Economic Sciences, University of Bordeaux, October 1967.

Vidal, J. E., "Vegetation of Laos, Parts I and II," *Work of the Forestry Laboratory of Toulouse*, School of Science, University of Toulouse, 1934-1960.

Vidal, J. E. and Lemoine, Jacques, "Contribution to the Ethnobotany of the Hmong in Laos," *Journal d'Agriculture Tropicale et de Botanique Appliquée*, Vol. XVII, Nos. 1-4, January-April 1970.

Vongvichit, Phoumi, *Laos and the Victorious Struggle of the Lao People Against American Neo-Colonialism*, Neo Lao Hak Sat Publications, 1968.

Yaj, Mim (Mee Yang), *Tsa Lub Neej* (Youth Facing Marriage), Vientiane, 1972.

Yaj, Txoov Yeeb (Chong Yeng Yang) and Yaj, Zoov Ntxheb (Zong Say Yang), *Zaj Tshoob* (Collection of Marriage Rituals), Vientiane, 1964.

Yaj, Zoov Ntxheb (Zong Say Yang), *Rog Paj Cai 1918-1920* (Collection of Testimonials About the "War of Pachay" 1918-1920), Vientiane, 1969.

—, *Caj Ces Hmoob Yaj* (Yang Family Tree), Vientiane, 1974.

Yaj, Zoov Ntxheb (Zong Say Yang) and Lauj, Tswb (Chue Lao), *Dab Neeg Hmoob* (Collection of 13 Hmong Folk Tales), Vientiane, 1963.

Yang, Dao, "Multiethnic Laos," *L'Etudiant Lao* (Lao Students' Bulletin), Paris, April 1970.

TABLES AND ILLUSTRATIONS

PHOTO CREDITS

Air America, photo 26; Catholic Mission of Laos, 9, 10, 13; (Courtesy of) Jerry Daniel, 27; Col. J. J. Devaux, 25, jacket; Sai Lee, 2; (Courtesy of) Tougeu Lyfoung, 24; (Courtesy of) Toulia Lyfoung, 21; Blong Moua, 32; National Information Service of Laos, 29, 30; Viliam Prasayavong, 23; Thaophia Saykao, 6; USIS, 14, 16, 28; Xinhua News Agency, 31; Za Kao Yang, 1, 3; Author, 4, 5, 8, 11, 12, 15, 17; Unknown, 7, 18, 19, 20, 22.

INDEX

165

Tobacco, 51

Tonkin, 53

"Tougeu Affair", 30. *See also* Lyfoung, Tougeu

Tounalom, Khammeung, 32n.17, 73, 74, 86n.52

Trân Ninh, 37, 42n.5; hemp yields in, 61. *See also* Xieng Khouang

Transportation, 124, 133; air, 8, 91, 94, 95; costs, 46, 95, 112, 125; of farm products, 92; infrastructure, 46, 58, 77, 114, 115, 117, 122; river, 8; Xieng Khouang Air Transport, 94. *See also* Roads

Trees, of northern Laos, 5. *See also* Forests

USSR: NPCC visit to, 155; in Second Indochina War, 41, 155

United Nations Educational, Scientific and Cultural Organization (UNESCO), 98, 131

United States: assistance to Laos, 105; Hmong population in, xvi n.2; in Second Indochina War, 41; withdrawal from Indochina, 142, 154, 155

United States Agency for International Development (USAID), 96; experimental farms, 146, 149; food assistance, 147; Long Cheng ADO, 150; Nam Tan irrigation project, 149

United States Central Intelligence Agency (CIA), 156

Unity of Laotian Ethnic Groups Radio (Long Cheng), 100-101, 101n.17

Urban development, 17

Vang Pao (General), 32n.20, 39, 40, 41, 42n.14, 68, 143, 152n.12, 152n.15, 154, 155, 156; evacuation to Thailand, 156

Vang Vieng, North Vietnamese troops at, 156

Vegetables, 50, 51, 52, 59, 60, 115; development potential of, 117; marketing of, 91, 94, 117; preservation of, 59; in resettlement sites, 147, 149

Vieng Say, 143, 146

Vientiane, 4, 17, 22, 41, 84, 88, 94, 95, 117, 120, 149; evacuation of foreigners to, 16; Hmong population of, 15; Hmong *tasseng* in, 27; markets in, 95, 97, 117; Mien in, 13; money use in, 79; neutralization of, 142; opium marketing in, 67, 68, 79; prohibition of tree cutting in, 116; refugees in, 15, 105; roads in, 8; salt deposits in, 7; temperature in, 4, *table 5*

Vientiane Agreement. *See* Agreement on Restoration of Peace and Achievement of National Reconciliation in Laos

Viet Bac (North Vietnam), 53

Viet Cong, 33n.24, 154

Viet Minh, 32n.11, 33n.24, 39

Vietnam, 67, 82, 110; fall of South, 155; troop withdrawal from South, 142

NORTH, 4, 7, 8, 12, 25, 56, 154; Chinese in, 66; Hmong in, 25, 32n.3, 56; Hmong irrigated rice growing in, 53; Hmong migration through, 60; Hmong population in, xvi n.2; "Madman's War" in, 36; opium growing in, 63; Tai in, xi; weekly markets in, 80

Vietnamese, in Laos, 16, 18, 67, 90, 91, 94, 97, 115; repatriation of, 90

NORTH: attacks on Long Cheng, 41; troops in Laos, 16, 32n.11, 32n.12, 104, 105, 154, 155, 156

Village: chief, 24, 31, 46; social organization, 46

Vinh (North Vietnam), 8, 117

Vongvichit, Phoumi, xii, 29, 156

Vue, Patchay, 37, 38, 42n.2

Vue, Shong Tou, 38

War: casualties, 32n.20; economic effects of, 91; Hmong involvement in, 34, 134; in northern Laos, 17, 21, 30, 32n.9, 39-41, 69, 95, 104-105, 129; population displacements due to, 22, 59, 82; royalist forces in, 104; troop demobilization, 150

Water, purification, 114

Water buffalo, 70, 123, 149, 150

Wheat, 116-117

Women, role of, 24

Xieng Khouang, 4, 17, 18, 38, 86n.48, 134; cattle in, 70, 123; coal deposits in, 7; commerce in, 94-95; corn yields in, 57-58; daily markets in, 91-92; deforestation in, 88; duck raising in, 69; ethnic composition of, 15; firewood price in, 127; forest products of, 6-7; gold in, 7; Hmong in Constitutional Assembly, 38; Hmong irrigated rice growing in, 50, 53; Hmong mortality rate in, 19; Hmong *muong* in, 30; Hmong population in, 8, 14, 15, 19-20, 30; Hmong population displacements in, 19, *maps* 20-21, 104; Hmong population survey in, 13-14; Hmong settlement in, 25, 90; Hmong *tasseng* in, 25, 26, 27; Hmong vegetable marketing in, 117; iron deposits in, 7; Khmou *muong* in, 30; Khmou rule of, 36; market economy in, 90-95; markets in, 78, 80; migration from, 88; opium growing in, 65, 68; opium marketing in, 67, 68; pear growing in, 60; periodic markets in, 92-93; Phouan in, xvi n.7; population of, 91, 92; potato raising in, 118; potential for vegetable raising in, 117; production cost of rice in, 55; refugee settlements in, 18, 21, 22, 93, 94; revolt of Hmong *kaitong* in, 36; schools in, 26, 98; survey of refugees from, 18; swine raising in, 69; temperature in, *table 5*; timber shortage in, 127; Touby Lyfoung in, 29, 90; war in, 21, 91, 105; wheat growing in, 117

Yang, Boua Fue, 147

Yang, Dao, 144, 152n.12, 156; in NPCC, 143

Yang, Fay Yia, 81

Yang, Za Nao, 119, 137

Yangzi River (China), xiii

Yao. *See* Mien

Yields, agricultural, 110, 114, 121

Yunnan, 8; piaster use in, 80

Zhou Enlai, 142